Studies in Economic History

RAILROADS OF NEW YORK

Published in coöperation with the Committee on Research in Economic History

RAILROADS

of New York

A Study of Government Aid

1826–1875

BY

HARRY H. PIERCE

HARVARD UNIVERSITY PRESS

Cambridge, Massachusetts

1953

Distributed in Great Britain by

GEOFFREY CUMBERLEGE
Oxford University Press
London

Library of Congress Catalog Card Number 52–5404
Printed in the United States of America

TO EDWARD CHASE KIRKLAND

Preface

THIS BOOK IS essentially a study of the part played by the state and its municipalities in financing the construction of New York railroads. It has been my objective to tell when, why, how, in what amount, and with what success these two branches of government contributed to the development of the railroad system of the state. In pursuit of this objective, I examined wherever possible all relevant private as well as public sources of information. Railroad companies deserve high praise for making their materials available to scholars. This industry has led all others in depositing and opening their records.

It is a pleasure to acknowledge aid given in the collection of material and the publication of this book. Financial help has been received from the Committee on Research in Economic History, the Social Science Research Council, and the Committee on Scholarship and Research at Syracuse University. To Paul Wallace Gates of Cornell University I owe a great debt of gratitude. He suggested the study and guided it through its various stages of development. Professor Arthur H. Cole of Harvard University not only acted as editor of my book but proffered many constructive suggestions and criticisms. I am especially indebted to Professor Carter Goodrich of Columbia University for his encouragement and his painstaking perusal of the entire manuscript.

Many scholars read the original manuscript or portions of it and made valuable suggestions for its revision. Without reflecting on the generosity of others I should like to express my thanks to Professor Merle E. Curti of the University of Wisconsin, Professor Arthur Sutherland of the Harvard University Law School, Professor Curtis P. Nettels of Cornell University, Dr. Blake McKelvey of Rochester, Professor David M. Ellis of Hamilton College, Professor Richard C. Overton of Northwestern University, Professor Thomas C. Cochran of the University of Pennsylvania, Professor L. Ethan Ellis of Rutgers University, Professor William P. Hotchkiss of Syracuse University,

Helen Marsh LaLonde of Utica, Samuel Hopkins Adams of Auburn, and the late Professor Elias Huzar of Cornell University. It seems hardly necessary to add that all errors of fact and interpretation should be laid at my doorstep.

Many of my friends helped me in nonprofessional capacities. Mr. Robert C. Hosmer of Syracuse and Mr. Dennis McCarthy of Utica, in particular, rendered valuable assistance by making it possible for me to examine town records in remote or isolated areas of the state.

H. H. P.

June 1952

CONTENTS

Foreword

HARRY PIERCE'S BOOK is an impressive contribution to the growing literature devoted to the role of government in the economic development of the United States. Recent reëxamination of the movement for internal improvements has indicated that government activity in the construction of railroads and other transportation facilities was greater in amount and continued for a longer period than is commonly realized, and that a very large part of it was carried on by local government agencies — cities and villages and counties — rather than by the states and the nation.

On each of these points the present study of public aid to railroads in New York gives striking confirmation. Professor Pierce's researches have brought to light a volume of governmental participation in railroad building in New York considerably greater than has been recorded before. Of this aid, three-fourths was contributed by local governments and only one-fourth by the state. No less than 70 per cent of the total aid in New York, moreover, was given in the years just after the end of the Civil War.

The last point is of particular interest. Other studies sponsored by the Committee on Research in Economic History have discussed the economic role of state governments in the period between the Revolution and the Civil War. Professor and Mrs. Handlin's book on Massachusetts, Professor Hartz's volume on Pennsylvania, and Professor Heath's forthcoming study of Georgia all show the state governments intervening actively in the economy and taking positive steps — wise or foolish — for the direct promotion of economic development. On the other hand, the period immediately following the Civil War has often been thought of as the one in which the triumph of laissez-faire doctrines was most nearly complete. Yet the present study shows that such doctrines had little effect in restraining the communities of upstate New York from committing the public credit for the building of the railroads they so eagerly desired.

Nor did community and civic interest in such development cease completely with the end of direct public aid. New York State prohibited local-government aid to railroads in 1875, as it had prohibited state investment in them in 1846. Yet communities in New York and elsewhere often continued to aid the railroads by collective though no longer official means. The process was illustrated in Mr. Pierce's own state while the book itself was in preparation. The old Midland Railroad, which he describes in its beginnings as zigzagging across the state in search of municipal bonds, was again in bankruptcy under its new name. In the communities along its line various civic bodies — chambers of commerce, boards of trade, and the like — were organizing a campaign to prevent the abandonment of the road. The agencies were no longer governmental, but their arguments were much the same as those recorded by Mr. Pierce, and their appeal was to a similar combination of private interest and civic spirit.

Two qualities are notable in the author's work. The first is the painstaking thoroughness of the research. His orderly tables and illuminating maps could only have been produced by means of a prolonged and exhaustive search of obscure town and village records and the books of the railroad companies. This is particularly true of the tables which establish profit and loss on railroad securities by tracing the town holdings down to the date of sale, sometimes even into the present century.

The second quality is impartiality. Mr. Pierce casts an equally critical eye on the failings of each of the participants of the drama which he records. His account misses nothing of the devices by which adroit promoters persuaded upstate farmers to mortgage their farms and bond their towns for the support of dubious enterprises. He is no less severe with the authorities of towns that repudiated their railroad bonds not because they were in economic difficulty but simply because they learned that there were technicalities by which their obligations could be evaded.

It was not the author's purpose to offer a general theory of public aid or to suggest the norms by which resort to the method of mixed enterprise should be judged. What he has given us is a valuable case study of the combination of private and public effort which has played, and in differing forms continues to play, a significant part in the development of the economy of the United States.

CARTER GOODRICH

La Paz, Bolivia
February 1952

RAILROADS OF NEW YORK

ONE

Sources of Railroad Capital

Unquestionably, the greatest economic factor in the transformation of American life during the nineteenth century was the development of the railroad. The railroad colonized the West and made 160-acre homesteads possible. Oil men depended upon the railroad for the transportation of crude oil to the refinery and refined oil to the consumer. For more than a half-century American steel production was geared to the demands of an expanding railroad network. The modern meat-packing industry owes its very existence to invention of the refrigerated car and the extension of the railroad to the Great Plains. And yet, despite the vital role that the railroad was destined to play in the development of the nation's economy, no industry ever presented as many or as great problems as those which attended its construction. Strange as it may seem to many today, there was, in the beginning, a considerable amount of human inertia and human prejudice to overcome. Some viewed the proposal to use steam engines for motive power as utterly impractical; while religious fanatics denounced the railroad as a device of the devil for leading immortal souls to hell. There were complex problems of technology, organization, and management. But the most perplexing of all the difficulties that confronted early railroad companies was the problem of finance. Railroading was a new and highly speculative business. In competition for capital with other transportation or industrial interests, it could not expect to attract the full financial support of those who had been accustomed to receiving substantial returns within a short period of time. Many early lines were relatively short and were located in areas where the population was dense. Funds for these roads were rather easily obtained. For the more extensive enterprises, however, especially where the traffic was slight, the financial risk involved was frequently greater than private capitalists were willing to assume.

The great transcontinentals which were built far in advance of both population and traffic were richly endowed by the federal government. In addition, thousands of communities and virtually every state encouraged railroad development by either building the roads themselves or by furnishing the cash and credit needed for private construction. Virginia took three-fifths of a company's stock as soon as the other two-fifths had been subscribed. Georgia financed the Western & Atlantic from Chattanooga to Atlanta and operated it as a state enterprise until 1870. Pennsylvania introduced its own railroad on the Pennsylvania system. As early as 1853, the railroad debt of Wheeling amounted to $1,100,000; Louisville, $1,500,000; New Orleans, $3,500,000; and Philadelphia, $8,154,000. In 1870, the city of Baltimore, which had furnished much of the early capital for the Baltimore & Ohio, had financial commitments for railroads aggregating $15,000,000. Cincinnati, prohibited by constitutional restrictions from lending its credit to promote corporations, built the Cincinnati Southern as a municipal enterprise.[1]

The large amount of capital required for the building of railroads in the state of New York, coupled with the unwillingness of private investors to risk their money in railroad securities, frequently made it difficult for companies to raise sufficient funds for important projects. New York was a wealthy and prosperous state, but the capital available for the development of its transportation system seldom kept pace with the demands of its promoters. The stock of the 90-mile Utica & Schenectady was oversubscribed seven times[2] and that of the 44-mile Tonawanda was taken up in a single day.[3] But these were exceptional cases. Both roads were launched during the boom years preceding the Panic of 1837. Furthermore, these early lines were rather flimsily built and required relatively small amounts of money for their construction. On the other hand, the failure of private capital to subscribe to the stock of important roads such as the New York & Erie and the Albany & Susquehanna delayed the completion of these enterprises for more than 16 years. The promoters of the Auburn & Rochester obtained enough money to conduct a survey of the route only by promising to run their line in a zigzag fashion through the towns of Canandaigua, Geneva, and Seneca Falls.[4]

It was common practice for construction firms to take part of their pay in securities of the road which they were building. The New York & Erie made an agreement with a company to furnish the materials and to build the 76-mile section of the road between Corning and Binghamton in return for "Income Certificates." [5] Between 1845 and 1849, the Erie issued approximately 15,000 shares of stock to pay for grading and for the purchase of locomotives, cars, and machinery.[6] The contract for the construction of the Albany & Susquehanna called for payment in $1,000,000 of the road's capital stock, $2,000,000 in cash, and $1,000,000 in the first-mortgage bonds of the company.[7] The contract for building the New York & Oswego Midland between Neversink and Walton carried the provision that payment was to be made $1,460,000 in the company's first-mortgage bonds, $1,625,000 in its second-mortgage bonds, $100,000 in town bonds, and $1,250,000 in the capital stock of the line.[8] Prior to 1875 more than a thousand railroad charters in the state were forfeited through the failure of promoters to obtain sufficient stock subscriptions. Nonetheless, by this date, approximately $400,000,000 had been invested in the construction of New York railroads.[9] Where did the money come from?

The national government, which contributed so heavily to the development of the nation's transportation network, gave only slight financial assistance. In 1834 the Erie appealed for a tract of 2,000,000 acres of public land in return for a contract to carry the mail without compensation for a period of 30 years, but Congress rejected the proposal.[10] Federal aid to railroads in New York was limited to the temporary remission of duties on railway iron and a preliminary survey in 1828 of a projected road between Hudson and Pittsfield, Massachusetts.[11]

Foreign capital, which did so much to stimulate the building of western lines, played only a minor role as an initiating force in financing New York roads. Prior to the Civil War, Europeans owned a comparatively small share of their securities. Benjamin Tibbits, one of the early promoters of the Hudson River Railroad, wrote to a London friend: "As long as we can continue to get your capitalists to take our R R Bonds our most remote borders will be made accessible by the R R tracks." [12] Yet, two years after the opening of the line, foreign investors held only $5,000 of the company's $3,740,515 capital stock and $928,000 of its $7,500,000 bonded indebtedness.[13]

In 1853, scarcely $350,000 of the Harlem's $8,000,000 stock and $150,000 of its $1,400,000 bonds were owned abroad. Approximately $200,000 of the first-mortgage bonds of the Buffalo, Corning & New York found their way into the London market but foreigners possessed only negligible amounts of securities in the Buffalo & State Line, the Buffalo & Niagara Falls, the Saratoga & Washington, and the Watertown & Rome.[14] European capital did not flow into the New York Central until the late 1870's. The Secretary of the Treasury reported in 1853 that none of the company's $22,858,600 stock or $2,111,824 outstanding bonds were held in Europe.[15] But this is probably a misstatement. The largest single stockholder in the Central line of railroads in 1850 was Benjamin Ingham, a citizen of the Two Sicilies, who owned 669 shares in the Utica & Schenectady.[16] Ten years later his investment in the stock and bonds of the New York Central amounted to $640,600.[17] Aside from Ingham's purchases, there was virtually no European investment in the lines that went into the New York Central consolidation of 1853. In 1857 John V. L. Pruyn, secretary and treasurer of the Central, established a London office for the transfer of the company's stocks and bonds, but the securities sold very slowly.[18] In the first six years only 212 persons, a majority of them residing in England or France, purchased stock in the company. Most of these were small subscribers who bought 50 to 100 shares. Among them was William Makepeace Thackeray, the famous English novelist, who purchased 50 shares.[19]

Baring Brothers & Company, the great English merchant bankers, refused to handle the securities of short, locally built roads.[20] European investors preferred to put their capital in trunk lines and land-grant railroads. "Pacific railroad bonds," declared the *Chronicle*, "appear to be regarded in Germany as a sort of semi-government security." [21] Only in the Erie of the New York lines did foreign investors hold a substantial block of securities. In 1853, two years after the completion of this road, $3,000,000 of its $10,000,000 capital stock and $7,000,000 of its $19,200,000 bonds were owned abroad.[22] By 1875, three-fourths of the company's common stock and a majority of its bonds were owned by Europeans.[23]

The purchase of New York state securities by foreigners indirectly aided in the promotion of railroads as it released private savings and bank resources for other investment. These, however, were government and not railroad securities, and their owners were not granted any share in the management of the road. The ownership of state stock issued for the construction of railroads was reported by the comptroller in 1843 as follows:[24]

Railroad	Held in New York	Other States	Europe
Delaware & Hudson	$ 409,316.88	$ 17,358.88	$373,324.24
Erie	2,587,000.00	251,000.00	162,000.00
Tonawanda	86,000.00	14,000.00	
Schenectady & Troy	100,000.00		
Long Island	80,000.00	3,000.00	17,000.00
Catskill & Canajoharie	86,000.00		114,000.00
Ithaca & Owego	82,000.00	12,000.00	221,000.00
Auburn & Rochester	188,000.00	11,000.00	1,000.00
Hudson & Berkshire	141,000.00		9,000.00
Tioga Coal & Iron	70,000.00		

During the last quarter of the nineteenth century the amount of foreign capital invested in New York railroads increased enormously. The character of this investment differed, however, from that made before the Civil War. During the latter period, funds from abroad found their way into the state's transportation system chiefly as secondary rather than as primary capital. The money flowed into the securities of lines that were already in operation; it helped to finance company improvements and company expansion. Relatively little was employed in the construction of new roads.[25]

Before 1875 there were no significant foreign holdings in the New York lines which compose the present-day Lehigh Valley, New York Central, Delaware, Lackawanna & Western, or the New York, Ontario & Western systems. By the close of the century a substantial volume of the securities of some of these companies had passed into European hands. When the New York & Oswego Midland (now the New York, Ontario & Western) opened for operation in 1873, none of its $6,798,211 stock and only about $2,000,000 of its $16,073,500 bonds were owned abroad.[26] A decade later, a majority of its $58,000,000 capital stock and an unknown amount of its $100,000 bonded indebtedness were held in England and Holland.[27] There were no important European investments in the Delaware & Hudson lines until 1871, when the company negotiated with Gilead A. Smith & Company for a loan of £600,000 for the purpose of improving and expanding the road's property.[28] Three years later, the New York & Canada, now the main line of the Delaware & Hudson between Albany and Montreal, sold £800,000 of its first-mortgage bonds in England.[29]

Following the Hepburn investigation of 1879, William Vanderbilt, who held 87 per cent of the New York Central's capital stock, decided to dispose of a large share of his holdings.[30] In 1880 a syndicate headed by Junius S. Morgan & Company marketed an estimated $25,-000,000 of Vanderbilt's stock in Europe. Within six years the number of New York Central shares owned by people living in England or on the continent rose from 94,974 to 317,296.[31] Moreover, in 1873, the Central floated an issue of $30,000,000 in registered first-mortgage bonds. With the exception of a $500,000 investment by the North British & Mercantile Insurance Company of London, these securities were purchased principally by the Vanderbilt family, American life insurance companies, and American savings banks. But a second issue in 1873 of £2,000,000 in first-mortgage bonds was sold wholly in England, and interest on them was paid in sterling from London.[32]

There is no way of determining precisely the amount of foreign capital invested in railroad securities. Figures on stock or bond holdings at a particular time give only an approximate indication of the actual money outlay. It is also difficult to ascertain the exact price at which investors purchased securities. The shares of many early railroads seldom reached par; their bonds frequently sold at a heavy discount. The New York & Oswego Midland, to which the British are known to have lent some £400,000, experienced great difficulty in marketing its bonds at 30. During the late 1840's and early 1850's, English investors were purchasing the bonds of the New York & Erie at less than one-half their face value.[33]

Unquestionably most of the funds used for the original construction of railroads in New York came from individual savings and from credit extended by American banks. Most people invested in railroad securities to make money; but thousands of small farmers and merchants purchased stock in projected enterprises mainly because they desired improved transportation facilities or hoped that the value of their lands would increase. In 1848, five years after completion of the Auburn & Rochester, approximately one thousand persons, most of them holding only five or six shares, owned the company's stock.[34] A few months before the opening of the Albany & Susquehanna in 1869, practically all of the privately owned stock of the company was held in small lots by people in the towns along the road.[35] The largest individual stockholder in the New York & Oswego Midland was the philanthropist and reformer Gerrit Smith, who owned 250 shares.[36]

The $2,000,000 capital stock of the Utica & Schenectady was apportioned among bidders in the following manner: Utica, 5500 shares; Schenectady, 2500; New York City, 5565; Albany, 5000; State List, 1435. In 1850 nearly 550 persons held stock in the road.[37] The directors of the Watertown & Rome reported in 1849 that they had received but "little aid from abroad" and that "a large proportion of our stockholders are farmers, whose means are not generally in ready cash." [38] By 1855 more than nine hundred persons, a majority of whom resided in communities along the route, controlled the company's stock.[39] The initial capital for building the Buffalo & State Line was furnished by small investors living in the towns of Ripley, Fredonia, Pomfret, Westfield, and Buffalo.[40] Funds for the construction of branch roads such as the Dunkirk, Allegany Valley & Pittsburgh, the Clayton & Theresa, the Utica Clinton & Binghamton, and the Rome & Clinton were subscribed mainly by local communities and persons of ordinary means who were seeking an outlet to markets or who viewed the undertaking as a patriotic venture.[41] One-half of the $1,600,000 required to build the Syracuse & Binghamton was furnished by some 2,000 stockholders living along the road.[42] In 1854, the Buffalo, Corning & New York reported that 1200 shareholders owned the $1,380,000 capital stock of the company.[43] These examples are, it is true, drawn almost entirely from short, parochially built roads. Nevertheless, the great railroad systems operating in New York today were created largely by combining, consolidating, or leasing these locally constructed lines. The Erie, the West Shore, and the New York, Ontario & Western are the only roads in the state with considerable mileage that were built by one corporation.

Although many early railroad companies suffered acutely from lack of adequate funds, there was no dearth of liquid capital in the state. Many large financiers and wealthy merchants, however, shied away from the slow and uncertain returns of local enterprises in favor of more remunerative opportunities in the West. Only a few were willing to devote a substantial amount of their savings to ventures involving great risks or requiring long periods to yield a return. Ira Davenport, a wealthy Steuben County merchant and land speculator, wrote to his brother in the fall of 1853:

No difficulty in making favorable loans in Mich. — money is worth 15 in Detroit on short time, good paying stocks cannot be had at par. Rail Road bonds are below par but what Bonds to buy is an uncertain affair — Illinois Central at 85 is low, N Y Central at 94 is not so good as loaning at 10 — If Charles Doutremont would go to Wisconsin and start a bank it would pay.[44]

The names of a number of well-known capitalists such as Erastus Corning, William H. Aspinwall, John V. L. Pruyn, Edwin D. Morgan, Cornelius Vanderbilt, and Russell Sage are closely associated with the early history of the New York Central. Yet none of these men, with the possible exception of Corning, invested heavily in the original lines from which it was formed. It was not until these roads had established themselves as going concerns, or until there were opportunities to make huge speculative profits through their consolidation, that these financiers acquired substantial blocks of securities. Corning, Pruyn, and Sage invested heavily in western lands and railroads. Following the gold rush of 1849, Aspinwall risked his fortune in the Pacific Mail & Steamship Company.[45] Morgan, who was an associate of Pruyn and Corning in plundering the Schenectady & Troy line, invested his money in the banking and brokerage business.[46] Publius V. Rogers, wealthy Utica banker, limited his investments in local projects during the fifties and sixties to a few thousand dollars while risking upwards of a quarter of a million in western lands and railroads.[47]

As a general rule, the great financiers of the state did not speculate heavily in New York railroads until the element of risk was substantially reduced. Before 1850 the pioneer capital for construction of railroads was furnished principally by small investors supplemented by state subsidies. After this date, particularly during the decade following the Civil War, the initial risk was assumed largely by the local communities through which the roads passed. In both periods public money rushed in where private capital feared to tread.

Since many early lines were built parallel to the Erie Canal or touched the same geographical centers, a bitter dispute arose over the state's policy toward railroad construction. Shortly after the opening of the Mohawk & Hudson in 1831, Governor Enos T. Throop warned the legislature that future roads should be authorized with caution lest their operation adversely affect the publicly owned canal system. He recommended that all railroad charters should reserve to the state "the right to take possession of them as public property" and should require "such rates of toll . . . as would secure canal revenues from loss and not retard the payment of the canal debt." [48] A few months later, an Assembly committee on internal improvements asserted its unbounded confidence in the superiority of railroad transportation, and urged the state to promote it by becoming "a stockholder in all leading routes." [49] To harmonize these diverse opinions and at the same time to assist in the formulation of a permanent public policy, the legislature appointed a commission to make a thorough study of the comparative merits of the two carriers. The investigation, however, did little to allay factional strife. The committee reported that railroads were better for passenger travel; but, it claimed, the construction and operation of canals was considerably cheaper and preferable for the transportation of freight.[50]

The conflict between railroad and canal interests resulted in the adoption by the legislature of two mutually contradictory policies. On one hand, the state sought to protect its investment in the Erie Canal by severely limiting the activities of railroads. On the other, it encouraged the building of railroads by authorizing municipalities to subscribe to their stock, and also by liberally subsidizing their construction — in some instances, assisting the very roads on which it had placed restrictions.

The original charter of the Mohawk & Hudson made the stockholders personally liable for all debts of the company and reserved to the state the right to purchase the line within five years upon the payment with interest of the amount expended on construction.[51] The New York & Erie, to which the state donated $6,217,096.86, was required to lay its entire track within the boundaries of New York and was prohibited from connecting with any line leading into Pennsylvania or New Jersey. This restrictive provision, intended to deny to neighboring states any benefit from the road's operation, deprived the company of the important terminus of the city of New York. The legislature forbade the Utica & Schenectady to transport "property of any description, except the ordinary baggage of passengers." [52] The law authorizing the Auburn & Rochester contained an ambiguous provision forbidding it to "transport merchandise or property in such a manner as to lessen the income of the Erie Canal during the time when the canal is navigable." [53] Freight might be transported over the Auburn & Syracuse, the Syracuse & Utica, and the Tonawanda lines, but tolls equivalent to the amount the state would have received had these goods been shipped by water had to be paid into the canal fund.[54] The railroad lobby was strong enough in the legislature by 1844 to liberalize the property clause in the charter of the Utica & Schenectady, but the policy of discriminating in favor of canals through the imposition of railroad tolls continued until 1851.[55]

Turnpike, plank-road, bridge, and steamboat companies also exerted a considerable influence in the legislature in opposition to the railroads. The charter of the Utica & Schenectady[56] compelled it to purchase the Mohawk Turnpike Company and to keep it in good repair, while that of the Syracuse & Utica[57] required it to compensate the Seneca Road Company for any damages the latter might suffer by reason of the railroad's construction.

State aid to private enterprise in New York was not new. For nearly 50 years the state had tried to promote its economic and social development by making generous loans or gifts to individuals, corporations, colleges, charitable institutions, and local governing units. As early as 1790, the legislature chartered the New York Manufacturing Society "for the employment of the honest poor" and directed the state treasurer to purchase 100 shares of its stock.[58] Aid to banking was initiated in 1797 when the legislature voted to acquire 50 shares in the Bank of Albany.[59] Educational institutions were natural recipients of governmental assistance. By 1820 Hamilton, Columbia, and Union colleges alone had received over $700,000 in state aid.[60] In 1792 the state donated $25,000 to the Western and Northern navigation companies to assist them in building canals in the Mohawk and Hudson valleys.[61] Loans to individuals on first mortgages, many of which were never repaid, were freely granted throughout the first quarter of the nineteenth century.[62] Prior to the Constitutional Convention of 1846, thirty-three corporations had received financial help from the state. In fact, the first substantial sum ever borrowed by the state was immediately loaned to aid the construction of manufacturing establishments.[63]

In 1827 the state inaugurated a policy of government aid for railroad construction by advancing the Delaware & Hudson Company a credit of $500,000.[64] This loan and all subsequent loans to railroads were granted in the form of state stock. These certificates of indebtedness, which were comparable to bonds, had to be auctioned off by the company within a specified time, usually three months. Any premiums realized on the sales reverted to the state comptroller for support of the public schools. A railroad receiving such assistance was required to set up a sinking fund and to pay into it annually a sum sufficient to meet the interest on the loan and the principal itself when it fell due. For its protection the state took a first mortgage on the road's property.

Consequently, when the New York & Erie appealed to the legislature in 1836 for a loan of public money, there was nothing unusual about the request. State aid for the promotion of private enterprise had been an accepted policy in New York for almost half a century. Moreover, the Erie petition was strengthened by the fact that, although the legislature had previously appropriated large sums for the construction of internal improvements, practically none of this money had been spent in those areas of the state through which the proposed railroad would pass. Supporters of the line contended that any aid extended to the company would be only a partial repayment of the onerous taxes they had paid for the development of transportation facilities in other sections of the state.

Without public aid, the outlook for building the railroad was exceedingly dark. The line was a highly speculative enterprise and funds for its construction were difficult to obtain. It was projected through a mountainous and isolated region marked by languishing industry and subsistence agriculture. Products of the area reached the great commercial markets of the East by long and circuitous trade routes through deep snow drifts at one season and treacherous mudholes at another. From one end of the proposed line to the other there was not a single community with a population of more than 3000 people. Piermont on the Hudson River was a desolate marshland; Dunkirk, a struggling village with an undeveloped harbor.

In the fall of 1835, the New York & Erie, with less than $200,000 in its treasury, began the construction of a project which the directors of the Company admitted could not be built for less than $6,000,000.[65]

Within a month, a catastrophic fire in the city of New York ruined some of its strongest financial supporters; two years later, the Panic of 1837 plunged a number of others into bankruptcy.[66] To avert the abandonment of the road, the company asked the state for a loan of $3,000,000, to be advanced in installments as the work progressed.

The legislature agreed to lend the Erie $600,000 as soon as it had constructed a section of the road 146 miles long.[67] It promised an additional $1,000,000 when the company completed a continuous line of double track from Piermont to Dunkirk. Unable to fulfill the first condition of the offer, the road never received any assistance under the terms of this bill. An appeal to the city of New York for a stock subscription of $1,000,000 also failed.[68] When the stringency of the money market during the depression years precluded any substantial help from private investors, the Erie petitioned the state for liberalization of the law of 1836. The legislature now agreed to reimburse the road with one dollar of state stock for each dollar raised and expended by the company. In 1839, it increased this subsidy to two dollars for each one spent by the railroad.[69]

Despite these credits, which amounted to $3,000,000, James Bowen, president of the Erie, informed Governor Seward in the spring of 1842 that unless additional aid were forthcoming the road would be forced to suspend work. In such a contingency, he declared, the company would be compelled to default on the payment of its state loans. The governor transmitted the letter to the legislature with a message stressing the gravity of the situation and urging it to advance sufficient funds to guarantee completion of the undertaking:[70]

The letter of the president of the New York and Erie Railroad Company . . . shows that if legislative aid is longer withheld from the association, it must desist from prosecuting its great enterprise; the laborers employed must be discharged; the interest on the three million state loan, which will accrue on the first of April next, will remain unpaid; the contingent debt will fall immediately upon the treasury; the capital invested in the enterprise by our fellow citizens will be lost; the New York and Erie railroad in its scarcely half-completed condition will be exposed to auction at the suit of the State; and the just expectation of immeasurable benefits to result from the enterprise will be suddenly and hopelessly disappointed . . . I will only add that no measure less favorable to the enterprise, than the past policy of the State, could now be effectual, while none, in my judgment, that would involve any sacrifice on the part of the State is necessary. Nevertheless the responsibility of conducting the enterprise to an early consummation seems to me to rest not with the New York and Erie Railroad Company, but with the State.

Wary of making additional loans to the project, the legislature refused to carry out the governor's recommendations.[71] Three years later, however, it agreed to release the company from its liability to the state on condition that the road be finished within six years. It also authorized the board of directors to issue $3,000,000 in first-mortgage bonds to expedite the work.[72] In May 1851 the New York & Erie reached its destination at Dunkirk and the state not only cancelled its mortgage but also assumed the interest on these securities, amounting to $3,217,096.86.

Between 1827 and 1878 the state of New York by loan, lease, or donation of money subsidized the construction of 16 railroads to the extent of $10,308,844.77.[73] Public aid for internal improvements during this period was a fundamental principle of the Whigs, but the Democrats often supported the program with more enthusiasm than did their opponents. In a few instances this aid proved to be a wasteful expenditure, but in the main the results more than justified the cost. Loans amounting to $1,570,000 made to seven railroad companies — the Auburn & Rochester, the Auburn & Syracuse, the Delaware & Hudson, the Long Island, the Schenectady & Troy, the Tioga Iron, Mining & Manufacturing, and the Tonawanda — were subsequently repaid without loss.

The state was not so fortunate in lending its credit to other lines. In 1840, the Ithaca & Owego, a 29-mile line designed to connect Cayuga Lake with the navigable waters of Pennsylvania, obtained a loan of state stock amounting to $315,700. At the same time a projected Catskill-to-Canajoharie road secured a similar credit of $200,000. Neither company was able to pay the interest on its obligation, and the state foreclosed on its mortgages. At a public sale held on May 20, 1842, the Ithaca line was bid off at $4,500 and the Catskill company for $11,600.[74] The Hudson & Berkshire road was built by a group of enterprising promoters who hoped to establish a trunk line to the West by linking the Catskill & Canajoharie with the Western Railway of Massachusetts. To aid this undertaking, the state lent the company $150,000. In the fall of 1846, eight years after construction began, the road became financially embarrassed and the legislature agreed to exchange its first-mortgage bonds for a lesser lien. But the business of the company continued to languish and, unable to meet the interest on its obligations, the road was auctioned off by the state comptroller for $155,000. The first-mortgage bondholders realized about 88 cents on the dollar, but the state's equity was completely lost.[75]

From the sale of these three roads the state received only $16,100 from mortgages amounting to $665,000. The lien on the Ithaca & Owego did not cover the rolling stock, and it would have availed the state nothing to take possession of the line. The agreement with the Hudson & Berkshire was far more rigidly drawn; but, as in the case of the New York & Erie, the state voluntarily waived its rights when the company found itself in financial difficulties.[76] Yet this money was not entirely wasted. The Ithaca & Owego was soon reorganized and became an important artery of commerce as well as a great source of profit to its owners. The Hudson & Berkshire, after many vicissitudes, is still in operation as a branch of the New York Central. The Catskill & Cana-joharie is the only railroad which received state aid that is not in operation today.

After 1840 the state's critical financial condition militated against further loans for railroad construction. The state debt, which amounted to less than $7,000,000 in 1837, rose to nearly $27,000,000 in 1842. Six per cent state stocks that brought a premium of 22 per cent in 1833 now sold at a heavy discount.[77] A loan of $200,000 to the Auburn & Syracuse in 1838 yielded $202,097.50; a similar advance to the Auburn & Rochester the following year netted only $182,990.[78] The New York & Erie experienced considerable difficulty in disposing of its state securities even at a discount of 22 per cent. The $3,000,000 state loan brought only $2,599,514.92 into the company's treasury.[79] The state comptroller concluded that "the impulse for internal improvements and local interest regardless of the condition of finances has pressed the state to the very brink of dishonor and bankruptcy." [80]

In 1841, Assemblyman Arphaxed Loomis of Herkimer County introduced a resolution which demanded in part that every bill providing for the issue of state stock should require the people's approval at a general election. The legislature looked on this measure as "visionary and dangerously revolutionary in its character" and refused to pass it.[81] The following spring, with the credit of the state at the lowest point in its history, the legislature enacted an emergency measure which suspended all public works and authorized a loan of $5,000,000 to meet the government's current obligations.[82]

The poor condition of the state treasury was not wholly the result of improvident loans to railroads. During this period the legislature floated large bond issues for expansion and improvement of the state-owned canal system without providing for either the interest or the ultimate redemption of the securities. Nonetheless, the successive failures of the New York & Erie, the Ithaca & Owego, and the Catskill & Canajoharie railroads, with an eventual loss to the state of more than $7,000,000, produced a sharp reaction against the use of public credit to aid private enterprise. This feeling became so strong that, without a dissenting vote, the delegates to the state constitutional convention of 1846 adopted an amendment prohibiting further loans to private corporations.[83]

The constitution of 1846 only restricted state aid to railroads; it did not forbid assistance altogether. The legislature might still subsidize the construction of railroads by donations of land or money or by the waiver of taxes. During the 1850's the promoters of the Albany & Susquehanna repeatedly importuned the legislature for help. This aid, solicited on the plausible pretext of developing the area's resources and justified on the ground that other companies had received such help, was blocked for several years by gubernatorial opposition. In 1863, under the exigencies of the Civil War, the state donated $500,000 to assist completion of the line. Four years later, it made an additional gift of $250,000.[84]

The success of the Albany & Susquehanna encouraged other lines to seek similar assistance. Between 1867 and 1874 the supporters of these measures, by adroit use of logrolling tactics, succeeded in driving through the legislature more than a score of bills providing generous grants for impoverished railroads. During the year 1869 alone, 17 corporations petitioned for subsidies amounting to $4,315,000.[85] But only the Whitehall & Plattsburg obtained any aid. In 1867 this company received a grant of $5,000 a mile for a length of road not exceeding 50 miles. Shortly thereafter the line was consolidated with the New York & Canada and the unexpended part of this appropriation, amounting to $73,090, was turned over to the latter company.[86]

In addition to direct cash subsidies, the state has granted many railroads a variety of indirect aids. In 1824, it authorized the Delaware & Hudson to set aside $500,000 of its capital and to engage in the banking business for a period of 20 years.[87] Railroads during this period were highly speculative ventures and many people were reluctant to invest in such undertakings. Banking was an established business. By combining the two enterprises railroad promoters found it much easier to dispose of their securities to a timid public. Moreover, banking privileges enabled companies to finance construction through the issue of their own bank notes.[88]

To aid construction of the Lake Ontario & Hudson River, the state sold the road and its corporate successors more than 1,500,000 acres of land at five cents an acre. These lands, which were heavily wooded with excellent pine timber, were made tax exempt for 25 years.[89] The charters of the Poughkeepsie & Eastern and the New York & Oswego Midland contained a provision waiving all property taxes on the roads "until a single track is completed or for a period not exceeding ten years." [90] The Cherry Valley, Sharon & Albany was exempted from the payment of taxes until it paid a semiannual dividend of 3 per cent. Shortly after its completion in 1870, the Delaware & Hudson leased the road. By reporting the earnings of the Cherry Valley and the Albany & Susquehanna road as one line, the company managed to avoid payment of taxes on the property for more than fifteen years.[91] The state also exempted from taxation the $1,291,000 in municipal bonds sold to aid construction of the Southern Central and the $5,704,707 issued on behalf of the New York & Oswego Midland.[92]

When the constitutional convention of 1846 prohibited the state from lending its credit to private corporations, railroad promoters turned with astonishing success to the localities for support. Burdens that the state was reluctant to bear were now assumed by hundreds of cities, towns, and villages. Between 1837 and 1875, 85 railroad lines were subsidized through funds raised by mortgages on entire communities. During this period, 315 municipalities in 55 counties advanced $36,841,390.69 in cash or municipal bonds to aid railroad construction.

The most common method by which municipalities aided in the building of railroads was by subscribing to their capital stock. Of the 315 communities that subsidized railroad construction, 297 assisted in this manner. The city of Buffalo, for example, purchased $1,000,000 worth of stock in the Buffalo & Jamestown, now a part of the Erie system.[93] The town of Theresa bought 600 shares of the Black River & Morristown, now a branch of the New York Central.[94] The city of Utica was the only community in the state that held "guaranteed stock" in a railroad company. In return for a $200,000 subsidy to the Utica, Clinton & Binghamton, the city received an equivalent amount of 5 per cent debenture stock guaranteed by the road's lessee, the New York & Oswego Midland, and by the New York, Ontario & Western and the Delaware & Hudson Canal Company.[95]

Only a few municipalities held railroad bonds. Promoters generally preferred that they should purchase common stock because bonds, which might be sold at discount, were comparatively easy to market. Nonetheless, nine communities in the state made loans on first or second mortgages amounting to $3,162,500.[96] To aid in financing the Troy Union Railroad, the city of Troy entered into a complicated arrangement with this corporation, the Rensselaer & Saratoga, Troy & Boston, Schenectady & Troy, and Hudson River lines. The Union road agreed to issue $30,000 of its capital stock; the city agreed to issue $680,000 of its 6 per cent bonds; and the four operating companies agreed to subscribe for equal amounts of the capital stock and to guarantee payment of the principal and interest on the community's securities. The city's investment was secured by a first mortgage on the carrier's property.[97]

The amount of public money donated for the building of railroads was relatively small. Local officials usually demanded that the company should exchange some kind of securities for their aid. The town of Schoharie, however, turned over to the Schoharie Valley road $20,000 in state bonds which had been given to the town because of an excess of volunteers furnished during the Civil War.[98] Johnstown contributed $175,600 for construction of the Fonda, Johnstown & Gloversville.[99] To aid in building the Glens Falls road, the town of Queensbury[100] donated $100,000 and the villages of Fort Edward [101] and Sandy Hill [102] an additional $55,000. A few communities like Albany, Bath, Sacketts Harbor, and Center Village made minor contributions.[103]

Only one municipality ever guaranteed an issue of railroad securities. In 1842, the city of Albany endorsed $100,000 worth of Mohawk & Hudson bonds to assist the company in relocating its line. These securities were subsequently retired without expense to the community, but the city's endorsement of the bonds constituted a contingent liability and, therefore, should be classified as an aid to transportation.[104]

There are a great many instances of New York railroads receiving public donations of land, buildings, bridges, or rights of way. No attempt has been made in this study to estimate the total value of these aids. Municipal land grants ranged in value from a few dollars to $285,-805.70 which the city of Buffalo contributed to construct the Buffalo Creek Company.[105] The city of Rochester built four bridges over its water mains for the Lehigh Valley and the state erected an equal number for the road over the Barge Canal at a total cost of $178,134.[106]

Municipalities have held a controlling interest in several New York railroads, but only one, the Schenectady & Troy, was entirely constructed with public money. This line, built by the city of Troy at a cost of approximately $700,000 was operated as a municipally owned project for more than 11 years. In February 1853, the city sold the road to a group of New York capitalists headed by Edwin D. Morgan and Erastus Corning, who included it a few months later in the New York Central system.

Were these various public grants for the promotion of railroad construction really aids? Some companies have vigorously denied that they were. The New York Central has contended that the state and local governments which made loans to railroads or guaranteed their securities "merely acted in the capacity of a banker or financial agency and that the railroad company received no more of an aid than if they had issued their own securities and sold them direct to the public or to a banking or financial agency." The Central has claimed that the sale of shares by railroad corporations to various cities, towns, and villages, was "merely a means of selling their stock and was no more of an aid than was received by them in the sale of the balance of their stock to individuals and companies." Only tax exemptions and donations (less disposal costs) are conceded to be subsidies.[107]

The record of public aid to railroads in New York does not support these views. On a strictly mathematical basis, the amount of assistance provided by a government through subscription to the capital stock of a railroad is the difference between the amount raised on the municipal securities and the amount that would have been received through sale of the stock to private individuals. Where a community lent its money or guaranteed a company's securities, the subsidy represents the difference between the interest actually accrued and that which would have accrued on the road's securities if they had been issued without public endorsement.[108]

It is impossible to say exactly what the alternative costs would have been, but it can be shown that many companies sold their securities to municipalities at much better prices than they could have obtained from private investors. Municipal railroad-aid bonds were almost invariably marketed at par or better. Scarcely a locality in the state was forced to sell at a discount. In the period from 1869 to 1875, when most of the local aid for railway construction was granted, municipalities were forbidden by law to market their bonds below par. Rare indeed was the company that could sell its securities at this price.

To aid in the construction of the Albany & Susquehanna the state of New York donated $750,000, 22 communities purchased $950,000 worth of its common stock, and the city of Albany lent the company $1,000,000 for 20 years. Was this financial assistance a subsidy? Or was it, as the comptroller of the Delaware & Hudson company later declared, "as much if not more . . . an 'Aid' to the Towns and State?" [109] It is true that the Albany loan cost the city nothing. It is also true that some communities, such as Cobleskill and Colesville, drew excellent dividends on their securities for a long period. Nevertheless, the company itself benefited enormously by the government's help. In fact, it owes its very existence to these subsidies. At the time the municipalities purchased shares in the road, the company's stock seldom brought more than 10 or 15 per cent of its par value. Its bonds could be marketed only at a great sacrifice.[110] A company memorial to the legislature in 1856 described its financial plight:[111]

Individual subscriptions can not be sufficiently increased to give the necessary cash basis, nor can bonds, as was originally contemplated, now be negotiated for that purpose. The experience of the last few years has not only thrown discredit upon such securities but has more than ever demonstrated the equity, propriety and safety of building railroads on local property, for then only are the holders comparatively independent of dividends.

On the $950,000 worth of municipal securities, however, the company realized a net income of $949,500. The Albany bonds sold at par.[112]

The importance of public capital in construction of the Albany & Susquehanna is indicated further by the proportion of the total stock held by the towns. Scarcely two months before completion of the line in 1869 the total paid-in stock amounted to $1,861,393.13, of which $950,000 was municipally owned.[113] Hobart Krum, a delegate to the Constitutional Convention of 1867 from Schoharie County, emphasized the significance of this aid when he declared:[114]

> Money was exhausted, every resource that could be thought of was exhausted, energy, skill and perseverance were exhausted until as a last resort that indefatigable and persevering man J. H. Ramsay applied to the legislature of the state of New York for a law authorizing towns along the line of that road to bond themselves in aid of its building. But for that law, but for that provision its building was an absolute impossibility.

Municipal aid played an even greater role in the building of other lines in the state. Sixty-seven localities subscribed to the stock of the New York & Oswego Midland and the Lake Ontario Shore roads at par when it was virtually impossible to sell these securities to private investors at any price. In 1873, the directors of the Midland were unable to market their 7 per cent first-mortgage bonds at 30.[115] Shortly before the road opened, the total paid-in stock amounted to $5,872,549.32, of which $5,704,707 was municipally owned. The Shore Line was still under construction when a constitutional amendment halted further municipal subsidies, but of the $1,857,106.45 paid in at that time, $1,772,500 was held by the communities through which the road passed.[116]

In a number of other roads the share of municipally owned stock was even greater. The town of Greene owned $198,700 of the Greene railroad's $200,000 capital stock. The communities along the Rondout & Oswego, now part of the New York Central, purchased nearly $1,000,-000 worth of its stock at par when the company's bonds were selling at ten cents on the dollar.[117] Lines such as the Utica, Chenango & Susquehanna Valley, the Rome & Clinton, the Carthage, Watertown & Sacketts Harbor, the Black River & Morristown, the Clayton & Theresa, and the Utica, Clinton & Binghamton were originally financed almost entirely by proceeds from municipal subscriptions.

Public subsidies should be assessed by their worth to the railroad as well as their cost to the community. The amount of financial assistance to the carriers is of great importance; but even more significant are the benefits the companies derived from the grants. A loan of $500,-

000 to the Delaware & Hudson in 1827 cost the state nothing but it saved the company from bankruptcy.[118] If the constitution of New York had prohibited state aid to private enterprise, the Erie railroad would never have been built. Not even its most optimistic supporters believed that private capital would furnish sufficient funds to construct the road. Company officials expected that most of the cost of the undertaking would be borne by the state.[119] As late as 1844, eight years after construction began, more than one-half of the money invested in the road had been supplied by the state. Public and not private funds assumed the initial risks in building the New York & Erie. In 1845, when the line was on the verge of bankruptcy, the state waived its $3,000,000 lien and authorized the company to issue $3,000,000 in first-mortgage bonds. Cancellation of the state loan produced a marked change in the road's fortunes. It did not solve all the financial difficulties of the enterprise, but it did restore confidence. From that time on, the company's ability to finish the work was no longer in doubt.[120]

It cost approximately $20,000,000 to build the New York & Erie.[121] The actual money outlay, however, was probably much less. The state stock, which sold at 86.3, brought only $2,599,514.92 into the treasury; the company marketed huge blocks of its stocks and bonds at heavy discounts.[122] Furthermore, the road's subpar securities were frequently pledged as collateral for loans at the rate of 40 or 50 cents on the dollar or were exchanged for services and supplies, especially iron rail from England, which the company was compelled to accept at inflated prices.[123] Since the discount on government bonds was considerably less than that on the company's securities, the use of public credit enabled the promoters of the enterprise not only to avoid inflated costs but to construct a greater mileage than would have been possible on the basis of private capital alone.[124]

When the Auburn & Syracuse appealed to the legislature for a state loan in 1838, the road was in difficult financial straits. During the spring and early summer of 1837, many subscribers refused to pay the calls on their stock and the company, in a frantic effort to meet its obligations, issued interest-bearing notes in amounts as small as $5.00.[125] Thomas Y. How, Jr., the line's treasurer, wrote to a friend:[126]

If by the failure of the stockholders in your city to pay the installments called and due we are compelled to declare ourselves unable to meet our engagements we must be sued not only of what we have expended lost entirely but the road itself the rail and fixtures sold on execution and the company in fact dissolved.

By January the company was unable to market its stock and the banks refused to honor its paper.[127] The road's desperate financial situation is revealed in a letter written by How to one of the directors:[128]

> Such is the condition of things here, that we are not able to realize from the notes of our stockholders half that sum . . . Money is not to be had . . . Is it possible that anything could be paid by Gov. Throop, Jno. L. Graham and yourself? Necessity compels me to ask the question. Can the forfeited stock be sold for anything . . . I am almost in despair, but my whole soul being given to the object I must have hope. Is there no sale for the stock?

At this critical moment in the company's history, the legislature authorized a loan of $200,000 to help it complete the undertaking. This state stock, which bore an interest rate of only 5 per cent, was sold by the road at a premium of $2,097.50.[129]

A few years later the Mohawk & Hudson, hard hit by the panic of 1837, found itself in similar difficulties. The stock of the company had slumped to 34, and its bonds could be sold only at a heavy discount. A bond issue of $35,000 in December 1841 brought only $25,375 into the treasury.[130] The outlook for the road became worse after November 1842, when a competitive line, the Schenectady & Troy, opened for business.[131] To retain its grip on western travel and to meet the Troy road's challenge, it was imperative that the company should remove the troublesome and expensive inclined planes at both ends of its line. For this purpose the directors turned for help, without success, to the state legislature and to the Utica & Schenectady. In desperation, the road appealed directly to the city of Albany for assistance. In 1842, this community guaranteed an issue of $100,000 of the company's bonds to remove the planes at Albany. The following year it lent the line $125,000 to do the same at Schenectady. The cost of this assistance to the Auburn & Syracuse and the Mohawk & Hudson lines was insignificant. Neither the state nor the city of Albany paid out a single dollar in cash.[132] To the railroad companies, however, the value of these subsidies was incalculable. They involved more than a saving on interest payments. They meant the difference between the success and the failure of the roads.[133]

Prior to 1875, 315 municipalities in New York advanced $36,841,-390.69 toward the construction of railroads. The state legislature granted an additional $10,308,644.77. No other state in the Union contributed so much.[134] Yet the importance of these subsidies lies not in their amount but in their timeliness. In practically every instance the aid was proffered at a critical moment in the company's history. It is significant that, with the exception of the city of Albany, neither the state nor any municipality ever assisted a railroad that was already in operation. Public money in New York always pioneered the way. It took the initial risk. It was never invested in a going concern. Government aid to railroads not only facilitated the raising of money, but also greatly reduced the cost of financing them. In many cases, particularly in the building of marginal lines, public subsidies made possible the construction of roads that would not otherwise have been built. In an even greater number of instances, it permitted the completion of projects at a much earlier date than would have been possible with private capital alone.

TWO

The Law of Municipal Bonding

Since local governments — counties, cities, towns, and villages — are creatures of the state, they had to secure permission from the legislature before they could subsidize the construction of railroads. Municipal corporations possess neither inherent nor implied power to create a debt to assist private enterprise without a specific grant of authority from the state. Prior to the passage of the New York municipal bonding law in 1869, the legislature conferred this authority freely by passing special enabling acts. These laws varied widely in content and application, but generally they provided for the submission of the question to the people, who were to determine by a special election whether such assistance should be extended. In addition to requiring some evidence of community support for the project, the legislature always restricted the amount of aid the locality might give.

In 1837, the village of Catskill was empowered to subscribe to 2000 shares of stock in the Catskill & Canajoharie Road if a majority of the qualified voters approved.[1] In the same year, the legislature authorized the city of Hudson to lend $50,000 on a first mortgage to the Hudson & Berkshire upon ratification by the "mayor, recorder, aldermen and commonalty of the city." [2] An act permitting Rochester[3] to aid the Rochester & Genesee Valley and another allowing Rome[4] to invest in the Ogdensburg, Clayton & Rome required the approval of two-thirds of the taxpayers representing two-thirds of the taxable property in the communities. In a more general way, the legislature permitted the village of Auburn to subscribe $100,000 to the stock of any railroad constructed between Lake Ontario and the New York & Erie or Cayuga & Susquehanna lines. Moreover, any town along the route chosen was allowed to invest $25,000 in the enterprise.[5] Despite the apparent severity of some of these laws, no community in the state of New York ever refused to bond itself on behalf of a railroad when the issue was placed before it at the polls. The city of Utica[6] voted by the narrow margin of 2701 to 2337 to extend aid to the Utica, Clinton & Binghamton; but the village of Rome[7] approved 450 to 1 a subscription to the capital stock of the Ogdensburg, Clayton & Rome, and the town of Binghamton[8] bonded in favor of the Albany & Susquehanna without a dissenting vote.

Defeated at the polls, the opponents of town bonding frequently turned to the courts for relief. They contended that the legislature had no right to authorize a municipality to invest in the securities of a private corporation. The jurisdiction of the legislature in this matter was questioned as early as 1840 by the Albany Common Council, but it was not until 1856 that a case actually appeared in the courts.[9] By 1852 the city of Rochester was blessed with three important railroads, the Tonawanda, the Auburn & Rochester, and the Rochester & Niagara Falls. It lacked, however, rail communications with the rich Genesee Valley and the important coal fields of Pennsylvania. To obtain these connections, as well as to provide an alternative route to New York, prominent business men and shipping interests in the community advocated the construction of the Rochester & Genesee Valley road to link the city with the Erie line at Portage.[10] At the request of the Rochester Common Council, the legislature amended the municipal charter to permit it to borrow $300,000 and, upon approval of the two-thirds of the voters, to invest the money in the road's stock. A special election overwhelmingly endorsed the plan, and the city promptly subscribed this amount to the securities of the company.[11]

Construction of the line had scarcely begun when a bitter factional dispute arose among the stockholders. Some wanted to build a standard-gauge road and run it in connection with the New York Central; others urged adoption of the broad gauge so that it might be operated in close association with the Erie.[12] The leader of the latter group was Freeman Clarke, a prominent Rochester businessman and politician. In a move to seize control of the enterprise, Clarke entered into a complicated arrangement with the Rochester Common Council which enabled him to gain command of the company's stock and made the city financially independent of the road's success or failure.

By the terms of a contract dated March 2, 1853, Clarke agreed to purchase all the city stock, payable $20,000 down, $2,000 each year for 20 years, and the remainder on January 1, 1873. Interest on the unpaid balance was fixed at 6 per cent. The city agreed to issue $180,000 worth of corporate bonds to Clarke, who promised to pay for them in cash as they were delivered. Title to the stock and scrip was vested in the city, but Clarke was to have all the dividends made by the railroad company. Furthermore, Clarke was allowed to anticipate his payments by surrendering an equal amount of bonds and might then call for a proportionate share of stock. Any failure by Clarke to pay as agreed was to terminate the contract and forfeit all his previous payments.[13]

After paying in some $41,700, Clarke was advised that the law and the subscription made under it were void and that the city could not give him a clear title to his stock on completion of the contract. Clarke then demanded that the city should cancel the agreement and refund his payments. When the Common Council refused, he brought an action to recover what he had paid.[14] The New York State Supreme Court ruled in his favor. Municipal corporations, it declared, had no power to hold stock in railroads or other private companies. It reasoned that, since the legislature was forbidden by the state constitution to lend its credit to private enterprise, it could not authorize a local or subordinate legislative body to make such loans.[15]

The case was of great significance because many communities, such as Buffalo, Auburn, Utica, Albany, Troy, and Binghamton, had invested heavily in the construction of railroads. If this decision were sustained on appeal, these bonds would be worthless and the municipalities would be compelled to repudiate them even though they might be in the hands of innocent purchasers.

The uncertain status of these obligations encouraged a group of Albany taxpayers to demand that the city should repudiate $300,000 of railroad-aid bonds issued to aid the bankrupt Albany Northern line.[16] The towns of Sterling, Venice, Scipio, and Genoa immediately challenged the validity of securities they had sold on behalf of the Lake Ontario, Auburn & New York.[17] The village of Rome, which had invested $150,000 in stock of the ill-fated Ogdensburg, Clayton & Rome, now refused to pay the interest on its debt.[18]

While the Clarke case was still under judicial advisement, the New York Court of Appeals passed on the legality of municipal aid for railroad construction. In a series of decisions[19] beginning in 1858 the court held that, in the absence of restrictive constitutional provisions, the legislature might permit a municipality to create a debt for public purposes which were not of strictly municipal character but from which the community as a whole would derive some direct advantage.[20] The court asserted that a railroad was a public improvement invested with the full right of eminent domain. The fact that a line was built under private auspices, it declared, did not divest it of the character of a public work; nor did the road's right to charge for transportation extinguish the public interest or make the enterprise a private one.[21]

The courts have consistently maintained that a law authorizing a municipality to assist the construction of a railroad does not delegate or surrender legislative power to a local constituency but is conditional legislation entirely within the legislature's jurisdiction. The act is effective when it leaves the lawmaking body, and all that is left for a locality to determine is whether or not to take advantage of its provisions.[22] For many years the United States Supreme Court declined to review state-court decisions on the validity of municipal aid to railroads. It was content to follow the ruling by the highest court of the state in which the case arose. These decisions were so conflicting, however, that soon after the Civil War the court agreed to review the question. Speaking for the court in *Olcott v. The supervisors,* Justice William Strong declared:

Whether the use of a railroad is public or a private one depends in no measure upon the question who constructed it or who owns it. It has never been considered a matter of any importance that a road was built by the agency of a private corporation. No matter who is the agent the function performed is that of the state. Though the ownership is private the use is public . . . That all persons may not put their own cars upon the road, and use their own motive power, has no bearing upon the question whether the road is a public highway. It bears only upon the mode of use, of which the legislature is the exclusive judge.[23]

Both state and federal courts have also ruled that, in the absence of constitutional restrictions, a state legislature may empower a community to issue bonds and donate the proceeds for the construction of railroad facilities. In May 1867 the legislature authorized the town of Queensbury in Warren County to borrow $100,000 and to donate the sum for the building of a line from Glens Falls to some point on the Whitehall & Saratoga road. Years later, the town brought suit in federal court to have its securities declared void on the ground, among others, that the legislature had no authority to order money taken from the people by taxation to be given to a private corporation. The case was carried to the United States Supreme Court, which held against the town. The Court pointed out that the legislation authorizing the gift was not mandatory but permissive and that its operation depended on the approval of a majority of the community's taxpayers. Since there was nothing in the state constitution prohibiting the passage of such a law, the court held that the act was valid.[24]

Prior to 1869, communities got permission to assist railroad construction through special legislative acts. For a while this procedure worked very well, but the large number of applications that poured into the Assembly and Senate after the Civil War not only encouraged fraud and favoritism, but also consumed entirely too much of the lawmakers' time. To reduce the pressure of local interests and to secure a greater degree of uniformity in bonding, the legislature passed the General Bonding Act of 1869.[25] The law provided that, whenever a majority of taxpayers in a municipality representing a majority of its taxable property requested in writing that their community be allowed to bond itself in aid of a railroad, the county judge must hold a public hearing to determine the validity of the petition.[26] If the application conformed to the requirements of the law, the judge was empowered to name three resident taxpayers to serve as municipal railroad commissioners. These officials were authorized to negotiate the sale of the community's bonds and represent it at all stockholders' or bondholders' meetings. Railroad-aid bonds might not be sold or exchanged for less than par, bore 7 per cent interest, and were limited in amount to 20 per cent of the assessed valuation of the community's property. The commissioners were empowered to dispose of the municipality's investment for par value or better at any time; but they could not sell its securities, prior to the retirement of its own bonds, for less than par without the approval of a majority of the taxpayers representing a majority of the community's taxable property. The law provided further that each locality should establish a sinking fund within three years after issuing its bonds and pay into it annually a sum sufficient to liquidate the debt within 25 years.

The framers of this bonding law hoped that its provisions would limit local aid to worthwhile enterprises and protect communities from unscrupulous railroad promoters. But the law never worked as its supporters planned. During the six years of its existence, a virtual epidemic of railroad construction swept over the state. Every city and hamlet considered itself entitled to modern transportation facilities, and speculators and contractors were at hand to promise them exactly what they wanted.

The experience of the city of Utica in bonding on behalf of the Utica, Clinton & Binghamton is an example of some of the difficulties encountered by other communities.[27] In 1871 the opponents of municipal aid to this line challenged the validity of the city's bonding petitions on the ground that many names on them had been irregularly or fraudulently obtained. The hearing before the county judge revealed the names of hundreds of disqualified people — property owners who were tax exempt, administrators, agents, executors, guardians, and trustees. Scores listed themselves as property owners and taxpayers by reason of owning bank, railroad, or other stocks. Some failed to indicate their first name, others signed as many as seven times. The court justified this latter action on the ground that a taxpayer might hold property in various parts of the city and "if he stands on the rolls as a taxpayer in three different wards, and is so counted, but is counted but once on the consents, then his name will be reckoned but once in favor of bonding and twice against it, which would be clearly contrary to his intention and most unjust in its result." The hearing was complicated further by the disclosure that the county judge before whom the case was being tried was one of the petitioners for public aid to the road. Nonetheless, the court approved the application and the city bonded itself for $200,000.

Many bonding petitions were challenged in the courts, but only a few were contested successfully. During the period in which the 1869 law was in operation, state courts, particularly the lower ones, ruled liberally in favor of the supporters of municipal aid in their interpretation of the law. Even petitions containing signatures of persons induced by bribes to sign were held valid.[28] A large number of early bonding cases involved the right of a petitioner to withdraw his consent. In the town of Greene, the opponents of municipal aid to a projected railroad from the Greene to Chenango Forks challenged the petition's validity on the ground that many persons who had originally signed it were not permitted to withdraw their approval. To the road's supporters the decision of the court was of utmost importance, for, if anyone were permitted to withdraw his consent, the application would lack the required number of names. The judge ruled that a signature on a bonding petition was in the nature of a vote and, having given his consent, the taxpayer could not revoke it any more than he could alter his ballot after it had been cast. To allow otherwise, the court declared, would mean that future hearings on bonding petitions would scarcely attain the dignity of a political caucus:

It is very easy to discover how, in a town with a population as large as the town of Greene, with a large number of taxpayers, honest men who desire to do in the premises what would be for the interest of the town, but influenced in their judgment and action by the arguments and opinions of their fellow townsmen, might be thus operated upon by the friends and opponents of the project and be led honestly to change their minds in regard to the propriety of aiding the railroad; and success would be apt to attend the efforts of the party which was the most vigilant and fertile in their powers of persuasion, and thus the desire of success would be the most absorbing question, while the real interests of the town might be entirely lost sight of.[29]

Since this was a lower-court decision, the opponents of local aid continued to challenge the validity of such bonding petitions. In 1873, an action comparable to that tried in Greene reached the Court of Appeals. The case was brought up on a writ of certiorari to review a decision of a Jefferson County judge in a proceeding to bond the town of Orleans on behalf of the Clayton & Theresa line. At the original hearing, opponents of municipal aid to the road had presented a statement signed by several taxpayers who had approved the petition but now asked the court to delete their names. The judge refused the request. In reviewing the case, the Court of Appeals ruled unanimously that a taxpayer who had signed a bonding petition had a right to withdraw his name at any time before the application was submitted to the county judge and, if he did so, his name and taxable property were to be excluded from the proceedings. Once the petition had been approved by the county judge, however, the signer could not withdraw his consent.[30]

According to law, a municipality that took stock in a railroad company acquired the same relation to the corporation as did an individual. Its commissioners might represent the community at meetings of the stockholders, vote for directors, and participate in other ways in directing the enterprise. Town railroad commissioners, however, seldom knew anything about railroad construction or corporate finance. Consequently, management of the company's business was usually entrusted to the promoters of the project. Shortly before the completion of the New York & Oswego Midland in 1873, 97 per cent of the road's capital stock was municipally owned. Yet, not a single town official held an office in the company or served on its board of directors. Rare indeed was the community that was fully informed about the finances of the road in which its money was invested.

For nearly fifty years municipal stockholders in the Southern Central failed to receive an annual report, a notice of a directors' meeting, or a financial statement of any kind from the company. During this period local interest in the road's affairs declined to such an extent that many communities forgot completely that they were stockholders in the line. In 1942, the city comptroller of Auburn, while rummaging through the attic of municipal building, discovered the 5000 shares of stock which the city had purchased in 1867.[31] A few days later search of the town safe at Moravia uncovered 337 shares in the line.[32] In 1921, the Supervisor of Owego accidentally came upon the 2900 shares owned by the community.[33] The town of Cato never bothered to exchange its holdings when the Southern Central was reorganized in 1895 and, in 1951, still retained its old stock certificate.[34] There is nothing in the records to indicate that the towns of Sterling, Ira, Brutus, Locke, Groton, Harford, Richford, Berkshire, or Newark Valley ever disposed of their securities. It is quite possible that this stock was destroyed. Or, what is more probable, it is lost in the debris of records that is characteristic of so many town clerks' offices.

The bankruptcy of the Pennsylvania & Sodus Bay in 1874 came as a complete surprise to the people of Seneca Falls, who had invested $200,000 in the enterprise. The town board immediately hired an auditor and ordered him to investigate the road's accounts, but the company's directors for some time refused to permit anyone to examine the books or to allow any of its papers to be taken for publication.[35] The Rochester, Nunda & Pennsylvania, in which seven localities had invested $505,000, operated for five years without submitting a single report to its stockholders. Embittered by the absence of dividends and by rumors of the line's failure, a taxpayers' association in the town of Nunda wrote to the road's officials denouncing the policy of secrecy and demanding a complete statement of the company's financial condition.

In nearly every instance, the committee complained, information released by the directors was "nothing more than idle gossip or reports set afloat to quiet an anxious and interested people." [36] When no report was forthcoming, the association called a meeting of towns along the route to discuss possible action against the officials. As as result, a committee representing the municipal stockholders confronted the management with a list of ten searching questions relating to salaries, debts, bonds, mortgages, stock, and the prospects of the line. But the officials of the company took the position that it was "not good policy to publish these facts to the world" and declined to answer any of them. The treasurer even refused to reveal the amount of money the officers had advanced to the road or what collateral was taken by them as security for the loans. The committee discovered that the company's outstanding debt totaled about $240,000, but in their report back to the towns the investigators confessed that they could not learn "to whom this sum was due, nor are we prepared to say that it is all the said directors are owing, but it is all the figures given or that we were able to get from the directors." Moreover, the committee declared, the directors had neither funds nor definite plans for the future, but sat around "Micawber-like, waiting for something to turn up." [37]

In an effort to spread the debt burden over several years and to assure holders of railroad-aid bonds that the obligations would be paid, the General Bonding Act of 1869 provided that all taxes (except those for schools and roads) collected on railroad property within a municipality should be turned over to the county treasurer, who was required to set up a sinking fund for redemption of the community's securities. This provision was based on the theory that, by bonding itself to aid railroad construction, a municipality created new taxable property and, consequently, it had a claim upon the taxes assessed on this property as long as its bonds remained unpaid. Supporters of local aid to railroads hailed this section of the law as evidence of the soundness of the bonding system. The promoters of the New York & Oswego Midland cited it frequently as an argument in favor of municipal aid for their road. A Norwich editor declared: "If the Midland be worth no more than fifty cents on the dollar at the end of thirty years the amount so realized, added to the sinking fund now provided for, will redeem the bonds in full and leave a surplus in the town treasury." [38] Once they had bonded themselves, however, few localities paid any attention to this statutory requirement.[39] In 1875 only 10 per cent of the communities in the state with outstanding railroad-aid bonds had made any provision for the payment of their obligations. Enthusiastic local officials freely predicted that the return on the stock would be more than enough to pay the interest on their bonds, but the Panic of 1873 plunged many roads into bankruptcy and dispelled forever most communities' hopes of receiving dividends on their investment.

Meanwhile, failure to adhere to the sinking-fund law cost the towns hundreds of thousands of dollars since the taxes collected on railroad property within the communities were diverted by the counties to pay their share of the state's general property tax. In 1888, several towns in Ulster county sued to compel the county treasurer to set aside such assessments for redemption of their bonds. After much litigation the courts affirmed the right of localities to all taxes that were collected from railroad property.[40] The counties, in turn, sought reimbursement from the state. In 1899, the Court of Appeals upheld their claim and the state refunded to 40 counties approximately $1,000,000 in illegally collected taxes.[41]

The failure to establish a sinking fund or to provide otherwise for amortization of railroad-aid debts affected adversely the financial standing of many communities. The town of Delhi, which had paid nothing on the principal of bonds it had issued in behalf of the New York & Oswego Midland, had to pay a premium of 2 per cent interest when they were refunded thirty years later.[42] In 1893 the town of Andes was obliged to borrow $120,000 from the state to meet delinquent railroad obligations.[43] The city of Oswego paid out $1,204,500 in interest before its Midland bonds were canceled in 1918.[44] Syracuse and Rochester spent more than $6,000,000 in interest on bonds issued for railroad construction. The latter city made no provision until 1918 for paying the principal on bonds issued to aid the Rochester & State Line and the Rochester, Nunda & Pennsylvania roads.[45] The town of Thompson, which bonded itself for $148,000 in 1868, owed $180,000 in 1929.[46] In some sections of the state, these railroad-aid debts still exist. As late as 1949, the city of Syracuse and the towns of Solon, Nelson, and Thompson were paying on obligations contracted over 75 years before.

The powers of railroad commissioners were strictly circumscribed by law. They were not permitted to bind a town by an act not done in strict compliance with the statutes nor could they obligate a town by waiving certain conditions or by agreeing to substitute other terms. Attempts of overzealous officials to protect their communities by adding subscription conditions beyond those contained in the original application often led to long and costly litigation. The town of Mt. Morris, for instance, bonded itself in 1871 for $75,000 on behalf of the Rochester, Nunda & Pennsylvania. After $45,000 of the securities had been issued, the railroad commissioners tried to safeguard the town against loss by turning over the balance of the bonds to the road's officials in exchange for the company's promise to construct a line between Nunda and Mt. Morris and to have it in good running order within a year. Liquidated damages were fixed at $30,000. The company failed to fulfill its part of the bargain and the town sued to recover its money. The court held against the community on that ground that the railroad commissioners were not officers of the town but were merely agents who had no authority whatever to make a contract not expressly authorized by statute.[47]

A comparable case arose in Steuben County, where the town of Wayne had subscribed $30,000 to the capital stock of the Sodus Bay & Corning line. As an inducement to speed up the issue of the bonds, the company's president signed a contract with the commissioners in which he promised to alter the route of the road so that it would pass through the center of the town. In case of failure, the bonds were to be returned and the town reimbursed for any loss by reason of their delivery to the road. Before this agreement could be fulfilled, the railroad passed into bankruptcy. The municipality instituted legal proceedings to recover the bonds and the interest paid out on them. Again the court held against the town, declaring that the railroad was entitled to the bonds without executing an obligation of any kind. The commissioners, it ruled, had no power to execute such a contract and, consequently, the agreement was not enforceable.[48]

Legal restrictions governing the sale of municipally owned stock usually worked to the disadvantage of the communities. The courts consistently held that, in selling their securities, the commissioners had to adhere strictly to the letter of the law. Municipalities were not allowed to sell "on time," make conditional sales, or accept other securities in exchange. A check in the business world is generally treated as cash. For the purchase of town stock, a check, even if offered by a responsible party, was not considered payment until the money was received.[49]

During the famous "Erie raid" of 1869 many commissioners completely disregarded the law and made conditional sales of their securities to the agents of Jim Fisk or Jay Gould. All of these transactions were subsequently invalidated by the courts.

A few years later a comparable situation arose during the reorganization of the New York & Oswego Midland. Town Commissioners, anxious to take advantage of a temporary upswing in the price of the company's stock, found it both difficult and expensive to secure the written approval of one-half of the taxpayers representing one-half of the taxable property in their community. In Oswego, a special committee of the city council spent more than $300 on canvassers without securing a sufficient number of signers.[50] When other localities along the road experienced similar difficulties, the state legislature aided the towns in disposing of their securities by amending the bonding law to permit the town supervisor and the county judge to sell the stock at their own discretion.[51]

After January 1, 1875, municipalities were forbidden by the state constitution to donate their property or lend their money or credit to any private corporation. They could retain, if they wished, their present holdings but they could not make any further investments or exchange their securities for those of another corporation. In 1893, the railroad commissioners of Watertown sold 3,000 shares of the city's stock in the Carthage, Watertown & Sacketts Harbor line for $25,000 in cash and $275,000 in New York Central bonds. The sale was obviously illegal and the parties to the agreement were subsequently compelled to modify its terms to meet the requirements of the law.[52] As late as 1944, the state comptroller refused to permit the town of Greene to exchange its stock in the Greene railroad for first-mortgage bonds of the Delaware, Lackawanna & Western.[53] The following year, he denied a similar request by the town of Cobleskill to exchange its holdings in the Albany & Susquehanna for securities of the Delaware & Hudson Company.[54]

Only a few communities managed to violate the law with impunity. Unlike Cobleskill, the town of Colesville, which held 250 shares of Albany & Susquehanna, refused to follow the comptroller's ruling. In 1945, the municipality exchanged its securities for 250 shares of Delaware & Hudson and $43,000 (market value) of Albany & Susquehanna 4½ per cent general mortgage bonds.[55] In 1914, the city of Dunkirk exchanged 625 shares of Dunkirk, Warren & Pittsburg for 235 shares of New York Central.[56] At the same time, Theresa exchanged 438 shares of Black River & Morristown for 790 shares in the Central.[57]

To the little restort town of Alexandria goes the honor of being the greatest speculating community in the state of New York and, perhaps, the entire United States. At various times between 1875 and 1942 this town purchased stock in the Gulf, Mobile & Ohio, the Black River & Morristown, the New Orleans, Texas & Mexico, the Mobile & Ohio, and the New York Central. It has held the bonds of the Virginia Railway, the East Tennessee, Virginia & Georgia, the Buffalo, Rochester & Pittsburg, the Canadian Southern, the Mobile & Ohio, the New Orleans, Texas & Mexico, the Chicago, Rock Island & Pacific, the Great Northern, the North Pacific, the Chicago, Burlington & Quincy and the St. Louis & San Francisco.[58]

It sometimes happened in New York especially among short or branch lines, that a company was consolidated or merged with another corporation before the municipality had issued its railroad-aid bonds. In such cases, the courts have ruled, if the new company is substantially the same as the old one, the community may exchange its securities for those of the new one. If the consolidated company is essentially different, however, the subscription is void.[59] The town of Leicester, for example, bonded itself for $40,000 to aid the Northern Extension Railroad Company on condition that the bonds should not be issued until the line was completed between the village of Leicester and the town of Caledonia on the New York Central. Shortly thereafter, the Northern Extension company was consolidated with two other roads to form the Rochester, Nunda & Pennsylvania, which followed a different route and contemplated a terminus different from that of the former road. A group of taxpayers in Leicester enjoined the railroad commissioners from issuing the town bonds on the ground that they were not authorized to subscribe to the stock of the new company. The railroad, in turn, instituted a counter action to compel the town to pay its subscription. The court sided with the township and refused to give the company the relief it demanded.

To permit the commissioners to subscribe for the stock or bonds in a different company, other than the one designated in the petition, is to disregard wholly the wishes of the taxpayers and to bind them by a contract into which they never intended to enter. No subscription having been made in behalf of the town of Leicester before the consolidation . . . it is not bound by the agreement of consolidation, or affected by the laws passed to confirm and enforce it.[60]

If a town refused to issue its bonds after a subscription to a railroad's stock had been made, the company could compel performance by securing a writ of mandamus.[61] Since most municipalities which refused to turn over their securities or to pay interest on their obligations claimed fraud or insufficiency of consents, action against the community often took the form of an appeal by the company to the state legislature. The power of the legislature retroactively to waive a requirement in an enabling act or to heal a defect in the issuance of railroad-aid bonds has not been settled decisively. The weight of legal opinion, however, tends to uphold this authority. In three important cases the state's courts have denied that the power of the legislature over municipalities is unlimited.[62] The legislature, the courts have reasoned, may compel a township to maintain public improvements such as highways or to enter into contracts of a purely public character but it cannot compel a locality to aid a business which, although public in some respects, is private in others.[63] Speaking for the court in *Dunkirk Railroad v. Batchellor,* Justice James Grover declared:

A railroad corporation is public as to its franchises but private as to its ownership of property and its relation to its stockholders . . . A municiple corporation, therefore, cannot be compelled without its consent or that of its taxable inhabitants, and against its will, to become such a stockholder, and a mandatory statute requiring it to issue its bonds . . . is unconstitutional.[64]

On the other hand, there are eight important cases in which the plenary power of the legislature has been upheld.[65] An early one involved the municipality of Duanesburg. In May 1862 the railroad commissioners of the town subscribed $30,000 to the stock of the Albany & Susquehanna. A few months later, the validity of the town's bonds was challenged on the ground that the petition did not represent a majority of the taxpayers. When this contention was sustained by the courts, the officials of the company appealed to the legislature to legalize the commissioners' action. The importance of such a law was stressed in the company's request:

It is very important, in the future prosecution of the work and the sale of the balance of the bonds of other towns beyond Schoharie, that all questions as to their validity should be put at rest; and where there has been a complication in the decisions of the courts, as in this case, the legislatures have, in repeated instances, legalized the proceedings, and thus prevented litigation and promoted the ends of justice.[66]

The legislature immediately declared the bonds "valid and binding upon the town without reference to the sufficiency of proofs." [67] The Court of Appeals upheld this action. Since the legislature could establish the prerequisites of municipal action, the court argued, it might also remit or modify these conditions.[68] Apparently, there was little difference between authorizing a community to bond itself and passing a law requiring it to do so.

The general bonding law was amended in 1871 to permit municipalities to impose as a condition precedent to subscribing for stock or bonds of a company that the road be constructed through a particular part of the community. Under this legislation the town of Ellicott authorized a subscription of $200,000 to the Buffalo & Jamestown, with the provision that the line should be built through the village of Jamestown before the town bonds were delivered. The company did not meet this condition until October 1875. Meanwhile, an amendment to the state constitution prohibiting a municipality from lending its credit to a private corporation went into effect. Upon completion of the road through the village, officials of the Buffalo line demanded that the town redeem its pledge and subscribe to the road's stock. When the railroad commissioners refused, the company instituted legal proceedings to compel the town to fulfill its agreement. The passage of the state constitutional amendment, the company protested, impaired the obligation of contract. The highest state and federal courts, however, supported the town. The agreement of 1872, the United Supreme Court declared, was not a contract since the town commissioners possessed complete freedom up to January 1875 to make or refuse a subscription to the company's securities.[69]

Only a few communities such as Ft. Covington, Bombay, Chazy, and Willsboro were prevented by constitutional restrictions from aiding the construction of railroads. By 1875, a sharp revulsion had set in against the use of public credit for internal improvements. The chief problem confronting New York communities at this time was not that of finding some legal means of subsidizing the building of railroads, but rather one of discovering how they might avoid payment of obligations already incurred on their behalf.

THREE

The Period of Promotion

The phenomenal rise of industry and agriculture in New York during the nineteenth century greatly stimulated public efforts to improve the transportation and communication systems of the state. Hundreds of communities, convinced that their material progress depended on an adequate network of railroads, contributed generously toward their construction. Many confidently believed that the presence of a line would convert their little hamlet into a thriving community and double or triple land values in the region through which it passed. Shrewd promoters in quest of town bonds fired the imaginations of the people with promises of trade, travel, and dividends. Railroads were hailed as the key to prosperity and the long-sought remedy for almost every kind of economic ill. They were superior to both turnpikes and waterways. They could carry freight or passengers with unprecedented speed through the snows of winter and the floods of summer to almost every corner of the land. No longer did a farmer need to be a jack-of-all-trades. By providing a market for his surplus products and bringing in manufactured goods, the railroad made possible the development of specialized agriculture and contributed powerfully to the breakdown of rural isolation. But aside from speed and continuous service, the motives prompting municipal subsidies to railroads varied with the needs and aspirations of the communities.

The argument most frequently advanced to win public support stressed the importance of modern transportation facilities to the business life of the community. Without rail connections many towns, particularly in the rural districts of the state, could scarcely maintain any commercial existence at all. Large parts of Chenango, Otsego, and Schoharie Counties, for example, were left virtually isolated after the completion of the Erie Canal and the New York & Erie railroad. Because of their unfortunate geographical position, the economic development of the communities in this area failed to keep pace with that of the localities along these great arteries of commerce. In a determined effort to restore their former prosperity, and to infuse new life into the region, 19 of the 21 towns in Chenango County, 15 of the 24 in Otsego, and 9 of the 16 in Schoharie bonded themselves for more than $3,000,-000 to obtain rail facilities. Only two of the 24 towns on the line of the 142-mile Albany & Susquehanna which was built through the area refused to purchase stock in the road. The city of Albany voted five to one in favor of lending the company $1,000,000. "Such a result," declared an opponent of the road, "under strenuous and organized opposition for the loan, and under so full a vote, exhibits in a striking manner the preponderance of the public sentiment, not merely in favor of the project itself, but in favor of the means proposed in aid of it." [1]

Proposals for the construction of railroads often evoked the wildest enthusiasm among people along their routes. A resident of Newburgh offered a company the right of way through any part of his property except his house.[2] An Oswego businessman reported that the people of this city were "unanimous for anything in the form of a railroad whether it goes crooked or straight they seem to have no care." [3] "Mr. Swartz," observed the *Ontario Times,* "thinks a man almost wild to oppose bonding for a railroad, even if we should have to go six or eight miles to a depot." [4] The town of Ithaca bonded itself on behalf of the Cayuga Lake line with the expectation that it would become part of a great transcontinental road. "There is no reason," declared a local editor, "why the direct route from San Francisco to New York City may not be through Ithaca." [5] Lyman Murdock, a promoter of the project, was even more optimistic about its future. Construction of the line, he exclaimed, would enable the people to "ride cheap every day of the year mostly on a level through America and this world and probably some ways into the next." [6] The village of Geneva was willing to aid any road through the town no matter what direction it followed. At one time or another it offered to subsidize the building of a railroad to Ithaca, Salamanca, Dunkirk, Corning, Binghamton, and New York. In the eyes of some enthusiasts, even short branch lines had unlimited possibilities. Any town, however remote and isolated, might become a bustling community on a trunk line across the country. In 1865 an innkeeper in the tiny village of Copperstown wrote to a nephew in Canada:

The rail-road is all the talk here now. They are now surveying the route from here to Colliersville 14 miles, and from here to Richfield Springs same distance. If they get it to Richfield, they are going to extend it to Utica & Rome & connect it with the Rome & Ogdensburg Railroad & so have a through route to Canada & your place. They are going to build a Railroad from Colliersville on the Albany & Susquehanna R. Road to Rondout on the Hudson River & so connect with New York. So you see there will be a through rout from Canada to New York through Cooperstown. If they can make this go, it is thought there will be more travel on this road than on the Central.[7]

The discovery of anthracite coal in Pennsylvania dates back to colonial days. The exploitation of these valuable deposits, however, was delayed for many years, partly because the cost of transportation was high and partly because no one knew how to use the fuel efficiently. By 1850 both of these obstacles had been overcome. Meanwhile, the rapid depletion of New York forests, the adaptation of steam power to manufacturing, and the steady growth of the state's population greatly increased the demand for coal. Moreover, the successful application of coal for smelting purposes led to a sharp rise in the production of iron and a concentration and specialization of mineral industries. Whole communities soon became dependent on a cheap and adequate supply of coal for domestic as well as for industrial uses. The vital importance of this commodity was a major factor influencing municipalities to pledge their credit for railroad facilities.

The success of the first industrial enterprises in Buffalo was due largely to its accessibility by water to the coal fields of Ohio and Pennsylvania. By 1854 the city possessed 13 ironworks as well as several copper and brass foundries, but it was not until coal reached Buffalo by rail that manufacturing became important.[8] The extraordinary growth of the community during the Civil War resulted in such serious fuel shortages that the city was virtually impelled to invest $700,-000 in Buffalo, New York & Philadelphia to provide an additional avenue for the importation of coal.[9]

As early as 1851, the city of Rochester tried to establish connections with the Pennsylvania coal fields by subscribing $300,000 to the stock of the Rochester & Genesee Valley. Three years later the road had reached the town of Avon, 20 miles away, and its promoters the end of their resources. The company soon passed into the control of the Erie, but, under the unprincipled direction of such notorious speculators as Gould and Fisk, it never attained any commercial importance. The failure to develop an independent artery to the coal mines soon placed the city at the mercy of Buffalo and Syracuse dealers. By the late 1860's the latter community was receiving large quantities of Lackawanna anthracite over the municipally subsidized Syracuse & Binghamton line. At the close of the canal season each year the price of coal, which was delivered to Rochester over the monopolistic New York Central, soared $4 to $5 a ton. During the Civil War, the establishment of a People's Coöperative Coal Yard saved its patrons a considerable sum on their fuel bills, but the enterprise was forced out of business shortly after the close of hostilities.[10]

In 1869 the fuel situation became so acute that petitions urging Congress to repeal the tariff duties on coal were circulated throughout the city.[11] Charges in the local press that a conspiracy existed to control fuel prices fanned popular indignation, but a committee of the Common Council appointed to investigate these claims and to suggest measures "to relieve citizens from the extortion of the coal monopolists" denied in its report that any conspiracy existed and recommended simply that closer coöperation should be established between the coal companies and the railroads to maintain prices.[12]

By the 1870's the economic independence of the city was imperiled to such an extent that the Common Council, in order to assure the community a cheap and continuous supply of coal, borrowed $750,000 to subsidize construction of the Rochester & State Line and the Rochester, Nunda & Pennsylvania. Both of these roads were plunged into bankruptcy by the Panic of 1873. But they were soon reorganized and the municipal stockholders compensated for their financial losses by the great commercial advantage derived from the operation of the reconstructed companies. By the 1880's, coal, lumber, and oil were being transported over these lines in great quantities.[13]

An agreement in 1870 between the New York & Oswego Midland and the Delaware & Hudson Canal Company for the distribution of the latter's anthracite coal led to the building of several short municipally financed branches to the Midland system. The Utica, Clinton & Binghamton, the Delhi & Middletown, the Rome & Clinton and the Utica,

Chenango & Cortland were built primarily as coal carriers. Promoters of the Rome & Clinton estimated that the construction of the road would save the people of Rome $40,000 annually in fuel costs alone.[14] In Utica, supporters of public aid for the Utica, Clinton & Binghamton stressed the difficulty of securing capital for any business in the community that depended upon steam power. The city's coal supply, they charged, was both uncertain and expensive, especially during the suspension of canal navigation when freight rates over the New York Central became ruinously high. The construction of a road to Binghamton, they contended, would "introduce to Utica the famous Lehigh coal, the Barclay coal, the Blossburg coal, and the Smith Valley coal from the Delaware & Hudson Co.; Utica would thus at once and by this single effort become the depot and distributing and competive point for every desirable variety of coal mined in Pennsylvania." [15] Upon its completion to the main line of the Midland in 1871, this road became the most important route for the delivery of coal and oil into the city. By breaking the fuel monopoly of the Syracuse and Albany coal dealers, it contributed greatly to the industrial development and economic independence of Utica.

The promise of cheap coal was the strongest argument put forth in support of public aid for the Syracuse & Chenango Valley, the Cazenovia & DeRuyter, the Buffalo & Jamestown, the Middleburgh & Schoharie, the Cherry Valley, Sharon & Albany, the Ithaca & Geneva, the Southern Central, and the Utica, Chenango & Susquehanna Valley lines. "Let us remember," exclaimed an advocate of the Pennsylvania & Sodus Bay, "that this is to be a coal road; that as a coal road alone it will pay for itself in a few years. We want a railroad to open a coal mine at our doors." [16] Slogans such as "Three Hours to the Coal Fields," "This is a Coal Road not Wood," and "Old King Coal" appeared frequently in the promotional literature of the times.

Many localities were induced to pledge their credit for railroad facilities by assurances that real estate values would increase sharply once the road was built. Hundreds of hypothetical examples purporting to show the salutary effect of railroads on land values appeared in the farm journals and in the press throughout the state. The promoters of the New York & Oswego Midland promised inhabitants of Preston, in Chenango county, an increase of at least $10 an acre if the line passed through their community.[17] Property values in the town of Delhi, in

Delaware county, were reported to have advanced 100 per cent on the "mere prospect" of obtaining a road.[18] Supporters of a railroad through Canandaigua estimated that if the village would bond itself for $50,000, its taxes would increase "only $500 per annum for twenty-five years, while the value of our lands would be increased at the very lowest computation not less than $75,000, at once." [19] The people along the route of the Cayuga Lake railroad were informed that if they built the line out of their own pockets and then gave it away, they would still profit heavily from increased property values.[20] During a debate in the New York State Constitutional Convention of 1867 over a resolution to prohibit municipal aid to private corporations, one delegate claimed that property values jumped 80 per cent in three years after the completion of a railroad through the town of Rhinebeck.[21] The promoters of the Albany & Susquehanna laid great stress on the effect that the construction of the line would have on the value of the land along the route. A prospectus of the company in 1855 declared: "The building of the road will add five millions of dollars to the taxable property of the several counties through which it will pass; and while the towns are only asked to subscribe one-fifth of that sum, they will have the benefit of taxing the whole value of the road." [22]

Agricultural journals frequently alluded to the rise in value of farm lands served by railroads and the steady decline in price of those without such connections. In 1848, the Jefferson County Agricultural Society predicted that if the towns would build a line from Watertown to Ogdensburg, the farmers in the area would profit by nearly $1,000,000 in the form of increased prices and land values.[23] The *American Agriculturalist* concluded that the appreciation of property resulting from improved transportation facilities was sufficient to pay the entire cost of all the railroads constructed in the county.[24]

Some towns with limited and expensive means of transportation feared that competition from their more fortunate neighbors would result in the emigration of their more enterprising residents. The people in Schoharie and Otsego counties were warned that if the Albany & Susquehanna line were abandoned because it lacked town support, their representation in the legislature would suffer severely after the next apportionment.[25] It was fear of depopulation that led the town of Lansing[26] to aid the Western Extension of the Midland and the town of Geneva to bond itself on behalf of the Geneva & Ithaca.[27] A Norwich editor described the consequences he feared would follow the failure of communities in Chenango county to subsidize construction of the New York & Oswego Midland:

Our population is decreasing. The value of our farm lands is depreciated, we have no accessions from without, and are being constantly drained of all our industrial and pecuniary resources. If we do not take measures, and that speedily, to remedy this, *we are ruined;* our villages will lose their inhabitants, and village property will be comparatively worthless—farm lands will decrease in value from year to year, and it will not, it cannot be long, before we shall be the center only of decay and material death while the world around us is engaging in the activities and progress of life, and reaping its certain benefits and rewards.[28]

Other considerations sometimes played an important part in winning community support for a projected road. The town of Greene, for example, agreed to build a railroad from the center of the village to Chenango Forks if the Delaware, Lackawanna & Western would lease it, upon completion, at an annual rental of 6 per cent on the capital stock.[29] The municipalities of Rome, Kirkland, and Westmoreland bonded themselves to assist the Rome & Clinton road with the understanding that the New York & Oswego Midland would operate the line and pay an annual rental of $25,000.[30] Utica refused to aid the Utica, Clinton & Binghamton until the company guaranteed the payment of 5 per cent dividends on the city's investment.[31] Middletown pledged $100,000 toward the building of the New York & Oswego Midland on condition that the company should locate its car-repair shops within the town.[32] The promoters of the Rochester, Nunda, and Pennsylvania had to offer the same inducement to secure a loan of $150,000 from the city of Rochester. These shops, the road claimed, would create 400 new jobs, stimulate home building, and increase the city's taxable property by $1,200,000.[33]

In appeals for public support, the prospectus that set forth in glowing terms the anticipated benefits to the community as well as the high hopes of the promoters played a significant role. These arguments were reiterated by newspapers in their advertising and editorial columns and by company speakers as they passed from town to town in search of funds. Surveys, allegedly conducted by prominent and experienced engineers and amply supported by maps and charts, were circulated to show that the proposed line followed easy grades and passed through areas rich in markets and raw materials. "It will be a great advantage," wrote the president of the Albany & Susquehanna, "if a map can be prepared showing the great line we make by the road from Little Valley, etc. to Cincinnati & St. Louis. *There is much in it.*" [34] A report on the Black River & Utica, which was projected through the barren and rocky Adirondack mountains, stressed the natural advantages of the country and the relative ease with which the line could be built.[35] Incredible as it may seem, the engineers who surveyed the proposed Midland road from Oswego through the desolate Catskill region to New York made the following report on the route they chose:

> It is ascertained from actual surveys to be more than 70 miles nearer from Syracuse to New York than by the Central to Albany with much lower grades than the Erie. There are no expensive bridges to be built, and no heavy cutting to be done on any part of the line. The country abounds in all material with which to build a road except iron. It traverses a belt of fertile country, densely populated with industrious people, thro' the central part of the state over 200 miles in length and 50 miles in breadth, full of water-power, substantially destitute of railroad facilities, crossing the Chenango Canal, the Albany & Susquehanna Railroad, and the valleys of Chenango, Unadilla, Susquehanna and the two Delawares at right angles, commanding their business for a long distance on either side and converting them into tributaries. No road in the State or in the United States, of its length would be better sustained by freight and travel than this. It neither runs through nor passes by any waste land or barren track or country, as does the Erie and Central.[36]

When such claims were questioned, prominent citizens and experts in railroad construction were frequently called to testify for the company. This testimony was followed by new efforts at pamphleteering and revised estimates of the road's business which were usually wilder and more visionary than the first reports. Occasionally a promoter arranged for an investigation. A visit to the coal fields of Pennsylvania convinced the Buffalo Common Council of the wisdom of subsidizing the Buffalo & Washington.[37] In Utica, a citizens' committee headed by Roscoe Conkling and John Butterfield inspected the proposed Black River & Utica route before the city bonded for its construction.[38]

But prospectuses and notices alone were seldom sufficient to induce whole communities to pledge their credit on behalf of a railroad. Virtually every company in the state had to conduct a systematic canvass for signatures to the bonding petitions. Some municipalities were designated as key towns — that is, communities whose decisions would profoundly influence the action of others. In Schoharie county, for example, Esperance, Richmondville, Schoharie, Seward, and Summit refused to bond themselves in behalf of the Albany & Susquehanna until they knew the outcome in Cobleskill. A director of the company, who was in charge of securing the necessary consents, informed the road's president that if "this town is secured the other towns in the county will go right into it and will take the amount proportioned to them very soon." [39] The communities along the Rochester & State Line threatened to withdraw their pledges unless the city of Rochester contributed toward its construction.[40]

Promotional literature was usually carefully prepared and skillfully disseminated. The greatest precautions were taken to show that the contemplated aid would create no financial burden on the taxpayers. On the contrary, the promoters declared, the failure to provide adequate railroad facilities would tell far more heavily on the property owner than the cost of their construction. No one expected, they reasoned, that the municipalities should bear the entire expense of the undertaking. All that the company was seeking, they would explain, was a public investment during the initial stages of the road's development large enough to entice private capital to support the project. Ezra P. Prentice, President of the Albany & Susquehanna, exhorted his canvassers to use the utmost care in presenting the company's case:

It is quite important that the explanation should be very *minute* and plain. In the country such documents are read more carefully than in the city, and there is not always the same basis of general information that would render the demonstration of axioms unnecessary — The farmer family lives in the kitchen, and at evening one of the boys who has been to school more than his parents had the opportunity to do, will read it aloud and the kitchen cabinet will discuss it, as it appears to them in all its bearings. I am as times go, a very good sort of a Democrat with a full party share of confidence in the masses, yet I would rather trust a genuine well turned sophism, stated with utmost confidence and frankness, and made very *plain*, to influence the *crowd*, than all the half-told truths that have been enunciated since tongues and pens came into general use.[41]

In towns where the opposition was particularly strong, officials of the road often did the canvassing themselves. The directors of the Albany & Susquehanna were expert solicitors. "Mr. Ramsay, Mr. Courter, Mr. Ford, and Mr. Northrup," wrote one of the officials of the company, "would carry every town they went into — They *go for that purpose* and they do not leave their work half done." [42] Ramsay, who eventually became president of the Susquehanna company, made hundreds of personal calls to win over those who were opposed to the line's construction. For this additional service he retained as his commission 2 per cent of the community's investment.[43] President William E. Pierson converted scores of farmers to support of the Pennsylvania & Sodus Bay by offering exorbitant prices for the right of way through their property. Special canvassers along this route were paid as high as $12 for each name they secured to the bonding petitions.[44]

Public meetings afforded promoters an excellent opportunity to arouse enthusiasm and influence the taxpayers. As early as 1831, a Goshen editor reported: "It is almost impossible to open a paper without finding an account of some railroad meeting. An epidemic on this subject seems to be as prevalent as influenza." [45] These gatherings were usually local affairs, but occasionally they involved several counties or states. In December 1865, delegates from a number of counties along the route of the New York & Oswego Midland convened in New York City and petitioned the legislature for permission to bond their towns for the road.[46] A prospectus of the Albany & Susquehanna stated that its directors proposed to hold "the following series of meetings for the purpose of recommending this important enterprise to the favorable consideration of the people of the counties of Schoharie, Otsego, Delaware, Chenango, and Broome . . ." [47] In 1869 delegates from several states and provinces in Canada convened at Oswego for the purpose of promoting a transcontinental road from Portland, Maine, through Oswego to the Pacific coast.[48] These gatherings frequently turned into community picnics replete with music, fireworks, and free beer. A meeting held at Sherburne to promote interest in a line between Utica and Binghamton "opened with the ringing of bells, firing a cannon and strains of music by the brass band; a procession formed at two o'clock and marched to the Free Church, which was filled with ladies and gentlemen." [49] The little town of Norwich closed an exciting three day convention by adopting the following resolution: "Resolved, as the sense of this meeting, that the town of Norwich will pay its due share of the cost of a railroad from Syracuse or Oswego to Newburgh or New York, passing through the town of Norwich UP TO THE SUM OF ONE MILLION DOLLARS." [50]

The local press always described these audiences as solid, thoughtful, taxpaying citizens who were genuinely interested in community progress; those who refused to endorse the enterprise were characterized as "ol' fogies," "Rip Van Winkles," or "sour bellies." Great care was taken to convey the impression that supporters of a projected road were a true cross section of local society. "Our meeting," declared the *Chenango Telegraph,* "was composed of men of every rank: The Banker and the Mechanic; the Farmer and the man of leisure; the Merchant and the Laborer; as well as the professional man, were all there, and evinced their interest in the great work in which they are about to engage." [51] Women were especially urged to attend these gatherings. Notices announcing a series of town meetings to promote the construction of a road through the Chenango Valley stated that "the presence of the Ladies at these meetings is most cordially invited. If the men are found wanting, they can and will build the road." [52]

The principal speaker of the day was usually a prominent local citizen. His presence inspired the crowd with confidence and helped to dispel suggestions of absentee control. He was followed by company spellbinders who presented carefully prepared statements about the cost and prospects of the road and the amount of aid expected from the town. The flamboyant DeWitt Littlejohn, President of the New York & Oswego Midland, had a reputation for being able to lead his audience right up to the point of "Hurrah for the Midland." The city of Oswego, which hesitated for two years to bond itself for $600,000, was reported ready to pledge $1,5000,000 after Littlejohn addressed a meeting there.[53] In Skaneateles, an observer declared that "his flowery speech bewildered the audience in such a manner that they were ready to bond immediately. The managers anticipating this result, had previously prepared to receive the signatures to the petitions." [54]

In their quest for town bonds railroad promoters capitalized heavily on intercity and intertown rivalry. Alternative routes were often surveyed through competing trade centers in order to get communities to bid against each other. All the towns wanted the railroad to run within their boundaries and those that offered the most financial support were the ones most likely to get the line. Where uncertainty existed, the promoters generally warned the towns to bond conditionally. The final determination of a route usually waited on the outcome of the bonding process. "The point seemed to be," lamented a Candor editor, "that if we would consent to bond for $60,000 the road would pass a little above the upper end of our village while if we did not bond, the road would pass somewhat further north and thus leave us out in the cold." [55]

When Rome, Utica, and Herkimer vied with one another to become the southern terminus of the Black River & Utica road, company officials announced that the route would be determined by the most favorable replies to two questions: First, what would be the cost of fifteen or twenty acres of land lying along the Erie canal? Second, what amount of public and private stock would the municipality pledge toward construction of the road? After a hectic campaign, the city of Utica secured the depot primarily because it subscribed $250,000.[56] The towns of Waterloo, Geneva, and Seneca Falls engaged in a spirited contest to become the northern terminus of the Pennsylvania & Sodus Bay. "If we are not prepared to say that our village may be fenced in, whitewashed and declared finished," declared the *Geneva Gazette*, "we should respond to overtures made for promoting our material interests by prompt and decided action." [57] But the community's bid of $100,000 was too low. Seneca Falls put up $200,000 and the company agreed to run the road through that town.

The selection of the New York & Oswego Midland's line, which zigzagged 250 miles across the state in search of municipal bonds, was delayed for more than three years by local rivalries. During this period the company repeatedly threatened to follow an alternative route in order to speed up the bonding process or to compel communities to increase the amount of their subscriptions. A communication addressed to people along the proposed route declared that the company was determined not to begin construction until enough municipal bonds were available. "If better lines can be found," the statement warned, "or towns withold their aid, we feel at liberty, in carrying out our determination . . . to reconsider our action and make necessary changes." [58] Syracuse, from which the Midland expected a subsidy of $750,000, resisted every attempt to bond the city. Out of sheer spite the company's officials then chose a circuitous route around Oneida Lake. "The idea of getting Oneida North Shore trade," complained an opponent of the road, "seems to make many foolish." [59] When the town of Hamilton, in Madison county, refused to subscribe to the Midland's stock, the line went "over the hill" by way of Eaton, principally because this community promised a subscription of $150,000.[60] The Midland's successor, the New York, Ontario & Western, corrected this mistake in construction by building a branch line around Eaton hill, which saved the company $10,000 annually in operating expenses.[61] The Utica, Clinton & Binghamton, a branch of the Midland, halted its track on the outskirts of Utica until the city subscribed $200,000 to the road.[62] In the spring of 1870, the town of Phelps in Ontario county bonded itself for $130,000 for construction of the Sodus Point & Southern on condition that the road should run through the village. After approximately $33,000 worth of the securities had been sold, the town officials refused to issue more on the ground that the petition bonding the municipality was invalid. The directors of the company promptly retaliated by altering the route so that it passed through a neighboring community.[63] "Let them [the towns of Livingston and Clermont] be told," wrote an official of the Rhinebeck & Connecticut, "that unless they co-operate the Pleasantville cut off will be made and thus they will loose [sic] the road. The line thence to Hudson may be mentioned to aid in waking them up." [64]

The local press was one of the most important elements in the promotion of local aid to railroads. Scarcely a newspaper in the state opposed the subsidy system. News space was given freely while editors aroused popular interest by frequent discussions of the proposed route, the anticipated business of the line, and the amount of public aid it expected to receive. During bonding controversy the press carried many items which extolled the part played by railroads in the growth of the nation's cities or which attributed the retrogression of certain communities to the lack of rail facilities. Advertisements featured the sale of municipal bonds or called people's attention to approaching railroad meetings. Enthusiasm was kept at fever pitch by exciting word pictures of the growth of the transportation network and iron-horse accomplishments. "When our sluggish blood," wrote an Ithaca editor, "purified by the steam breath, is driven, dancing, through the iron arteries of trade, to all the palpitating surfaces and extremities of this wonderful land, we may say we *live*." [65]

In Ontario County, the opponents of local aid charged that the *Geneva Courier* and *Geneva Gazette* published only material favorable to town bonding.[66] John H. Selkreg, proprietor of the *Ithaca Journal* and a director of the Ithaca & Athens, refused to print any communications attacking that road's management.[67] Editorials in Oswego newspapers urging the building of the New York & Oswego Midland often surpassed the claims of the company's most rabid supporters. Neither the *Palladium* nor the *Times-Advertiser* would publish any material opposing the line's construction. "Mr. Littlejohn," wrote one critic of the road, "is still working at his Midland. There is an increasing opposition to it in this place but we can get no publications against it by our newspapers." [68] When Gerrit Smith, the famous abolitionist and wealthy Oswego landowner, attacked the road by circulating printed letters, the *Times* assailed him as an enemy of the city and canceled his subscription to the paper.[69]

Many individuals aided in bonding of their communities. Some were motivated by the merits of the project; others did so out of self-interest. Clergyman and professional people were especially urged by promoters to become actively identified with the construction of the road. The association of prominent and respected local citizens with the company tended to encourage small farmers and merchants, who were generally reluctant to speculate in railroad securities, to vote in favor of subsidizing the undertaking. Dr. John M. Cook, who directed the bonding of the town of Worcester for the Albany & Susquehanna, reported to the president of the road: "A. Beecher, Esq. is now ackting [*sic*] with us and we think the town safe — his influence will be felt for good in other towns in this county, and also in Schoharie County. He has published an article in favor of the road. You will find it in the *Republican & Democrat* signed Taxpayer." [70] Gerrit Smith distributed thousands of broadsides and printed letters urging municipal aid for the Lake Ontario Shore road. "It is provoking," wrote one of his business agents, "that Oswego takes so poor hold of the Lake Shore Road leaving you to do about as much as the remainder of Oswego." [71] The *Ithaca Journal* attributed the bonding of that community for the Geneva & Ithaca to Merritt L. Wood, "through whose indomitable energy, perseverance and unanswerable arguments the requisite number of names have been procured and some to spare." [72] John Lutes and Charles W. Briggs, mayors of Rochester, often appeared before the Common Council to urge public aid for railroad facilities. James Wadsworth, the mayor of Buffalo, spearheaded the drive to obtain a municipal subsidy of $150,000 for the Buffalo, Brantford & Goderich.

Some companies were fortunate enough to have men in the state legislature on their payrolls. Joseph H. Ramsay, president and moving spirit of the Albany & Susquehanna, was for several years chairman of a Senate committee on railroads. "For more than ten years past," declared the *Albany Evening Journal*, "he has haunted the capitol from the beginning to the close of every session converting Senators and talking with Assemblymen until the projects for granting aid to the Susquehanna came to be known as Ramsay's bills." [73] Senator Henry R. Low, of Middletown, and Speaker of the Assembly DeWitt C. Littlejohn, of Oswego, worked hand in glove to obtain special favors for the New York & Oswego Midland.[74] Principally because of their leadership in the legislature, all municipal bonds issued in behalf of the Midland were exempt from taxation, and savings banks for the first time were permitted to invest in these securities. Railroad rings exerted enormous influence in the legislature. In 1870 state aid was voted to five railroads with a tacit understanding that the friends of each should vote for all.[75]

Prior to the panic of 1873, the opposition to municipal aid for railroads was numerically small and ineffectively organized. It was composed mainly of tax reformers, friends of rival railroads, conservative groups who raised the cry of socialism, and a number of well-meaning persons who deplored the use of public funds for the promotion of private enterprise. Some even felt that the extension of public credit, if continued and expanded, would ultimately weaken and destroy the American system of private property. Speaking in support of a resolution to restrict the borrowing powers of municipalities, John Ramsay, a delegate to the Constitutional Convention of 1867 declared: "Towns are not organized for the purpose of creating railroads, it is no part of their business to do so, and railroads should be organized and created and put in operation, entirely without the aid or without the action, to any extent, of the corporate powers of the towns or counties." [76] "I must confess my surprise," cried another delegate, "that any gentleman can stand on this floor and deliberately, for any length of time, argue and contend for the proposition that there is any principle whatever which will justify one class of men in taking away the property of another." [77] Gerrit Smith, an outspoken critic of the New York & Oswego Midland, offered the city of Oswego $20,000 "in case it can and will by fair means prevent the construction of the Midland." Smith estimated that the tax burden resulting from the city's proposed subsidy of $600,000 to the line would reduce the value of his $750,000 real estate holdings by nearly $200,000.[78] But so overwhelming was the sentiment in favor of the enterprise that Smith's business manager reported that "Oswego could not raise a single man to oppose Littlejohn's Midland legislation." [79]

Canal interests, as well as the owners of stagecoaches, turnpikes, bridge companies, and other transportation enterprises, were natural opponents of municipal aid. The most vigorous opposition to the Pennsylvania & Sodus Bay came from the owners of the Seneca Steamship Company, which pledged $10,000 to defeat the project.[80] Lake-boat operators, wagoners, and tavern interests conducted a house-to-house canvass against public assistance to the New York & Canada. A small segment of the press, notably the *New York Times, New York Tribune, Albany Argus, Albany Evening Journal, Buffalo Commercial-Advertiser, Utica Observer,* and the *Nation,* opposed the subsidy system, partly on principle but chiefly on the ground that it led to the needless multiplication of short marginal lines. Where additional railroad facilities are needed, they argued, private capital would build them without government help. The *Evening Journal* was particularly hostile to town bonding. "Thaw of the Journal," declared a canvasser in Otego, "has done much harm — his insinuations & Bugaboos are taken by the enemies of the road as facts. It takes a powerful influence to overcome it. I must say it looks doubtful whether the requisite amount can be had from the town." [81]

The bankruptcy of some lines, particularly those in which fraud or mismanagement contributed to the disaster, was sometimes offered as evidence of unsoundness of municipal bonding system. The profits, complained the opponents of local aid, go to the promoters; the losses always fall on the communities. Efforts to bond the town of Varick for the Geneva & Ithaca road failed when a court investigation disclosed that canvassers were being paid as much as $40 a name for obtaining signatures on petitions.[82] "Shall we follow the example of Sterling," cried an opponent of the Midland, "that has shortly to pay $60,000 on its bonds for a railroad owned by schemers who fooled the people of Little Sodus into debt? Shall we imitate Troy which owns the Union Railroad and pays $28,000 per annum for the privilege?" [83] The few shovels of dirt thrown up at the opening ceremonies of the Buffalo & Belmont, the Lake Ontario, Auburn & New York, the Delhi & Middletown, and the Utica, Ogdensburg & New York might well have been the only earth moved as far as any value or use came from the roads.[84]

The retirement, in 1938, of a number of municipal bonds issued for construction of railroads that were never completed inspired the editor of a Cooperstown paper to write:

> Fates of railroads now remind us
> We should make our plans to stay,
> And, departing, leave behind us
> Kinds that time won't take away.
>
> When our children pay the mortgage
> Father made to haul the load,
> They'll not have to ask the question
> Here's the bond, but where's the road? [85]

The Albany Northern, to which the city of Albany loaned $300,000, was selling its bonds in England before it had even purchased the right of way.[86] The heavily subsidized Syracuse & Chenango Valley was plundered by a construction ring which had secured, by dubious means, a contract for building the road. At the printer's office this wily clique changed the wording of the agreement to its own advantage and company officials, having once seen the specifications, considered it unnecessary to re-read the document before giving it their approval. These alterations subsequently cost the city of Syracuse more than $100,000.[87] The construction of the New York & Oswego Midland was accompanied by shameless profiteering. The promoters of the road planned to make their fortunes from building the line, not operating it. Accordingly, they charged exorbitant fees for negotiating the sale of town bonds. The treasurer of the company, Walter M. Conkey, made as high as $100,000 a year in commissions.[88] In January 1873, just a few months before the Midland passed into bankruptcy, the salary of President Littlejohn was set at $12,500 for the years 1866 and 1867 and $25,000 for the period 1867 to 1873.[89]

Although the publicity associated with the bankruptcy of these lines failed to halt the movement for town bonding, it did cause many communities to give more careful consideration to the merits of the project in which they were about to invest. The town of Seneca bonded itself for $150,000 in favor of the Geneva & Ithaca only after a bitter factional fight between the people living in the rural areas, who opposed the road, and those who resided in the village of Geneva, who favored the line. After the vote was taken, the opponents of the project demanded that the Ontario County Board of Supervisors separate the village from the rest of the township. The board agreed. It stipulated, however, that the rural town of Seneca was to pay one-third of the railroad-aid debt.[90] Scores of localities, alarmed by the unhappy experience of their neighbors, tried to safeguard their investments by compelling railroad companies to execute certain guarantees before handing over their bonds. Some demanded that the entire amount of the subsidy be spent within their township or that they be given representation on the board of directors or that the corporation raise a certain proportion of its capital from other sources. The laws permitting the city of Rochester to aid the Rochester & State Line stipulated that $100,000 should be turned over to the company when it had obtained the right of way, another $100,000 when the road was graded, and $200,000 when the road was in running order from Rochester to Salamanca.[91] The city of Buffalo agreed to a $1,000,000 subsidy for the Buffalo & Jamestown with the understanding that the money would be delivered in installments of $75,000 for each five miles of track completed.[92] Legislation authorizing the towns north of Weedsport to aid the Southern Central required that the road should be completed between Weedsport and Lake Ontario before any municipal bonds were issued.[93] Few railroad companies were able to fulfill all the conditions laid down in these contracts. Local officials, however, were usually persuaded to ignore the restrictive provisions of the agreement either on the ground that the companies had complied with the spirit of the law or that they had completed an equivalent amount of work.

Every community had its opponents of local aid, but it was not until 1873 that their numbers became significant. As a result of the panic in that year, more than three-quarters of the publicly subsidized railroad mileage in the state passed into receivership. Scores of municipalities, where only a few years or even a few months before bonding enthusiasm had reached a fever pitch, now found themselves burdened with debt and with nothing to show for their expenditures but worthless stock certificates or abandoned railroad beds. In 1872 the railroad-aid debt of the town of Diana was equal to 80 per cent of the assessed valuation of the community's property. In Liberty it amounted to 42 per cent, in DeRuyter 42 per cent, and in Ithaca 30 per cent.[94] Munici-

pal aid to railroads in 1872 amounted to $5,631,862. The following year
it dropped to $90,000, or the lowest level since the Civil War.[95]

The reaction against the subsidy system was strongest in the rural
areas. Irate farmers, smarting under the increased weight of taxation,
seized company property or clamored for the repudiation of their
community's obligations. Local editors, who once supported municipal
bonding with almost fanatical zeal, now lashed out at railroad corporations as fraudulant monopolies and excoriated their promoters as financial adventurers. At its first annual convention the New York Grange
demanded the end of railroad subsidies and the repeal of town bonding laws which, they charged, operated only in the interests of monopolies and "have already drawn millions of dollars in taxes from the
taxpayers to the pockets of designing and corrupt men, without any
corresponding advantages in return." [96]

In the Constitutional Convention of 1867, the opponents of public
aid proposed a number of amendments which would have prohibited
further grants of money or property for the construction of railroads,
but the delegates refused to adopt them. Five years later, however, a
Constitutional Commission recommended, and the voters in the general election of 1874 approved, an amendment to the State Constitution
which forbade both the state and its municipalities to give their property or lend their credit to any individual, association, corporation or
private undertaking.[97]

FOUR

A Municipally Owned Railroad

Before the Erie Canal became an important factor in the internal development of New York, the city of Albany commanded the major share of trade from the northern and western parts of the state. With the completion of the canal in 1825, however, this commercial pre-eminence was threatened because Troy, rather than Albany, was selected as its main eastern terminus. Not to be outdone, Albany attempted to assure its economic supremacy by constructing in 1831 the Mohawk & Hudson railroad between Albany and Schenectady. The successful operation of this line started a wave of retaliations and recriminations lasting more than a quarter of a century as the two rival cities vied to become the great entrepôt of western commerce.[1] When Albany capitalists sought to divert the northern trade by building a line from Schenectady to Saratoga, the Trojans countered by financing the Rensselaer & Saratoga from Troy to Ballston Spa.[2] The Ballston road languished from the outset. It was supported only by the people of Troy, possessed no lateral supplies of business, and had no agreement with its rival for the exchange of passengers and freight. Business interests in Troy then deemed it necessary to construct a railroad to Schenectady if the city was to maintain its commercial position.

At the time the Schenectady & Troy line was proposed, its sponsors were confident that they could easily obtain the active support of the moneyed men of the community. Private capital, however, viewed the project as a hazardous financial undertaking. The length of the road, the paucity of local traffic, the rivalry of the Mohawk & Hudson, and the competition of the state-owned Erie Canal presented obstacles which they considered too difficult to overcome. Consequently, when private investors refused to assume the initial financial risk, the municipality of Troy agreed to advance the necessary funds. In 1836, the state legislature authorized the city to sell $500,000 of its bonds and to invest the proceeds in the stock of the road.[3] But the Panic of 1837 shook the confidence of the Troy Common Council in the enterprise. Almost four years passed before any construction was undertaken.

Early in 1840 the Trojans began to act. The prime mover and guiding spirit of Troy's railroad ventures was Jonas C. Heartt, Whig mayor of the city. Shortly after his election in the spring of 1840, he called the common council into special session to demand prompt sale of the city's bonds and immediate construction of the road. "The Western Railway," he declared, "has taken measures to ensure the completion of the whole line from Boston to Greenbush during 1841 and the time has arrived for Troy to take action and become the connecting link between the West and the East." [4] By fall, the route was surveyed and the contracts were let. But construction lagged. The laborers repeatedly struck for higher wages, iron rails purchased in England were delivered late, and the city experienced unexpected difficulty in obtaining the right of way.[5] Moreover, the cost of building the road greatly exceeded the original estimates and Troy was compelled to borrow $100,000 from the state and obtain legislative approval to increase the capital stock of the company to $650,000.[6]

Although the Troy line was only 20 miles long, it was one of the best roads in the nation. It was equipped with the latest T-shaped iron rail, followed easy grades, and crossed the Hudson River into the city over the Rensselaer & Saratoga railroad bridge.[7] The Mohawk & Hudson, on the other hand, used wooden rails, employed a complicated scheme of inclined planes to overcome heavy grades, obtained entrance into Albany by horse-drawn cars, and transferred its passengers and baggage across the Hudson by slow and cumbersome ferry boats.[8] Well might the *Troy Whig* boast that the Mohawk & Hudson would soon be abandoned in favor of a branch line from Albany to the Schenectady & Troy road in West Troy.[9]

The directors of the Mohawk & Hudson viewed the construction of the Schenectady & Troy with mounting fear and suspicion. The financial position of their road, which had never been very strong, grew steadily worse after the Panic of 1837. The operation of inclined planes at both ends of the line was a heavy expense to the company as well as a source of annoyance to the passengers. "These prolific sources of expenditures," declared an executive committee's report, "might be dispensed with by changing the termination of the road at both ends; but such changes would necessarily involve a large expenditure of money, at least $200,000 which your committee hesitate to ask or recommend at this time when the pressure is so severely felt in the money market, and in view of other existing circumstances." [10] The financial position of the company was weakened further during the summer of 1841 when a new stage line, which offered drastically reduced fares, opened between Albany and Schenectady.[11]

To meet this competition the directors of the Mohawk & Hudson adopted a policy of sharp retrenchment. Jobs were consolidated, salaries were cut, and a large number of employees were laid off.[12] But this was not enough. The company needed more money. The line's physical condition was poor. The roadbed and the rolling stock required thorough reconditioning. Declining revenues during the depression precluded purchase of the latest technical improvements and even of some necessary replacements. The successful operation of a rival line, supported by the financial resources of a thriving community, might readily force the Mohawk & Hudson into bankruptcy and establish Troy rather than Albany as the commercial center of all trade passing through the Mohawk Valley.[13]

As early as July 1838 the Mohawk & Hudson asked the Utica & Schenectady for a loan to make some badly needed repairs. The Utica line rejected the plea on the ground that it had no legal right to make such a grant.[14] The following February, the state legislature refused to lend the company $350,000 in state stock or to endorse an equal amount of the road's first-mortgage bonds.[15] Rebuffed by the legislature, the Mohawk & Hudson turned once again to the Utica & Schenectady, from which it tried unsuccessfully to obtain a guarantee for a large issue of improvement bonds.[16] At this critical moment the city of Albany, by extending prompt and generous financial assistance, saved the Mohawk & Hudson and with it, perhaps, the future prosperity of the community. In the summer of 1842, it guaranteed a $100,-000 issue of the company's bonds to remove the inclined planes at Schenectady. A year later, the city lent the road $125,000 for a similar purpose at Albany.[17] These changes enabled the line to double its speed and reduce the fare between Albany and Schenectady from 75 cents to 50 cents.[18]

The company then moved to strengthen its competitive position by negotiating with the Utica & Schenectady a series of agreements which provided for mutual preferential treatment in all matters relating to the exchange of passengers and baggage, sale of tickets, operation of through trains, and planning of time schedules.[19] This community of interest was the greatest obstacle which the Trojans faced. Their inability to break this combination or to compete successfully with it was the primary cause of their road's failure. Instead of placing business on a competitive basis by offering equal facilities to both lines, the Utica road used its power to divert trade and travel over the Albany route. It made no concessions to Troy. Its hostile policy was never relaxed or modified.

The Utica & Schenectady was by far the richest and most powerful of the railroads in operation between Albany and Buffalo. Built through a settled and prosperous area, it was able, by virtue of its strategic location, to exercise considerable influence over other companies making up the Central line of roads. But why should this line, in a position to profit heavily from the rivalry of railroads leading to Albany and Troy, seek to destroy the competition by aiding one road at the expense of the other? The explanation lies in the political and economic interests of those who controlled the company's policies. Five of its thirteen directors lived in Albany, where they had large mercantile and real-estate interests. One of them, John V. L. Pruyn, the shrewd attorney who later drew up the New York Central consolidation agreement, was not only treasurer of the Utica & Schenectady but also director, secretary, and chief counsel of both the Utica and the Albany roads. Another, Erastus Corning, the Utica & Schenectady's dominating figure and only president, was a leading citizen of Albany, having been three times elected mayor of the city. His financial interests in Albany were very great. He was president of the New York State Bank and the Albany Pier Company, and he owned an extensive iron business, from which he is reputed to have amassed a fortune of $3,000,000 by 1860.[20] When the Mohawk & Hudson was in financial difficulties during the early forties, Corning and Pruyn helped to obtain its Albany loans.[21] Later, as officers of the Utica road, they lent the Albany line more than $85,000.[22] By the latter action, the Utica & Schenectady was, in effect, underwriting the Albany road's success, for now the company as well as its officials had a stake in the future of the line.

Shortly before the completion of the Troy road, the Mohawk & Hudson proposed that the Central lines should operate as a unit in handling passenger traffic. As a result, an elaborate scheme covering immigrant travel, baggage, and mail cars was placed in operation between Albany and Rochester. Administrative costs were adjusted at the end of the year according to the mileage of the common cars; expenses for new cars and losses from fire were similarly prorated.[23] For many years, passenger travel provided the chief source of income for railroads. To protect its revenues the state restricted the transportation of property over railroads paralleling the Erie Canal either by prohibiting such traffic or by requiring the carrier to pay tolls equal to those it would have paid if the freight had gone by canal. Furthermore, most early roads were poorly constructed and were not properly equipped to haul heavy loads. In 1839, the directors of the Mohawk & Hudson resolved to abandon the transportation of freight unless this business could be made profitable.[24] With the enlargement of the Erie Canal, they predicted, freight traffic by rail "will disappear even if the rates were the same or even less." [25] Unlike the Albany line, which was required to pay tolls, the Schenectady & Troy was empowered to carry freight without restriction. This concession was an empty one, however, since way trade was negligible and through commerce was barred by a clause in the Utica & Schenectady's charter which forbade transportation of any property save baggage.[26] Under these circumstances, competition for passengers, especially through travelers to the West, became extremely keen because this traffic was the life blood of the rival roads.

During the 1840's, political and economic conditions in Europe caused immigrants to come to the United States in unprecedented numbers. In New York, "runners," who were usually paid on a commission basis by a canal or railroad company, competed for the business of transporting the newly arrived to their destinations. As this traffic increased, immigrant companies with agents in the principal European cities made contracts with American railroads to carry passengers at special rates in exchange for an agreement that the companies would not sell tickets to immigrants over competing lines.[27] Untold thousands of these people passed through the Mohawk Valley on their way to the West. Corning, who for many years handled all negotiations with the immigrant companies for transportation of their clients over the Central lines, usually required that the immigrant must travel by way of the Mohawk & Hudson. Passengers reaching Schenectady over the Troy road had to return to Albany to obtain tickets if they wanted to continue on their way.[28] Trojans frequently complained that the Utica line started its train for the West when the Troy cars were "within hearing distance, and sometimes before their advertised time of departure." [29] The high degree of operating harmony that existed among the several roads between Albany and Buffalo enabled Corning to drive hard bargains with immigrant companies and to obtain favorable terms from river- and lake-boat owners.[30] Heavy investments by the Central lines in western railroads during the early 1850's gave Corning even greater bargaining power.[31] Eastbound travelers were subjected to similar embarrassment and inconvenience. When the Schenectady & Troy tried to capture this traffic by reducing the fare between Schenectady and Troy from 50 to 25 cents, the Utica and Albany roads agreed to charge passengers the same fare from Utica to Albany as from Utica to Schenectady and refused to alter this policy until the Troy line raised its price. Within a few weeks the Trojans were compelled to submit.[32]

Even Troy's efforts to acquire mail contracts were frustrated. Reports that the Trojans were moving "heaven and earth" to obtain the award prompted the Mohawk & Hudson to appeal to Corning to intercede with the postmaster general to halt such an agreement. The president of the road wrote to Corning: "If you can suceed [sic] in bringing such influence on the department, our Line will take it at any rate without regard to compensation. It would be in the extreme mortifying to have the mail lost on the river and railroad." [33] The necessary political pressure was applied, and the Albany road retained the contract without any reduction in compensation.[34]

Efforts on the part of Troy to deal with this discrimination were always weak and ineffective. At first the Trojans tried to persuade the Albany road that its policies were unfair to the public and offered to pool all passenger receipts in a common fund to be divided on a 75–25 basis.[35] When this appeal was rejected, they sought the support of the lines west of Utica. These roads, particularly the Utica & Syracuse, were never very friendly to the domineering Corning and they would gladly have aided the Troy line had they not feared retaliation by the powerful Utica & Schenectady. In the summer of 1843, officials of the

Schenectady & Troy traveled throughout the western parts of the state to enlist the aid of hotel porters and forwarding agents in checking all baggage via the Troy line.[36] The response was so great that agents employed by the Mohawk & Hudson asked Corning to take immediate countermeasures. "Passengers to Albany," wrote one baggageman, "don't care which way they go and 9 out of 10 will go to Troy if asked." [37] At the eastern end of the line, they leased small steamers which drew alongside the New York packet ships as they approached Albany and solicited passengers to proceed by way of Troy. This pirating of business brought some increase in travel, but it disappeared when the river boats passed under control of the Central lines.[38]

Unable to divert a substantial amount of traffic to its road by these means, Troy carried its case directly to Corning: "We intend to ask for nothing," wrote the mayor of the city, "but what we then and now think was clearly right and due our road . . . We most respectfully *insist* upon our right to *claim* from your company, equal facilities, in every respect with the Mohawk & Hudson." [39] Corning refused to consider this and similar pleas on the ground that he did "not feel at liberty to answer them not being authorized to do so." [40] Appeals to the Utica & Schenectady's board of directors were equally unrewarding. "The public," the board replied on one occasion, "are too much interested in the benefits of the contract to have it broken up." [41] The Utica company did promise some slight concessions involving the sale of tickets and the employment of "runners," but these pledges were no sooner made than they were broken.

After the removal of its inclined planes in 1846, the Mohawk & Hudson's business showed marked improvement. Dividend payments were resumed and a fund was established for replacing the old wooden rails with iron ones. But traffic over the Schenectady & Troy continued to lag. While freight earnings did increase, the all-important passenger travel continued almost unchanged, and an operating deficit, which appeared for the first time in 1844, mounted steadily.[42] Consequently, in the spring of 1846, Troy again asked the Utica road for the same privileges that it afforded the Albany line. If their request were granted, the Trojans declared, they would try to compose all differences between the two companies and to discontinue any practice injurious to the Utica road. If it were rejected, they threatened to petition the state legislature for redress.[43]

The appeal was referred to a committee of directors consisting of Alonzo C. Paige of Schenectady, Gardener G. Howland of New York City, and James Hooker of Poughkeepsie. This board reported unanimously that the interests of the Utica & Schenectady, its stockholders, and the public required that all matters in dispute between the two roads should be compromised and that equal facilities should be extended to the Albany and the Troy lines. The committee also urged that the Troy road should be made a party to the existing passenger contract on the same terms as was the Mohawk & Hudson. To carry out these proposals, the board recommended the appointment of a special committee, none of whom should be residents of Albany. The plan was summarily rejected by the company's board of directors but the committee members promised the Troy road that they would press for its adoption at a future meeting and, if necessary, would appeal directly to the stockholders for support. Apparently no such appeal was ever made and, in desperation, Troy turned to the state for aid.[44]

In May 1847, the legislature passed a law requiring every railroad that intersected two or more competing lines to grant each of them equal privileges and accommodations. If any road felt that it was being treated unfairly, it was authorized to petition the governor for appointment of a commission to examine its grievances and to prescribe methods to redress them.[45] The city of Troy immediately asked for a hearing, which Governor John Young set for June 21. Over strenuous objections from the Utica & Schenectady representative, the governor named a commission consisting of John Wilkinson, Timothy Childs, and Samuel Works.[46] This board granted Troy substantially the same facilities as the Paige committee had recommended the previous May. The Schenectady & Troy was permitted to acquire an interest in any passenger or freight car jointly owned by the Utica and Albany roads, equitable time schedules were to be arranged, and the soliciting of passengers by "runners" or agents west of Utica was prohibited. The legality of this award was confirmed by the New York State Supreme Court, December 7, 1847.[47] But the business and benefits anticipated by the Trojans were never realized. The Syracuse & Utica immediately announced that it would abide by the verdict; but the rest of the Central lines, realizing that the decision's vagueness and ambiguity would make enforcement difficult, laid plans to circumvent it.[48]

In 1848, the joint operation of mail, baggage, and passenger trains was ended and the Albany & Schenectady undertook for a period of five years to supply the other roads with all necessary cars. The Troy line was excluded from this contract on the ground that the route by way of Albany was more direct.[49] This action nullified that part of the award which allowed the Troy road to participate in any joint car agreement; but it left in force those provisions aimed at the Trojans which forbade the use of "runners" to influence the direction of travel. In the same year, Wolf & Rischmiller Company, which held a monopoly of the immigrant business over the Central lines, forwarded their passengers exclusively by way of Albany.[50]

Meanwhile, the Albany road's strategic position as a link on the through route to Boston was beginning to tell heavily in its favor. With the opening of the Albany & West Stockbridge in 1842, a continuous although disconnected line of railroads extended from Buffalo to Boston. The Schenectady & Troy's lack of favorable eastern rail connections was a matter of deep concern to the city. Local traffic over the Troy line never promised to be of much importance and through trade would have to pass over the Albany lines unless such a route were built. A railroad was, therefore, built from Troy to connect with the Western Railway at Greenbush, a distance of six miles. The press of the city characterized the line as the most important ever undertaken for the interests of the community.[51] The *Whig* declared: "The Troy & Greenbush road is absolutely necessary as a feeder to the Troy & Schenectady road. Those persons, therefore, who are so fearful of an increased taxation to pay the cost of the Schenectady & Troy road should to prevent such an event, contribute liberally to the construction as the only way of avoiding the evil they apprehend." [52] The city of Troy, already heavily indebted for railroad facilities, refused to extend any financial assistance; but public meetings stirred up enthusiasm, and the road was constructed by private capital in the fall of 1845. When the trade continued to follow its customary course, the Troy & Boston was built, but this railroad was no more successful than the Greenbush road in winning for Troy the commerce of the East or the West.[53]

The Trojans now made their last and most determined bid to end their isolation and to provide their little road with favorable trade connections. "Their circumstances," declared the president of the Albany

& Schenectady, "are desperate and they will make desperate efforts to do something to better their condition." [54] In 1846, a group of enterprising businessmen formed a company to extend the Troy line along the southern bank of the Mohawk river to Utica. By joining at this point with the friendly Syracuse road, the Trojans would break the monopolistic position of the Utica & Schenectady and might disrupt harmony among the Central line of railroads.

In support of their application for a charter, the Trojans sent hundreds of memorials to the legislature, charging discrimination and unfair treatment by the Utica & Schenectady.[55] One observer reported that the city was so thoroughly canvassed that there was "scarce a business or railroad man in Troy who hasn't signed." [56] To win support from the western part of the state, the Trojans circulated petitions advocating transfer of the capital from Albany to Syracuse.[57] The Utica line responded with long protests and signed affidavits denying the validity of the allegations and charging that the construction of a parallel road would violate its rights.[58]

Public opinion in this instance generally favored the charter, and few people outside the Albany area gave the Utica & Schenectady's supporters any sympathy.[59] Frantic stockholders harassed Corning with demands for immediate action to check the projected rival road. Some pleaded that a large number of shares were held by widows and orphans who would suffer grievously if their value declined; others urged him to pacify the city of Troy "by running a line of cars especially for her accommodation." [60] While the bill authorizing the road was under legislative consideration, the stock of the Utica company fell sharply. Furthermore, the board of directors felt obliged to reduce fares drastically in order to conciliate the opposition.[61]

The Utica & Schenectady, however, had strong political friends and business allies. Livingston & Wells, a large express company, promised to exert its full influence in the legislature and "at our expense secure the services of George E. Pomeroy who shall if desired devote the whole of his time to protect the interests of the company." [62] This prominent expressman and lobbyist invented a story, which he spread in newspapers and among the legislators, that the stock of the projected Mohawk Valley road would be purchased largely by Bostonians for the purpose of developing a through line from Buffalo. The construction of the railroad, he asserted, would promote Boston at the expense of New York City. "I admit," he informed Corning, "this is a little falacious yet it will answer us a good purpose . . . The watchword here is: the N. Y. interest all are jealous of this." [63] Other friends of the Utica line offered to write articles in their local newspapers or to exert pressure on their representatives at Albany. So effective was this opposition that, when the bill came up for consideration in the Senate, its opponents were able to defeat it.[64]

This setback did not end agitation in behalf of the line, and support for the undertaking continued to grow. In 1850, a bill chartering the Valley road was again before the legislature. By this time feeling in favor of the project had become so strong that Nicholas Devereux, a prominent Utican and a director of the Utica & Schenectady, found it impossible to obtain a single signature of consequence to a remonstrance protesting its passage.[65] The following year, the legislature authorized the Mohawk Valley Railroad to construct a line along the southern bank of the Mohawk River between Schenectady and Utica. The president of the new company was a former state comptroller, Azariah Flagg, while the board of directors included such prominent names as James Roosevelt, John A. Dix, Ward Hunt, and Francis Spinner. Many Trojans felt that the millennium was at hand, the city would soon become the commercial center of the state, and their "worthless little railroad at once an 8% stock." [66] In this hope the people of Troy were doomed to bitter disappointment.

The officials of the Utica & Schenectady had not been able to prevent the chartering of the new line; but, by skillfully rigging the Mohawk Valley's securities, they might still manipulate the road to their own advantage. The outstanding capital stock of the company at this time amounted to approximately $1,250,000, upon which the first call, or 10 per cent, had been paid.[67] Outright purchase of a controlling interest, therefore, would require a substantial investment of money. In the spring of 1852 the directors of the Utica & Schenectady hit upon a plan to obtain control of the line with a minimum expenditure of capital. Francis Spinner, the secretary and treasurer of the Mohawk Valley, and Benjamin Carver, one of its most active directors, were persuaded to approach the stockholders and to induce them to cancel or reduce substantially the amount of their subscriptions. The stock was to be turned over quietly to Erastus Corning or his associate, John V. L. Pruyn. When enough had been surrendered, these two schemers were to use it to capture control of the road.[68] Spinner and Carver executed their assignment with such speed and thoroughness that by the middle of July the amount of outstanding stock had been reduced nearly 50 per cent. Only the final details of the conspiracy remained to be carried out. On July 21, Pruyn advised Corning when and how the blow would fall:

The New Board will meet here next Wednesday, when we must be prepared to name the parties to whom the surrendered stock is to be trans- ferred, and the persons we wish elected Directors — There was a disposi- tion to take an earlier day, but I named Wednesday to enable you to get home and to have time to arrange our plans somewhat before the time of meeting. It is a matter of consideration who we will take as the stockholders, and how many directors and who shall be made President, etc.[69]

On July 28, at a stockholders' meeting of the Mohawk Valley Railroad in Albany, the old board of directors was turned out of office and a new one, composed mainly of the officials of the Utica & Schenectady, took its place. Pruyn was immediately elected President while Spinner and Carver were rewarded for their services by seats on the board of directors.[70]

The position of the new management was strengthened during the ensuing weeks by additional cancellations of stock. Spinner informed Corning that all the subscription books were probably returned; but if some were not, they certainly were in no place that could do any harm. "Those from New York," he wrote, "are received, as are those from Troy, and what is better, all the subscriptions in the latter place, except the three of $1,000 each, that were legitimately subscribed came here *cancelled and erased by the parties themselves.*" [71]

Corning and his associates had scored a double victory. They eliminated the construction of a competing line; and, under the agree- ment providing for consolidation of the New York Central a year later, the Mohawk Valley's stock was taken in at a premium of 55 per cent, or $866,250. Pruyn, who had advanced only the requisite 10 per cent on his 337 shares, then paid the balance, and, for his trouble in bring- ing about the marriage of the Utica & Schenectady and the Mohawk Valley roads, he received a like amount of New York Central stock plus $18,535 in 6 per cent, 30 year bonds.[72] Corning, who held 403 shares, did even better.[73] Handsome profits, indeed, on a railroad that was never built. The final negotiations which led to the demise of the

Mohawk Valley Line were scarcely mentioned by the Troy press. That unhappy community had been preoccupied since 1850 with the financial condition and disposition of its own road.

At the time the Schenectady & Troy was projected, the cost of the undertaking was placed at $500,000. This estimate was subsequently revised to more than $700,000, largely because of a rise in the cost of materials and the slow sale of the city's bonds. To help meet the increased expense, the city obtained a state loan of $100,000.[74] Although the city expected that this debt would eventually be retired by the road's profits, the state required it to establish a sinking fund and to pay $20,000 into it annually.[75] By following this formula, the City Chamberlain was able to show a substantial reduction in the funded debt of the line at the close of each fiscal year. In 1849 the commissioners of the sinking fund reported that the obligation had been reduced from $695,000 in 1843 to $549,000.[76] Except for the annual statement, which reported the kind and amount of traffic, these figures were the only ones ever mentioned in the newspapers or discussed at meetings of the common council. The road was managed under its own charter, and the details of its financial condition did not appear on the books of the city officials.

The Trojans, of course, were deeply disappointed by the failure of their road to pay any dividends, but they attributed this condition to the hostile policy of the Utica & Schenectady and consoled themselves with the thought that, at least, the line was not losing any money. Consequently, an address by Mayor Day O. Kellogg, in March 1850, stating that the Schenectady & Troy Railroad was operating at a loss and that the floating debt of the company would soon reach $50,000, took the people of the city completely by surprise.[77] The mayor estimated that an annual appropriation of $15,000 for five years would be required to meet this deficit and pay for some necessary repairs to the road.[78] The speech touched off a spirited discussion over responsibility for the debt, the value of the road to the city, and the advisability of its sale.

While the mayor refused to assess any blame for the road's plight, the *Budget* charged that full responsibility for this "hidden debt" lay with some half dozen men, such as Russell Sage, who were interested primarily in depressing the line's value with a view to its ultimate purchase.[79] The *Whig*, on the other hand, denied that there was any attempt to conceal the debt from the people and claimed that these men had been consulted by the directors of the road simply because they were prominent citizens and leading taxpayers. They had always recommended, the paper asserted, that it was better to run the road at a small loss than to discontinue operations and thus to lose all connections with the West as well as the city's entire investment.[80]

The city of Troy had long been interested in railroad development. Although heavily taxed for the construction of their own Schenectady & Troy, many of its citizens had contributed liberally to the building of other connecting lines. In these undertakings, the people of Troy were animated by a belief that the larger the number of railroads that passed through their city, the greater would be its trade and commerce. With each new line, the Trojans expected increased prosperity, a rise in the value of real estate, and a more rapid growth of the community. Real estate did advance and business did become more prosperous; but some felt that these increases were not commensurate with the money expended while others contended that construction of the municipally owned railroad actually retarded rather than advanced the city's development. Between 1842 and 1850 the city tax rate doubled, with more than one-half of the increase going to pay the interest on the railroad debt.[81] Even the *Whig*, an early advocate and staunch supporter of the road, questioned whether it would ever repay the cost of the investment. "Real estate," it declared, "staggers under the heavy load of taxation — business languishes, for an iron hand annually takes large sums from its coffers for 'local improvement' — ; foreign capital and enterprise cannot be induced to locate here and to contribute to our growth — for with the continual drain upon it, its location here cannot be made to pay." [82]

A number of plans were advanced for solving the city's difficulty. There was support for the immediate sale of the road, a change in the board of directors, and the construction of additional connecting lines. Perhaps the most novel proposal was the so-called scrip plan advocated by State Senator Thomas B. Carroll. This scheme would have required the common council of the city to furnish each taxpayer with scrip for the amount he had been compelled to pay in taxes for the cost of the road. It further proposed that any future appropriations for the line should be kept separate from the ordinary municipal levy and that additional scrip should be issued when the annual taxes were paid.[83]

Supporters of the plan argued that its adoption would triple the value of real estate and predicted that "merchants, forwarders and manufacturers will no longer move away from Troy because of its high tax rate." [84] Opponents of the scheme protested that the distribution of the railroad's capital stock among taxpayers would be unfair to those who paid rent and that its effect would be to transfer the control of the company to the banks and a few wealthy landowners. This view was strengthened when speculators appeared among the city's 10,000 or 15,000 small taxpayers to prospect in scrip at 4 to 10 per cent.[85] The common council remonstrated vigorously against passage of the Carroll bill but it was approved by the Senate without a dissenting vote. Before the Assembly could act, however, the legislature adjourned.[86]

While the Trojans were debating the various proposals for alleviating the financial distress of their railroad, other groups not so concerned with the city's welfare began to take an interest in the fate of the Schenectady & Troy. At this time two rival lines, the New York & Harlem and the Hudson River Railroad, were being constructed northward from New York to the village of Greenbush opposite Albany. Both of these companies were anxious to secure control of the Troy road in order to obtain a crossing over the river at Troy and thus to form an unbroken line of communication with the West. In February 1851, the Hudson River Railroad extended its line to the city by leasing the Troy & Greenbush.

This was the very time that opponents of the Utica & Schenectady were pressing for construction of the Mohawk Valley road. The prospect of a through route, by-passing both the Albany and the Utica lines, drove Corning to threaten the Hudson River company with drastic consequences if it tried to use this new connection to enhance the position of Troy at the expense of Albany. "If East Albany [Greenbush]," he warned its president, James Boorman, "is to be proclaimed as a mere dropping place for passengers, and Troy the great starting place, I cannot but think that your road will be placed in an unsatisfactory position. The Albany & Schenectady, and the Utica & Syracuse Roads, will have in self defense to unite with Albany and thrown their whole strength into the Harlem and the Steamboats." [87]

Boorman replied that his road had no intention of giving Troy an unfair advantage. His company had leased the line, he explained, simply to obtain a greater share of the northern travel.[88] In no financial position to fight a combination of the Harlem and Central roads, the Hudson River company never moved to extend its control over the Schenectady & Troy. After this brush with Corning, Boorman exerted himself to bring about closer coöperation with the Central Lines and to block any arrangements that the Harlem might make with the Troy road.

When the Hudson River road failed to press its advantage, Troy signed a tentative agreement with the Harlem by which the latter promised to build a line from its terminus at Chatham to the city in return for the exclusive right to transport all passengers and freight passing from Schenectady to New York.[89] Furthermore, the Schenectady & Troy entered into negotiations with the Rensselaer & Saratoga, the Troy & Boston, and the New York & Harlem to construct a jointly controlled Union railroad through the city. Such a line would permit the easy transfer of rolling stock and obviated the necessity of horse-drawn carriages to convey goods and passengers from one road to another.[90]

The Hudson River company protested vigorously that these agreements prejudiced its rights and interest. Edwin D. Morgan, a director and subsequently president of the company, informed Boorman: "If this arrangement is perfected with these three concerns at Troy with the Harlem and we are compelled to connect with the roads leading from Troy by omnibusses we are in a bad box." [91] In the local elections held during the first week of March 1852, supporters of the Hudson River company campaigned actively against those candidates known to favor the Harlem scheme. The new city council showed little enthusiasm for the proposed contracts, and the bid of the Harlem for a western connection by way of the Troy road ended in failure.[92]

In the meantime, the Schenectady & Troy continued to operate at a loss. A statement from the City Chamberlain, covering its financial operations to February 1852, revealed that the floating debt of the road had reached $59,000 despite an annual appropriation of $12,000 for the preceding three years. The opponents of the line then began to agitate for its sale as a means of relief from taxation. On July 1, 1852, a group of 88 taxpayers petitioned the common council to sell the railroad because the city was no longer able to support it. The council referred their petition to a special committee of ten headed by Russell Sage, a director of the Troy road, with instructions to make a thorough

examination of the line's condition and future prospects and to recom-
mend a course of action.[93]

But who would buy this anomalous and unprofitable little road?
The Albany & Schenectady was anxious to see it pass into bankruptcy.
The Harlem was interested, but the city had just repudiated an agreement with that line, and it seemed most unlikely that the same common council would now negotiate a new contract. The Utica & Schenectady had never been favorably disposed toward the Troy line as an
independent company, but it might, conceivably, consider purchasing
the road as an investment.

To forestall such a move, Ezekiel G. McIntosh, a director of the
Albany & Schenectady, submitted to Corning a plan for consolidating
the Utica and the Albany lines. He estimated that the plan would result in an immediate saving to the Albany & Schenectady of $25,000
and an annual profit of $175,000. This would allow the road to pay 8
per cent dividends and still permit a substantial reduction in its fares.
A similar arrangement with the Schenectady & Troy, he claimed, not
only would leave a large deficit but also would necessitate heavy
expenditure for double-tracking the line and restoring it to good physical condition.[94]

When Corning refused to take this drastic step, McIntosh tried to
lessen the strategic value of the Troy road by promoting closer coöperation between the Central lines and the Hudson River Company. Unable to bridge the Hudson River because of opposition from interests
in Troy, McIntosh began to agitate for the construction of a tunnel to
permit establishment of an unbroken road between New York and
Buffalo. Shortly after Edwin Morgan became president of the Hudson
River railroad, McIntosh urged Corning to impress upon him the importance of this project. "It is their salvation," he declared, "and will
kill off all round-about projects much to your comfort and mine." [95]

Unless strong assurances of fair treatment could be obtained from
the Utica & Schenectady, the Trojans preferred to sell their property
to the Hudson River company because this road connected directly
with the city of New York. The Hudson River line had long cast a
covetous eye in this direction, but the Greenbush affair had taught it
that such an undertaking would be a hazardous step without the approval of Corning.

While the committee appointed by the common council was con-

ducting its inquiry, Russell Sage, its chairman, was doing some pros-
pecting on his own. In a confidential letter to Edwin D. Morgan, he
disclosed that the earnings of the Schenectady & Troy had increased
sharply since the opening of the Troy & Boston; and he expressed the
conviction that, if Morgan were interested, they could probably purchase the line on very favorable terms. The future of the road, Sage
noted, appeared unusually bright:

Our S. & T.R.R. is still on hand, and can be got to make money, *no
mistake* . . . I think this matter worthy of your consideration, both as
regards the H.R.R. Road, and as a money making operation . . . I talked
with Mr. Wilkinson in relation to the Road, and he said there could be no
mistake about its paying. He further said, he thought it very important for
your road to have it, that with it, you could control not only Passengers but
he thought ¾ of the freight, and if we choose, we might compel the Albany
& Schenectady Road to pay no dividends or they could not pay any. Suppose we should put the fare to 25¢, they would be compelled to, or else
we should get nearly all the travel, and if so, how could they pay 8% on
$1,700,000 while we should only have to pay on $200,000.[96]

Six months later this honored and trusted public official urged the
city to dispose of the road on terms identical with those he had suggested to Morgan the previous July. His committee's report was accepted unanimously by the common council, and Sage was appointed
to a second committee to negotiate the sale.[97] On January 24, 1853,
despite a higher bid by the New York & Harlem, this group recommended that the city should accept an offer of $200,000 from Morgan.
The common council approved the sale 14 to 3.[98] The terms of the
contract were extremely liberal, but a provision requiring that five
residents of Troy, including the mayor and city recorder, should be
ex officio members of the board of directors caused some apprehension
among the purchasers. Morgan, however, advised his associates that
this requirement could be easily "circumvented during the present year
for the security of myself and the persons who sign with me." [99]

The decision to sell the railroad was received by the Troy press
with mixed reactions. The *Times* felt that the sale of the line would
"have an immediate effect in advancing the interests of Troy . . . and
[would] save the city directly $30,000 or $40,000 a year." [100] The editor
of the *Whig* declared that the transfer of the road was made in accordance with the wishes of an overwhelming majority of the people
and would prove highly advantageous to the city.[101] The *Budget* pre-

ferred to withold judgment until the new owners could take possession.[102]

But who were the new owners? Since Morgan was president of the
Hudson River railroad, many assumed that he was simply acting as
agent for this company. In Schenectady, the *Reflector* contended that
the purchase was a bold move on the part of the Hudson River road
to by-pass Albany and that the capital city would soon be compelled
to tunnel the river in self-defense.[103] Rumors emanating from New
York that Corning and other Albanians were associated with Morgan
in purchasing the line were categorically denied. "All doubts on this
point," declared the *Whig*, "we presume are now put at rest. We should
think, also, that the true policy of all parties in the transaction was
clearly enough indicated." [104]

Was Erastus Corning apprised of the negotiations? Corning not
only was fully informed, but he was an important figure in all the
deliberations leading to the line's purchase and its subsequent consolidation into the New York Central some four months later. Acquisition of the Troy line as a speculative venture had been considered by
Corning as early as 1850. At that time Daniel Gardner, former city
recorder of Troy, informed him of a conversation with Mayor Kellogg,
who had declared that, if absolute secrecy were maintained, they
could buy the road for about $220,000. He suggested that the line
could then be resold "so as to leave us $40,000 to divide for our
labor." [105] Two years later, Gardner wrote again, predicting that
$50,000 or more could be made from the deal and promising that
Corning's name would not need to appear in connection with the
sale.[106] By this time, however, there was developing a situation that
offered purchasers of the Schenectady & Troy an opportunity to obtain
a much greater profit than that proposed by Gardner.

For many years a close community of interest had existed among
the several lines from Albany to Buffalo. By 1852, a number of railroad
developments made it advisable that this coöperation should be continued and if possible strengthened. In May 1851, the Erie was completed across the southern part of the state to Dunkirk; a few months
later the Hudson River line was opened to East Albany. Competition
for the trade passing between the Great Lakes and New York City
became at once possible and inevitable. Officials of the Rochester &
Syracuse feared that the opening of the Erie Railroad would drastically

reduce their profits. "Were we not officers of the company," they declared, "we would dispose of every cent we own in it as soon as possible." With the fare between Dunkirk and New York only $7.50 over
the Erie and $9.10 by way of Albany, considerable passenger travel
was being diverted from the Central route.[107] Scarcely less disturbing
was the construction of several lines into the West through states south
of New York and through Canada. In 1852 the Pennsylvania was completed over the Alleghenies to Pittsburgh, and a year later the Baltimore & Ohio opened to Wheeling. In 1853 the Grand Trunk of Canada
joined Montreal with Portland, Maine. To retain their control over the
western trade and to prepare for the competition of their rivals, the
Central roads drew up a plan to consolidate their lines into one system.
In January 1853, a bill authorizing the move was introduced in the
legislature.

The Trojans strongly opposed the measure lest the promoters of the
scheme make Albany rather than Troy the Hudson River terminus.
After passage of the bill, however, the city was converted and the
Common Council petitioned Morgan to take immediate steps to have
the Schenectady & Troy included in the consolidation.[108] Morgan
needed no urging, for his associates in the purchase of the line were
Erastus Corning, Dean Richmond, Hamilton White, John V. L. Pruyn,
and possibly Ezekiel McIntosh, John Wilkinson, James Boorman, and
Russell Sage.[109] These men were either officials of or held a controlling
interest in the companies to be consolidated. Even before the Sage
Committee recommended that Troy should sell its railroad, this group
had agreed upon the purchasers, the price, and its subsequent absorp-
tion into the New York Central system.[110]

In Morgan, the leaders of the proposed consolidation found an ideal
partner and agent to negotiate the transaction. The consolidation bill
needed support in the legislature; Morgan was a state senator from
New York City. The officials of the Central lines were prominent
Democrats; Morgan was a leading Whig. Most important of all, the
people of Troy were seeking a purchaser who could provide them with
favorable trade connections and break the commercial isolation of the
city; Morgan was president of the Hudson River Railroad and a close
friend of Russell Sage, vice-president of the Troy & Boston. Robert B.
Doxtater, the superintendent of the Rome, Watertown & Ogdensburg,
wrote to Corning: "I find that with Mr. Morgan a party to the arrange-

ment the matter can be accomplished, without him it can not. The Troy people are determined that the Hudson River Railroad shall have something to do with it." [111]

The principal motives for consolidation of the New York Central were commercial, but the opportunity for large speculative profits was not lost on the parties to the agreement. In fact, it may have been the decisive factor that enabled conflicting interests to reach an understanding. The stock of each of the consolidated companies, save the Schenectady & Troy, was taken in at a premium varying from 17 to 55 per cent. The stock of the Troy line was accepted at par upon payment of $25 a share. Despite this assessment, the admission of the Schenectady & Troy into the consolidation created considerable dissatisfaction, particularly among the companies in the western part of the state. Somewhat disturbed by this turn of affairs, Morgan offered to withdraw from the consolidation; but Corning remained adamant, and the line was taken in without any change in the rate.[112] Under the terms of the consolidation agreement, Morgan and his associates received, on their $362,500 investment, 6500 shares of New York Central stock (selling at 119 within two weeks) and the assumption by the New York Central of the state loan to the Schenectady & Troy of $100,000.

The people of Troy were elated by the inclusion of their road in the consolidation. The great commercial prosperity envisioned by the line's promoters appeared about to be realized. The editor of the *Times* exclaimed: "Troy, for the first time, and after years of fruitless struggle and personal and corporate sacrifices to obtain this result, is now placed in position to command her just share of the trade and travel of the great and growing west." [113]

But the Trojans were merely indulging in wishful thinking. They counted too heavily on the strategic value of their bridge to divert the course of East-West traffic through their city. For more than forty years they had successfully defeated every proposal to span the Hudson at Albany. The New York Central, however, was a power in state politics and could count on widespread support for its undertakings. In this instance the formula for success was suggested by Horace White, a director of the company. "If we move for the bridge," he wrote to Corning, "we ought to circulate the petitions and pour these in strong upon the Legislature upon the opening of the session — then it will be an easy job to carry it through with a little *greesing* [*sic*] of the wheels." [114] Despite repeated charges by Troy interests that the Central was bribing the legislature, a bill chartering an Albany bridge was enacted in 1856.[115] Bitter over the treatment accorded them by the new owners of the road, the Common Council of the city petitioned the legislature for a thorough investigation of all matters relating to the sale and consolidation of the Schenectady & Troy.[116] But the legislature refused to act and the New York Central operated the road as a mere branch line in its system for almost a century.

Although the Schenectady & Troy was not constructed until ten years after the opening of the Mohawk & Hudson, the people of Troy hoped to share, if not to monopolize, the vast trade that was developing between the West and the Atlantic seaboard. Possessed of an energetic, industrious, and prosperous people, the city gave liberally to make its road one of the finest lines in the country. Yet this little railroad, for which the future seemed to promise so much, never paid a dividend, hovered constantly on the brink of bankruptcy, and finally was sold for a fraction of its cost to those chiefly responsible for its failure. The success of its rival, the Mohawk & Hudson, was not due to the natural advantage of Albany over Troy, nor can it be set down as a simple demonstration of the superiority of private over public ownership. Indeed, geography favored the Troy route. Moreover, government subsidies to railroads during this period were not uncommon and, in the case of the Schenectady & Troy, occasioned little or no discussion. At times the Troy road did suffer from its character as a government enterprise, but in the aggregate the victory of the Mohawk & Hudson was the result of far-sighted management, financial juggling, bribery, ruthless competition, and an effective alliance between business and politics.

FIVE

Repudiation of Railroad-Aid Bonds

Repudiation by government of its financial obligations is probably as old as the practice of public borrowing. The United States, by constitutional amendment in 1868, declared illegal and void all debts contracted by the Confederacy for the prosecution of the Civil War. During the early forties, Illinois, Indiana, Arkansas, Pennsylvania, Maryland, Michigan, Louisiana, Mississippi, and the territory of Florida defaulted on bonds issued principally for internal improvements. A number of other states, such as Ohio, avoided economic catastrophe at this time only by extraordinary efforts. Again, during the reconstruction period, Florida, North Carolina, Alabama, South Carolina, and Tennessee repudiated or drastically scaled down public debts contracted by carpet-bag governments. In the North, Minnesota refused to honor securities issued for the construction of railroads.[1]

Although the panic of 1837 forced many states into temporary insolvency, scarcely a municipality in the country failed to meet its obligations on time.[2] One of the principal reasons for this excellent financial record was that municipal bonds had not yet begun to appear on the market in sizable amounts. The entire municipal debt of the nation in 1840 did not exceed $25,000,000.[3] It is not known precisely when the first municipal bonds were issued in the United States, but it was probably early in the nineteenth century. New York City floated securities in 1812 and again in 1837 and 1838 to build its water system.[4] Within a few years a number of towns and most of the large cities had issued bonds. In New York State, for example, the city of Albany (1838–1841) sold $1,000,000 worth of its securities to aid in the construction of the Albany & West Stockbridge railroad. Across the river, Troy (1840–1842) borrowed $550,000 to build the Schenectady & Troy line. Between 1840 and 1880 local indebtedness in the country multiplied 33 times, or from $25,000,000 to $821,000,000. The per capita debt rose 14 times, from $1.17 to $16.37. During this same period state debts increased only 50 per cent, or from $175,000,000 to $275,000,000. Moreover, the per capita state debt for these years decreased from $10.25 to $5.48. In 1840 municipal debts were one-seventh the amount of state debts; in 1880 they were three times greater.[5]

In New York the tremendous expansion in local debts was due partly to the payment of bounties to soldiers in the Civil War, but principally to popular demand for water works, sewers, bridges, and improved transportation facilities.[6] When the New York constitution of 1846 prohibited the state from lending its credit to private corporations, railroad promoters turned with astonishing success to the local communities for support. Burdens that the state was unwilling or unable to bear were now assumed by hundreds of cities, towns, and villages. So intent were these municipalities on obtaining better means of transportation that more than 20 per cent of the municipal indebtedness of the state in 1875 was for railroad construction.[7]

When municipal railroad-aid bonds first appeared on the market they were highly regarded by investors both at home and abroad. From an income point of view these securities, which usually bore 7 per cent interest, were better than United States government 5–20's, which paid only 6 per cent. Moreover, many bonds, such as those issued for construction of the New York & Oswego Midland and the Southern Central railroads, were exempt from state taxation when held by citizens in the counties through which these lines passed. A contemporary investor's guide assured its readers that American municipals were "the most remunerative and least precarious of all the opportunities which offer themselves for the profitable employment of money." [8]

Municipal bonds issued to aid railroad construction seldom sold for less than par value. Rochester marketed $100,000 worth of its obligations in 1853 at 104.6.[9] Bonds issued by the city of Buffalo in 1852 for the Buffalo, Brantford & Goderich and by Utica in the following year for the Black River & Utica were sold at par.[10] Furthermore, all of the 22 communities that aided construction of the Albany & Susquehanna disposed of their securities at par.[11] Even during the period of financial stringency following the panic of 1837, when New York State stocks were selling at discounts ranging as high as 22 per cent, the city of Albany sold $1,000,000 par value of its bonds for $990,-775.65, including the brokerage commission.[12] After 1869 municipalities were forbidden by state law to dispose of their securities at a discount.[13]

To the investing public the most valuable characteristic of municipal bonds was their safety. In this respect the record of New York communities was, until the 1870's, almost unimpeachable. Before this time only five defaults, involving $255,000, are known to have occurred in the state, and in none of these cases did the bondholder suffer any loss.[14] Yet, between 1870 and 1890, 57 towns and villages had repudiated securities having a par value of $4,152,382. With a single exception, involving only $10,000, all of these bonds had been issued to aid the construction of railroads.[15] Many communities that a few years before would have decried the thought of defaulting, now repudiated their debts without any sign of compunction or hesitation. In town after town the people showed a contempt for the conventions of finance and an indifference toward public obligations unparalleled in the history of the state.

There is no direct evidence to show that this wave of repudiation was associated in any way with the agrarian revolt of the 1870's. Only chronology makes such an argument plausible. The Granger movement was never strong in New York, and the farming population played only a minor role in bringing about the Hepburn investigation in 1879 and the law creating the Railroad Commission in 1882.[16] Nor can this phenomenon be explained solely on financial grounds. No community in the state of New York ever repudiated an obligation because of its inability to pay. While many communities were heavily bonded and their taxes burdensome, none was bankrupt. The underlying motive that induced municipalities to repudiate their debts was psychological rather than financial. It stemmed from a sense of being cheated. The people were convinced that they had not gotten their money's worth. Scant consideration was given to the fact that it was the railroad promoters or directors, and not the bondholders, who were responsible for their plight.[17]

Several localities, for example, defaulted on bonds issued to build the New York & Oswego Midland, the most ambitious and, in some respects, the most tragic of all the publicly subsidized lines. Proposals for its construction aroused such enthusiasm from the people along the route that 50 communities subscribed $5,704,707 to the capital stock of the company. But the enterprise was doomed to failure from the outset. Much of the road was projected through a sparsely settled area possessing neither great markets nor thriving industries. The company, therefore, encountered extraordinary financial difficulties in raising funds for its construction. Moreover, the estimated cost of building and equipping the road rose from $10,000 per mile in 1866 when construction began to $80,000 in 1873.[18] In addition to these physical and financial difficulties, the road suffered seriously from mismanagement. For some unknown reason the energies of the directors were not confined to completing the main line as originally intended. Hundreds of miles of branch roads were constructed, purchased, or leased without increasing the volume of traffic sufficiently to justify the additional expense.[19] In September 1873, four months after its opening, the Midland road passed into bankruptcy. In the reorganization which followed, the common stock of the company was virtually wiped out and the municipal shareholders were forced to dispose of their holdings at four to six cents on the dollar.[20]

With the reopening of the Midland line, the primary objective of the subsidizing communities, namely, the improvement of their transportation and communication facilities, was achieved. Nonetheless, a number of towns along the route were greatly dissatisfied with the result. The benefits actually obtained did not measure up to their expectations and a bitter feeling of disappointment and disillusionment followed. These localities felt that, while they had paid for the road, they did not own it. Small farmers and businessmen who had mortgaged their property to purchase stock in the company with the hope of increasing their trade now discovered that their securities were worthless. Moreover, their taxes were heavily increased to pay the bonds that had been issued to finance the line. Hard times following the panic of 1873 aggravated their condition. Instead of being a harbinger of prosperity, the Midland had proved the forerunner of a depression. Obligations that once appeared trifling now seemed unbearable. Although the debt was the same the ability of many to pay had diminished greatly. A reaction comparable to that experienced in the towns along the Midland followed the failure of the Syracuse &

Chenango Valley, the Pennsylvania & Sodus Bay, and the Lake Ontario, Auburn & New York.

Communities were particularly incensed when fraud or chicanery was associated with the failure of their line. In 1873 the town of Attica agreed to aid the construction of the Attica & Arcade as soon as the directors raised through private subscription 10 per cent of the authorized capital stock, or an amount equal to $1,000 per mile. On the basis of an affidavit filed with the secretary of state that the company had complied with this condition, the municipality bonded itself to assist in building the road. A short time later, the railroad passed into receivership and the people of Attica demanded an explanation. Upon investigation, it was discovered that no portion of the private subscription had ever been paid. All payments allegedly made by individuals were in the form of promissory notes and checks. Some subscribers had no funds in the bank on which their drafts were drawn; others presented their checks with the understanding that they were not to be cashed. In the light of these disclosures, Attica promptly voted to repudiate its securities.[21]

The town of Seneca Falls defaulted on $200,000 worth of its bonds after an investigation of the ill-fated Pennsylvania and Sodus Bay revealed that the company's directors had diverted the proceeds of the municipal subscriptions to their own use.[22] Some localities, such as Greenwood, Andes, and Delhi, repudiated their debts when the projected road which they aided was not constructed; whereas Solon, Taylor, DeRuyter, and several others did so because their line was abandoned and junked soon after its completion.

When repudiation was decided upon, towns used almost every legal technicality as an excuse to avoid payment of their bonds. Most of them contended that the petition bonding their community did not represent the required amount of property or that it did not contain the necessary number of taxpayers. The town of Phelps, for example, claimed that its petitions lacked sufficient legal signatures. Many persons signed only their initial instead of their full given name. "J. Smith," the municipality pleaded, "might mean James Smith, Joseph Smith or Jacob Smith."[23] In other instances similar names were counted as representing the same person as "Wormer and Van-Wormer, Owen and Owens, Frank and Franklin." When Sarah A.

Reynolds signed her name "Widow Sally Reynolds" the legality of her signature was denied.[24] There was no intentional fraud. Each of these persons was well known to the county judge before whom the petition was presented for approval. Nevertheless, the highest tribunal in the state held the bonds void. A similarity of names, the court ruled, was only *prima facie* evidence that they were the same persons and the county judge could not call upon his own personal knowledge to establish the identity of a signature.[25]

Other fine points of the law were used by the towns of Mentz, Caneadea, Potter, and Northampton, which repudiated their indebtedness because their petitions did not state that they represented a majority of the taxpayers "not including those taxed for dogs and highways only." [26] The town of Hume successfully challenged the validity of its securities on the ground that its petition failed to show that the amount of aid extended to the Buffalo & Belmont line did not exceed 20 per cent of the taxable property of the community.[27] Greenwich defaulted on $60,000 worth of its bonds because they were made payable in 20 instead of 30 years as required by law.[28] A few years later, Seneca Falls advanced a similar argument in an unsuccessful attempt to avoid payment on $200,000 of its securities.[29]

A few communities, aided by shrewd lawyers and self-styled specialists in railroad-bond suits, advanced even less tenable reasons for refusing to meet their obligations. The village of Fort Edward contended that the publication of an election notice for only eleven days violated the statute requiring publication for twelve days.[30] Thompson repudiated on the ground that the town railroad commissioners exchanged its bonds directly for stock in the company instead of selling them for cash as the statute directed.[31] The creditors of the town of Lansing lost their entire investment because the petition bonding that municipality for the Cayuga Lake road failed to state whether the money so raised was to be invested in the stock or the bonds of the line.[32]

In their search for a legal loophole the communities of Yates, Solon, Taylor, and Springport discovered that their bonds were not properly sealed.[33] The town of Taylor did not own a seal so the railroad commissioners simply signed the bonds at the left and opposite to the letters "L.S." printed within scrolls. On this flimsy basis the securities of all these towns were invalidated by the lower courts. Moreover, in each instance, the bondholders were forced to carry their cases to the state Court of Appeals or to a federal tribunal for relief.

An interesting case of a community's repudiating its railroad-aid bonds and one unique in the annals of New York municipal finance involved the town of Greenwood in Steuben county.[34] This small agricultural community of about a thousand people bonded itself in 1872 for $30,000 to aid the construction of the projected Rochester, Hornellsville & Pine Creek line. The road was expected to raise the town to the height of financial prosperity and commercial greatness, but it failed in its purpose for the reason that it was never built. While a few sections of the proposed line were graded, no part of it was ever placed in operation. In their search for some technicality by which they might escape payment of their obligations, the town officials, aided by adroit attorneys, discovered that the petition authorizing the issuance of the community's bonds failed to state that the railroad was a "corporation in this state." On this slight irregularity the state Court of Appeals held the bonds void.[35] Here the case might have ended, but the bondholders obtained from the legislature a law which freed the securities from any defect associated with their issuance.[36] The creditors thereupon renewed their suits and this time the courts held unanimously that the bonds were a legal obligation against the town and must be paid.[37]

The legislature's action compelling the payment of a debt which the highest tribunal in the state had declared to be illegal infuriated the people of Greenwood. At the request of their representative on the Steuben County board of supervisors, all railroad-aid taxes assessed on the community were recorded separately from the regular levy so that every property owner could tell at a glance his share of interest on the bonds.[38] Each year thereafter when the town taxes came due, the people paid their state and county charges but refused to pay any part of their assessment for the Pine Creek railroad.[39] Unable to raise the interest on the bonds by ordinary means, the tax collector for the town was forced to adopt a system of levies and sales on the property of private individuals. People who refused to pay the full amount of their taxes were notified that on a certain date some part of their property would be sold to satisfy the debt. On the day appointed for the sale, however, hundreds of townspeople, spurred on by martial music, marched to the auction place, determined that the scheduled proceedings should not be carried out. There was no rioting or outright intimidation, but the implied threat of violence was sufficient to restrain even the boldest from bidding. Since no one dared to bid on any of the advertised articles, the collector regularly adjourned the sales and reported the tax as noncollectible.[40]

Those resisting the railroad tax were exceptionally well organized and were a power in local politics. Consequently, the tax collector, who was an elected official, had to be careful about the manner in which he conducted the sales. Bondholders frequently charged that he hurried across the countryside to the auction place ahead of the bidders and then postponed the sale on the ground that nobody was there to bid. Moreover, they declared, he was in the habit of offering property for sale in language calculated to arouse the emotions of the crowd and to discourage any possible buyers. "How much am I offered," he would say, "for this poor man's cow which is to be sold for taxes for the Pine Creek Railroad?" Or, "Who will bid for this horse owned by a poor man with eight children to support?"

In an effort to slow up the sales, the collector frequently spent the whole day auctioning off a pig or a horse. Once he permitted a taxpayer to withdraw a cow that had been selected for sale and to "substitute in its place a truss which the poor old man wore for a rupture." [41] On another occasion the collector showed his resourcefulness against a bondholder's representative who threatened to bid on every horse or cow offered for sale. For a time it appeared that several Greenwood farmers were destined to lose some of their finest livestock. However, the collector came to their rescue by announcing that his bond had expired and that it would be necessary for him to renew it before any further sales could be made. The auction was then adjourned for two weeks.[42]

This procedure was repeated at regular intervals over a period of several years without the town's realizing more than a few hundred dollars to pay its debts. In desperation, a committee of the bondholders appealed to Governor Alonzo B. Cornell for help. The governor immediately declared the town of Greenwood in a state of insurrection and forbade any assembly or gathering that might interfere with the collection of taxes. Further levies and sales were ordered and the local officers were directed to enforce the law to the limit of their authority.[43]

Accordingly, the collector, assisted by the sheriff and his posse, held a new series of auctions on the property of delinquent taxpayers. The first sales held in compliance with the governor's proclamation were described by a reporter who attended the proceedings:

> The Sheriff and a posse of 30 men arrived early in the morning. The mother of the collector died yesterday, but this did not prevent the sale. The first chattel sold was to have been the horse of a widow, but, on the arrival of the sheriff at the house, it was found that the widow had sold her property on Saturday night. The crowd, which was very large, then proceeded to the house of another widow named Mrs. Lydia McGraw. Here a horse was offered for sale. A man named Bennett bid $5. but it was sold to another for $8. The next place visited was the house of an old man where a cow was sold. The old man is in destitute circumstances and took the sale very much to heart. The bystanders were moved to tears by the sorrow the sale caused him.[44]

Resistance to the payment of these taxes continued. It required nearly six months to raise the full amount of interest owed to the bondholders.[45] Finally, worn out by years of litigation and controversy, the creditors agreed to compromise the entire debt, which by this time amounted to $46,000, for $41,000.[46]

The strength of repudiative sentiment in some municipalities is revealed by the vote authorizing the town officials to default on their securities. A referendum in Hancock approved by 335 to 2 a resolution to resist further payment on its bonds.[47] De Ruyter renounced its indebtedness with only three dissenting votes.[48] The towns of Seneca Falls[49] and Delhi[50] repudiated by acclamation. Most communities took action against their creditors only after prolonged debate. This delay permitted local bondholders in towns in which the repudiationists appeared to be a majority to sell their securities before the market collapsed. In De Ruyter the town meeting which voted to contest the community's securities was postponed repeatedly until local investors disposed of their holdings to outside parties.[51] For this action the people of De Ruyter were bitterly denounced in the press throughout the state.[52] The local editor, however, vigorously defended the course pursued by the town and assailed as hypocritical those who ventured to criticize its conduct:

As we cast our eyes over some of our fraud crying sister towns we behold them with their despondent and sanctimonious faces just above the water, their eyes with frenzy rolling and their clenched hands raised toward heaven; and as we listen we hear them shout 'DeRuyter repudiates,' and then with an agonizing groan, inwardly exclaim 'Oh! how I wish we could.' [53]

Who owned these defaulted securities? The answer to this question can be given only in a very general way. Many, undoubtedly, were owned by individuals in municipalities that offered the securities for sale. During the promotional period, local editors frequently urged the people of the community to support the railroad by purchasing the town's bonds. Newspaper advertisements were directed especially to the small home investor.[54] A default or the threat of one frequently disclosed the ownership of a municipality's securities. A rumor that Norwich would repudiate its bonds revealed that many of these obligations were held by small local property owners. The *Chenango Telegraph* declared:

The scare developed a fact not generally known that thousands of dollars of our local bonds are held by people of ordinary means, in and around our own village, who have sought in them an investment deemed safe beyond per adventure showing how widespread would be the effect of any repudiation in Norwich. It would not affect the wealthy, but widow and orphan funds, as the investments of the prudent laborer, would be swept away and there is no telling the misery and woe that would follow in the wake of any failure of these bonds.[55]

The wave of repudiations that swept over the state during the 1870's caused a number of small bondholders to dispose of their investments. At the time Hancock defaulted, practically all of its securities were owned by individuals living in the town or in nearby Chenango county.[56] Some years later, when the municipality compromised with its creditors, the bonds were held almost exclusively by out-of-state speculators, mainly lawyers.[57] Banks and trust companies also held large amounts of railroad-aid bonds. The Williamsburg, Bowery, and German Uptown savings banks of New York, the Union Bank of Rochester, the Syracuse Savings Bank, and similar institutions often appeared as plaintiffs in lawsuits. Heavy investments in repudiated railroad-aid securities led to the failure of the Oswego County Savings Bank in 1879.[58]

When a community refused to pay the interest or principal on its securities, the bondholders were frequently forced to institute court action to obtain relief. In adjudicating such cases, the state courts, particularly the lower ones, showed a marked tendency to support the municipality at the expense of the public creditor.[59] As a general rule they held that, unless every step in the bonding process had been strictly in accordance with the law, the bonds were invalid. So favorably did the courts construe the law on behalf of the defaulting communities that almost any defect or irregularity in the proceedings was accepted as a defense against their creditors. Purchasers of municipal securities were always held chargeable with knowledge of the statute authorizing their issuance. Moreover, at no time, not even in the face of hostile decisions by the United States Supreme Court, did the New York judges relax the stringency of the rules that they had adopted. The doctrine of *caveat emptor* was never more fully accepted by the courts.

This rigid interpretation of the bonding law profoundly influenced the course of action pursued by both the defaulting towns and their creditors. Some municipalities that had shown no intention of repudiating decided, in view of the position taken by the state courts, to challenge the validity of their securities. A great many more, encouraged by decisions favorable to other localities, voted to continue litigation already begun.[60]

Perhaps the most disturbing decision handed down by the New York courts involved the town of Hancock. In 1871 this community subscribed $100,000 to aid the construction of the New York & Oswego Midland. The largest taxpayer in Hancock at this time was the Erie Railroad. Apparently irritated by the prospect of paying on bonds issued to build a rival line, the Erie goaded the town into repudiating its securities.[61] In the litigation which followed, the main point of the inquiry involved the conclusiveness of the local assessor's affidavit that the petition bonding the town contained the number of signatures required by law. The bondholders contended that this statement was incontrovertible evidence that the requisite consents had been obtained. The filing of it with the county judge, they maintained, was in the nature of a judgment which estopped the municipality from contesting the legality of the bonding proceedings. Numerous opinions of federal tribunals, including the United States Supreme Court, were cited in support of this argument.

The highest court in the state, however, held against the bond-holders. Such an affidavit, it asserted, was merely presumptive evidence that the town had met the requirements of the law. The attorneys for the town were permitted to go behind the affidavit of the local officials and, by comparing the bonding petition with the assessment roll, to show that less than one-half of the property owners in the community had signed for the railroad. With reference to similar cases in the Federal courts the New York tribunal declared: "There are undoubtedly decisions of the Federal Courts holding in favor of bona fide holders of such bonds a different doctrine but these decisions have not been regarded as controlling authority in this court." [62] Under this ruling, the sufficiency of every bonding petition in the state was subject to reëxamination by the courts at the instance of the municipality involved. Since a number of communities had bonded themselves with great speed or by very narrow margins, many bondholders were gravely concerned over the safety of their investments.[63]

Within a few weeks after the Hancock decision almost every locality that had aided construction of the Midland called a special town meeting to consider the wisdom of contesting its securities. The threat of wholesale repudiation terrified the bondholders. In Norwich, rumors that the city would refuse to honor its obligations precipitated a panic among its creditors. The *Chenango Telegraph* reported that

timid bondholders rushed hither and yon advising with everyone who knew anything about the matter, fetching up finally at the office of the railroad commissioner of the town who was quietly paying off the bonds as they were presented at par and accrued interest with the surplus money which the town had on hand. This was continued until eleven o'clock Monday morning when the money on hand was exhausted and the commissioner stopped paying. Then the panic increased and the bonds were freely offered, and taken by outside speculators at from 70 to 90 cents on the dollar.[64]

In three days the town of Guilford purchased at par, from frightened investors, $80,000 worth of its Midland bonds, which still had 20 years to run.[65] At Hancock the municipality's securities were freely offered at 40 and 50 cents on the dollar. Many of them passed into the hands of out-of-state lawyers and speculators who purchased them with a view to bringing suit in federal court.[66]

After waging a losing battle against repudiating communities in the state courts for many years, the holders of defaulted bonds turned with great success to the federal courts for relief. Federal judges, holding life tenure and far removed from local influence, almost invariably ruled for the bondholders. So favorable to the creditor group were these decisions that within a short time nearly all the litigation was drawn into the federal courts. Most of the cases arose under the federal Constitution's diversity-of-citizenship clause. The holders of disputed securities usually disposed of them to a relative or a speculator residing in another state. Occasionally, small bondholders pooled their investments for the purpose of establishing jurisdiction or reducing legal fees.[67] In passing on the genuineness of these assignments, the federal courts usually held that, whenever the transfer appeared real and not simply colorable, they would not question the motives that actuated the sale. Where it could be shown that the purchase was not made in good faith, however, and the exchange was accomplished simply to get the suit before a federal judge, the court usually dismissed the action and remanded the case to the state in which it arose.[68] Since collusion and conspiracy were difficult to prove, almost anyone who held a municipal bond was considered a bona fide purchaser.

This conflict between the two court systems is extraordinary in that federal rulings involving the construction of a state law ordinarily follow the views of the highest tribunal of the state in which the case arises. The construction given to a state's statute by its highest court is usually considered to be part of the statute and as binding on the federal courts as the text of the law itself. Consequently, the attorneys for defaulting municipalities, in defending their clients, pleaded that these judges should yield their own convictions and accept the position taken by the New York courts. This the federal judiciary refused to do. They justified their action by reasoning that the issue under consideration was not one of local policy or custom but one of general principles and commercial law.[69] Only when the question before the court involved a clear-cut case of statutory construction did the federal courts follow state decisions. They were ready to accept the rulings of the New York courts on the initial bonding of a community, but they refused to be bound by the state decisions after the bonds had been issued.[70]

As a result of this conflict between the federal and the state courts, many defaulting communities found themselves liable to citizens of other states even though they were not obligated to those of their own state. In *Murdock v. Town of Venice,* for example, the United States Supreme Court sustained the validity of the town's securities despite the fact that this and similar bond issues in other municipalities had been declared void by the New York Court of Appeals. Justice William Strong (1870–1880), asserted:

> We are aware that in the state of New York it has been held adversely to the opinions we have expressed. It was so held in Starin v. Town of Genoa, and in Gould v. Town of Sterling . . . These decisions are in conflict with the rulings of the court in Bissel v. Jeffersonville, 24 How (U. S.) 287; Knox County v. Aspinwall, 21 How (U. S.) 539; Mercer County v. Hackett, 1 Wall (U. S.) 83, and other cases which we have cited. They are in conflict with the decisions in other state courts . . . But assuming that what was ruled . . . is still the doctrine of the New York courts, we find ourselves unable to yield to it our assent. It is against the whole current of our decisions as well as against the decisions made in other states; and we think it is not supported by soundest reasons.[71]

In their adjudication of municipal bond suits the federal courts considered only two questions of decisive importance. Did the state legislature authorize the community to issue the bonds? And, if the bonds had been issued irregularly or fraudulently, what consideration should be given to innocent purchasers who bought them without knowledge of their defects? On the first question, the federal and state courts agreed that purchasers of municipal bonds could not force payment if there was a total absence of statutory authority to issue them. The mere recital on the face of a bond that it had been issued according to law did not preclude a community's denying its validity. In 1871 the legislature authorized the New York & Oswego Midland to extend its road westward from some place along the main line to Lake Erie or the Niagara River.[72] To aid the construction of the project, the towns of Lansing and Genoa subscribed $75,000 each to the company's capital stock. Before any of the road could be built, however, the Midland, embarrassed by the financial troubles of 1873, passed into the hands of a receiver.

The town of Lansing, embittered because it had received nothing more for its money than a partially completed roadbed, refused to pay the interest on its obligations on the ground that the course of the road had not been completely located at the time the community was bonded. The lawsuits which ensued lasted nearly fifteen years, but the state and federal courts consistently upheld the town's contention that a complete survey of the entire route and terminus was a necessary precedent to aiding the enterprise. In the absence of such a survey, the United States Supreme Court declared, the municipality had no authority to issue its bonds and, consequently, it could not protect an innocent holder of these securities even though they were regular on their face and stated that they were issued pursuant to law.[73] Genoa paid the interest on its bonds regularly for 16 years before repudiating them. In this instance, the precedent of a long line of adverse decisions failed to deter the bondholders, who sued without any success until 1903.[74]

The municipalities of Mentz and Northampton, whose railroad-aid bonds were invalidated by state and federal courts, presented a somewhat different problem. In 1869, the legislature authorized the town of Mentz to invest $30,000 in the stock of the Cayuga Northern, a little 35-mile line running between Ithaca and Auburn. Before the local officials had taken any steps to bond the community, the state's general bonding law was amended to require, as a condition precedent to voting municipal aid, that the petition should set forth that it contained a majority of the taxpayers appearing on the last assessment roll "not including those taxed for dogs and highways only." [75] Following the bankruptcy of the Cayuga road in 1873, the town refused to pay the interest on its securities for the reason that the petition bonding the community failed to contain this particular clause.

To the bondholders, the omission of these words seemed trivial and they pressed their case against the municipality with great vigor. The state courts held in favor of the town.[76] In the federal courts, however, the judges disagreed sharply over the interpretation that should be placed on this provision of the law. Were such bonds invalid at their inception for the want of power to issue them? Or was the omission of this phrase a mere irregularity not affecting their negotiability? Speaking for the court in *Rich v. the Town of Mentz*, Circuit Judge Coxe bitterly assailed the town for seeking to repudiate its debt on such a slight technicality:

The federal courts, which have with great unanimity sustained the validity of municipal bonds, should hesitate long before accepting the forced and narrow interpretation contended for by the defendant. These solemn obligations, issued to invite the investors of the world, should not be invalidated except for grave and serious infirmities. Even if the question were a doubtful one, a construction should be given to the statute which upholds the bonds, rather than one which turns them to ashes in the hands of a bona fide holder.[77]

The town of Mentz immediately appealed this decision to the United States Supreme Court, which reversed the verdict of the lower tribunal. The court held that the omission of the phrase rendered the bonding petition defective and the whole proceeding before the county judge void. In its review of the case, the Supreme Court considered itself bound by the ruling of the New York Court of Appeals, which had previously held the bonds invalid. The question at issue, the federal tribunal asserted, was clearly one of statutory construction and in the determination of such actions "the decisions of the highest tribunal of a state are entitled to great and ordinarily decisive weight." [78]

Although the court expressed the hope that the decision would end all discussion involving this point, the town of Northampton repudiated its securities on similar grounds after paying interest on them regularly for more than 20 years.[79] The bondholders pleaded that the payment of interest for such a long period of time amounted to recognition by the town that its securities were properly issued and that the community should not be permitted to take advantage of a slight omission in wording to escape further payment of its just obligations. Both the state and the federal courts, however, rejected this argument and held, as they had in the case of *Rich v. the Town of Mentz*, that failure to include this clause rendered the petition invalid and any bonds issued as a result of it void.[80]

Only a few cases carried from the New York to the federal courts involved the statutory power of a municipality to issue bonds. Most of the litigation was concerned with the question of whether the local officials had complied with the terms of the statute providing for their issuance. In considering this problem the federal judiciary exerted itself in behalf of the bondholder almost to the point of trespassing on the rights and powers of the state courts. The biased and dogmatic position taken by the United States Supreme Court in municipal-bond cases during the 1860's and 1870's was decried by Associate Justice

Samuel F. Miller (1862–1890). On February 3, 1878, he wrote to a friend:

Our court or a majority of it are, if not monomaniacs, as much as bigots and fanatics on that subject as is the most unhesitating Mahemodan [*sic*] in regard to his religion. In four cases out of five the case is decided when it is a suit to enforce a contract against a city, or town, or a county. If there is a written instrument its validity is a foregone conclusion.[81]

A few months later he remarked:

The decision by Swayne is a most slovenly one — but on the question arising out of these municipal bonds — the current has set so strong against all defenses it is impossible to resist it. There is no use to attempt the rehearing of the case.[82]

The New York doctrine, that unless the bonding of a community were perfect in every respect its securities would be held void, was summarily rejected. In their zeal to protect municipal creditors, the federal courts cast aside all strict interpretations of the law and ruled that railroad-aid bonds in the hands of a bona fide holder were valid negotiable instruments except where the securities were void for want of power to issue them. Indeed, the fact that many municipal bonds had any value at all was due mainly to the course of adjudication pursued by the federal courts.

Who were these bona fide holders that were privileged to invoke the protection of the law? Chief Justice Morrison R. Waite (1874–1888) described one as a "purchaser for value without notice or the successor of such a purchaser." [83] Justice Joseph P. Bradley (1870–1892) said, "One who purchases railroad bonds in an open market, supposing them to be valid, and having no notice to the contrary will be deemed a bona fide holder." [84] The courts, however, never accepted this doctrine of "innocent purchaser" and refused to recognize as binding on a town any bonds with whose issuance some irregularity had been associated.

The most common technical defect seized upon by municipalities that defaulted on their obligations, and, at the same time, the most contentious issue in the conflict between the state and federal courts, involved the sufficiency of signatures on the bonding petition. The bonding laws of New York permitted municipalities to lend their credit in aid of railroads only on approval of a certain number of property owners. In accordance with the decisions of the state courts, failure to obtain this assent voided the bonds. The federal courts, on the other hand, ruled that such a condition was merely an irregularity and that the securities were valid in the hands of a bona fide holder.

In 1852 the towns of Genoa, Venice, Scipio, and Sterling were authorized, with the approval of two-thirds of their taxpayers, to aid construction of the Lake Ontario, Auburn & New York.[85] Petitions signed by the assessors and supervisors of the communities stating that these conditions had been fulfilled were filed with the county clerk as required by law. Shortly afterward, the projected road passed into bankruptcy; and the towns, angered by this turn of events, repudiated their bonds on the ground that the petitions lacked the required number of consents.

The bondholders promptly brought suit, contending that they were bona fide holders for value. The affidavit of the local officials, they claimed, was sufficient proof that the towns were legally bonded. The state Court of Appeals held against them and ruled that this statement was merely prima facie evidence of the fact and that the security holders must prove affirmatively that the required number of assents had been obtained. In other words, the court maintained that, in an action against a town, the burden rested on the bondholder to show not only that the petition contained sufficient names but also that every signature was genuine. Failure to provide such proof, it ruled, was fatal to recovery.[86]

About fifteen years later the creditors of these towns again brought suit on their securities. This time the actions were instituted in the federal courts, which upheld their claims.[87] In *Venice v. Murdock* the United States Supreme Court assailed the rulings of the New York judges, and declared that the question, whether the preliminary proceedings precedent to bonding a community had been carried out according to law, was for the local officials to decide and not a matter for judicial consideration. This was answered affirmatively by the assessor and supervisor, it asserted, when they issued the bonds. The court's opinion was delivered by Justice Strong:

It is very obvious that if the act of the legislature which authorized an issue of bonds . . . intended that the holders of the bonds should be under obligation to prove by parol evidence that each case of the two hundred and fifty-nine names signed to the written assent was a genuine signature of the person who bore the name, the proffered aid to the railroad company was a delusion. No sane person would have bought a bond with such an obligation resting upon him whenever he called for payment of principal or interest.[88]

Despite these rulings by the country's highest tribunal, the New York courts adhered to their position that, in cases involving the sufficiency of signatures on a bonding petition, the burden of proof rested on the bondholder. Moreover, they continued to permit attorneys for municipalities to go behind the affidavits of local officials to show that the petition was deficient either in the number of signers or in the amount of taxable property it purported to represent. After the United States Supreme Court ruling in the *Town of Venice v. Murdock*, the towns of Hancock, Andes, Lyons, Orleans, and a number of other communities had their securities invalidated in the New York courts because the bonding petitions were insufficient. In each instance, however, the creditors of these towns carried their cases to the federal courts, where the decisions were reversed.[89]

Municipalities that repudiated their bonds for other reasons suffered a similar fate. The towns of Thompson, Shawangunk, Ontario, Yates, Potter, Lewiston, Phelps, and Springport all experienced the great joy of having their railroad-aid debts wiped out by state courts and the intense anger and depression of having the rulings reversed by the federal judiciary.[90] In reviewing these cases, federal courts rejected all claims of fraud, bribery, and other irregularities, and considered only the question of whether the owner of the securities was a bona fide purchaser for value.

The uncompromising position taken by the federal courts in favor of bondholders, not only in New York but also in other states, led to demands in Congress that the jurisdiction of these tribunals should be restricted. Senator Augustus H. Garland of Arkansas introduced a bill which provided that "No city, town, village, county or other municipal or public corporation shall be sued in the courts of the United States." [91] Congressman Richard W. Townshend of Illinois urged the passage of a similar measure in the House of Representatives.[92]

Gestures like these won great applause in debt-ridden communities but the conservative interests of the country viewed with concern every proposal to weaken the federal judiciary. Many leading journals vigorously opposed such legislation. The *Nation* argued that, instead of interfering to make repudiation easy, it was the duty of Congress to compel delinquent municipalities to pay their obligations.[93] The *New York Times* declared that the protection of many communities' bondholders would be a tedious, if not a hopeless, proceeding if their sole dependence were the local courts:

In this state . . . Federal courts are being brought into requisition to obtain quicker redress than could be hoped for in dealing with the defaulting towns. The interminable delays which are the bane of local practice, and which knavish debtors know how to profit by at the expense of creditors, may thus be prevented. The DeRuyter class of towns will have some of their calculations upset by the prompt appeal to Federal administrators of justice.[94]

The New York *Tribune,* alarmed by the steady growth of municipal debt and the widespread tendency to repudiate obligations incurred for the construction of railroads, suggested a different approach to the problem. Instead of curbing the power of the federal courts, the *Tribune* urged the federal government to insure the payment of all municipal debts. With this additional guarantee, the paper predicted, creditors might be willing to accept a reduction in the rate of interest and even in the amount of the principal.[95]

In the New York legislature a movement was initiated to have all railroad-aid debts assumed by the state. Most of the proposed measures provided that municipal creditors might exchange their holdings for state securities bearing interest at 5 per cent. The municipalities, in turn, would issue new 7 per cent bonds to be deposited with the state treasurer. Five per cent of this interest was to be used to pay the creditors and 2 per cent was to be set aside in a sinking fund to redeem the communities' bonds at maturity.[96] Thus, as one local editor put it, "Our town will rid itself of debt without paying more than it pays at present for interest alone." [97] Legally, the bondholders could not be compelled to accept any reduction in the yield on their securities, but many rural communities voiced the threat that the alternative to conversion was repudiation or protracted litigation.[98] The combined opposition of representatives from the city of New York and those from localities that had no railroad debts was enough to defeat these proposals.

The state of New York never assumed any direct liability for municipal debts, but it did provide some indirect assistance. In 1881 the legislature passed a refunding law which permitted any community to refinance its maturing obligations (and, with the consent of the creditors, those not maturing) by issuing new bonds bearing interest at not more than 5 per cent. Most communities with railroad-aid debts eventually took advantage of this legislation.[99] Moreover, in response to the pressure of debt-ridden localities and for other reasons, the legislature lowered the legal rate of interest in the state from 7 to 6 per cent.[100]

Many of the municipalities that repudiated their railroad-aid bonds did so with the expectation of avoiding all payments on them. Some, however, defaulted in order to compel their creditors to compromise and to scale down the amount of the debt. Small bondholders, particularly, were frequently willing to settle their claims for a few cents on the dollar. Others, exhausted by years of controversy, preferred to compromise their demands rather than continue tedious and expensive litigation. Seneca Falls, which had repudiated $200,000 of securities issued to build the Pennsylvania & Sodus Bay, kept its case alive in the courts for more than nine years without winning a single decision. Yet the town steadfastly refused to acknowledge the debt unless its creditors agreed to modify their demands. Finally, in 1883, the parties reached a settlement under which some of the bondholders exchanged their 7 per cent 30-year bonds for 5 per cent 20-year securities with back interest payable at 5 per cent. Others agreed to surrender their securities in return for the principal amount and defaulted interest. This agreement eventually saved the community more than $100,000.[101]

The holders of bonds issued by the town of Phelps to aid construction of the Sodus Point & Southern line sued for 26 years before accepting a settlement of 20 cents on the dollar.[102] After 10 years of litigation, the creditors of Angelica exchanged $62,100 in 7 per cent 30-year bonds for $42,300 in 5 per cent securities.[103] Ontario compromised a debt of $85,000, which had been in default for 17 years, at 40 to 60 cents on the dollar.[104] In Orleans the bondholders surrendered $80,000 of the town's obligations for the principal and defaulted interest for 10 years.[105] Andes paid the interest on its bonds for 10 years, defaulted for 10 years, and then compromised with its creditors for the balance at the rate of 60 cents on the dollar.[106]

In 1880 there were 27 separate actions pending against Hancock in the courts. Cases brought before federal tribunals were generally compromised by the town before going to trial. Those instituted in the state courts, however, were always contested. This procedure was followed without exception after 1881, when the municipality's bonds were invalidated by the New York Court of Appeals. In 1887, after 15 years of ceaseless litigation, costing the town more than $30,000 in legal fees, the community voted 270–128 to compromise all outstanding obligations at 58 cents on the dollar.[107] The town of Northampton repudiated $30,000 of its securities after paying interest on them regularly for 20 years. The bondholders, reluctant at first to carry their case into the courts, offered to settle the debt for $18,000. The town officials were willing to accept the proposal, but, in a special election called to determine the community's sentiment, the people voted overwhelmingly to refuse payment. These bonds were subsequently held void by the United States Supreme Court.[108]

Controversies between the towns and their creditors frequently became an issue in local politics. Rival candidates for public office vied in promising the voters reductions in their bonded indebtedness or its complete abolition. In Andes, Hancock, Seneca Falls, Greenwood, and other municipalities in which the repudiationist sentiment was strong, candidates for local offices invariably included in their campaign speeches vigorous denunciations of the community's bondholders. For many years the only member of the Democratic party to be elected in De Ruyter was the town supervisor. While Republican candidates captured other local offices by wide margins, Democratic supervisors George F. Annas and Byron Bryant invariably won by overwhelming majorities largely because of the skillful manner in which they compromised or scaled down the town's debts.[109] They generally carried on negotiations with the security holders in secret. Just before an election, however, these officials would announce the amount of bonds they had canceled during the past year. Commenting on the election of 1889, the editor of a De Ruyter newspaper declared:

Supervisor Bryant cancelled $2500 of old bonds the day before election . . . which was noised about and had its influence in his favor . . . The confidence all have in his ability to handle the bonding question accounts for his big majority which is the largest ever received by a democrat.[110]

The following year the paper reported: "As it was last year, Supervisor Bryant cancelled some $1,500 worth of old bonds a few days before election. Everything helps." [111] Over a period of 13 years, claims against the town amounting to more than $150,000 were settled at 50 cents on the dollar by these two men without resort to the courts.[112]

By 1900 the repudiation of railroad-aid bonds in New York had practically ceased.[113] Only the securities of Genoa and Northampton remained in litigation. Between 1856, when the first default occurred, and 1903, when the last dispute was settled, 56 communities in the state had repudiated railroad-aid bonds with a face value of $4,242,-382. The securities of 16 of these localities, involving $805,000, were subsequently invalidated by the courts.[114] Of the remaining 42 municipalities that defaulted, at least one-half of them compromised or scaled down the amount of their debts. This widespread repudiation of bonds issued for the construction of railroads stands in marked contrast to the record of New York communities in meeting obligations incurred for other purposes. From 1850 to 1950, only 15 municipalities, with bonds amounting to $4,408,000, failed to pay the principal or interest on time.[115] Furthermore, in none of these cases was the community in default for more than a few weeks nor did the bondholders suffer any loss. During the depression of the 1930's, many New York localities found themselves in serious financial difficulties. But not even in this period of unprecedented hardship did the number of defaults approach the proportions of the railroad-building era.

SIX

The Sale of Stock

One of the most important characteristics of transportation development in New York during the last quarter of the nineteenth century was the combination of many short, disconnected lines to form the great railroad systems of the state. At the close of the Civil War, the New York Central was an end-to-end consolidation of a number of small roads between Albany and Buffalo. By 1900 this company had expanded its lines longitudinally by acquisition of the Harlem, West Shore, and Hudson River roads and laterally by inclusion of the Rome, Watertown & Ogdensburg with its 643 miles of track. Meanwhile, great anthracite companies such as the Lehigh, the Delaware & Hudson, and the Delaware, Lackawanna & Western sought, partly by construction but principally by leasing small independent roads, to increase the market for their coal throughout the state and in Canada. During this same period, the Erie, the Pennsylvania, and somewhat later the Baltimore & Ohio extended their systems to reach Lake Ontario and thus to establish connections with the rising industrial cities of Rochester and Buffalo.

Many of these leased lines had been municipally aided and their association with rich and powerful corporations had a profound effect on the localities through which they passed. For some of these communities, location on a trunk line provided not only a more effective link between the centers of production and distribution but it also invested their railroad stocks with considerable value. In 1851, the legislature chartered the Albany & Susquehanna to construct a road between Albany and Binghamton, a distance of 142 miles. Designed primarily as a branch line, it was laid out on a broad gauge to serve as a feeder to the New York & Erie. Since the road passed through an area almost barren of agricultural or industrial resources, it was extremely difficult to obtain funds for the undertaking.[1] Private capital refused to support the enterprise, so the communities along the route subscribed nearly $2,000,000 and the state donated an additional $750,000 to aid the company in building the road. Despite this liberal assistance, the project, described by one observer as a "very contractor's Golgotha," moved slowly toward completion.[2] It was not until February 1869, sixteen years after construction began, that the line opened for traffic.

In the meantime, a number of important changes had taken place on the railroad map of the state. In 1850, when the Albany & Susquehanna Company was organized, the Erie was the only road over 100 miles long. The future New York Central consisted of a dozen disconnected lines extending from Albany to Buffalo. By 1869, the Central and the Erie had become major trunk roads and were competing fiercely for through traffic between the Great Lakes and tidewater. The management of the latter company at this time was vested in two notorious stock gamblers, Jay Gould and Jim Fisk. During the late 1860's, these unscrupulous operators turned their attention to the carrying of coal.[3] In the Fisk-Gould scheme of things, the great anthracite companies which were beginning to branch out as carriers would be forced back into the mines while the Erie railroad, from its strategic central position, would become the indispensable link between the producers and the consumers of coal. The success of this plan depended on control of the Albany & Susquehanna. As an independent company, this road might easily become a major competitor; as part of the Erie, it would provide the system with an entrance into Albany as well as a direct connection with the vast coal markets of eastern New York and New England.

Early in the summer of 1869, the two men made elaborate plans to capture control of the Susquehanna line.[4] At this time, the stock of the company was divided among three classes of owners: three New York capitalists, Samuel Thompson, David M. Groesbeck, and Dabney Morgan & Co.; hundreds of individual owners; and 22 communities along the route.[5] The transactions by which Thompson, Groesbeck, and Morgan acquired their securities requires some explanation. While the line was under construction, a large number of shareholders, discouraged by the road's slow progress, refused to pay the calls on their stock. Many others repudiated their subscriptions altogether. Lawsuits to compel the payment of these obligations generally resulted in favor of the railroad, but the publicity aroused by the litigation created so much ill-will that the company made no further attempt to collect from those who would not pay.[6]

In July 1868, the directors of the Albany & Susquehanna ordered forfeited 7970 shares on which payments of 10 to 40 percent had been made.[7] In anticipation of this action the board had negotiated with Thompson to purchase $160,000 of its second-mortgage bonds at 80 with the option, subsequently exercised, of buying 600 shares of forfeited stock at 25. Soon afterward the company sold to Groesbeck $800,000 of its second-mortgage bonds at 70 with the additional right of purchasing 2400 shares of forfeited stock at 25. Morgan & Company held $500,000 in second-mortgage bonds and 1000 shares of stock which it obtained at prices comparable to those paid by Thompson and Groesbeck.[8] When Gould and Fisk sought to obtain control of the Albany & Susquehanna, in July 1869, the stock of the company was divided approximately as follows: subscribing municipalities held 9500 shares; individuals along the line owned 10,500 shares; Thompson, Groesbeck, and Morgan had 3000 shares, with subscription rights to an additional 2400 shares; 4970 forfeited shares were in the company's possession; and 12,030 shares authorized by the charter had not been sold.

The opponents of Erie domination were led by Joseph H. Ramsay, president, political agent, and guiding spirit of the Susquehanna company. After struggling against overwhelming odds for more than 15 years to complete the line, Ramsey was determined not to surrender his road to figures as disreputable in the railroad world as Fisk and Gould. Late in July, both sides began to buy up stock in anticipation of the contest on September 7 for control of the board of directors. For election purposes, the books of the company closed on August 7, since stock transferred after this date did not carry voting privileges.

Before the summer of 1869, Albany & Susquehanna stock had been selling at about $10 to $15 a share. Under the sudden demand of the rival interests, however, the price mounted rapidly to 80, 90, and even par value.[9] After a few days of feverish buying activity it became apparent to both sides that the disposition of the stock held by municipalities along the line would decide the fate of the road. Ramsay had counted heavily on town support. The possibility that Gould or Fisk would purchase these securities seemed very remote. The laws permitting communities to bond themselves for railroad construction provided that municipal stock must be sold by the towns for cash at par and forbade them to dispose of it at a discount unless authorized to do so by a vote of the people.[10] Obtaining control of the Susquehanna through the purchase of town stock was too much like paying for the road. Certainly, neither Gould nor Fisk would do that. Ramsay, however, underestimated the resourcefulness of his opponents. On the evening of July 29 word reached him in Albany that Gould's agents had purchased the stock of the town of Summit at par and that Schoharie, Davenport, Esperance, and other communities were being solicited to sell their holdings.[11]

Towns that would gladly have sold their stock a few days before at $10 a share were suddenly confronted with offers of par or better. Ramsay paid cash. But the agents of Fisk and Gould rarely made outright purchases. They simply agreed to buy the stock at par after September 7 if the town railroad commissioners voted in the election as the Erie party wished. For the fulfillment of these contracts Gould and Fisk gave their private bond. In town after town, commissioners were called upon to accept or reject this offer within a matter of hours.[12] It was a choice between control of the railroad and the abolition of the town debt. The decision was not easily reached. Some officials arranged immediately for transfer of the stock; others remained open for negotiation.

Ramsay succeeded in purchasing the stock of Richmondville, Sidney, Harpersfield, and Seward, but the rest of the municipal stockholders preferred to negotiate with Fisk and Gould. Milford, Unadilla, and Colesville took Gould's check for $10,000 and his bond for the balance. The people of Maryland felt that they did even better by securing Gould's bond for the principal amount of their stock and his check for $8,000 as a premium. In Davenport, the commissioners held out for cash and got it. Before the stock could be transferred, however, the treasurer absconded with the company's books. In Westford the situation was thrice confounded. One commissioner wanted to sell to Fisk, the other to Ramsay. To break this deadlock, Gould's agent gave the local authorities his bond for the stock and a cash bonus of $4,000. An attempt by the commissioners to retain this premium as their commission for negotiating such a favorable transaction subsequently resulted in protracted litigation.[13]

In some localities railroad commissioners were threatened with the loss of their jobs or political oblivion if they supported one faction or the other.[14] The Albany Common Council removed its representative on the board of directors for supporting the Erie cause.[15] At Colliers a public meeting censured the railroad commissioners for selling to what it called "a rapacious, forceful and fraudulent monopoly."[16] In Milford and Oneonta the officials were forced to resign for negotiating with Gould's agents.[17] On the other hand, the opponents of Ramsay in Otego petitioned the county judge to remove the commissioners on the ground that they refused to sell to Erie interests.[18] Many of the Gould-Fisk purchases were obviously illegal and Ramsay warned the treasurer of the road, William L. M. Phelps, against transferring the stock on the company's books.[19] On August 3, Gould's agents appeared at the Susquehanna office in Albany and demanded the transfer of their securities. Phelps refused. The next day some town stock which had been legally purchased was transferred but a series of injunctions obtained by Ramsay restrained Phelps from making any further changes.[20]

By August 5 all the municipal and private securities that could be purchased were in the hands of one party or the other. Ramsay, who up to this time had been waging a desperate battle for control of the road, now resorted to tactics comparable to those employed by his adversaries. Approximately 12,000 shares of the authorized capital stock of the company had never been issued. Shortly before the books of the company closed, he entered into a secret arrangement with a number of individuals whereby 9,500 of these shares were disposed of to friendly interests. For the most part these newly created stockholders were men of no more than average means. Minard Harder of Cobleskill, who purchased 500 shares, declared a few months later that he did not own sufficient property to pay even the requisite 10 per cent down.[21] John Eddy of Milford, who subscribed for 1000 shares, stated that he bought the stock with the understanding that it was to be transferred to other parties who would pay all the necessary costs.[22] Who were the other parties? As early as 1866 the Delaware & Hudson Canal Company recognized the strategic importance of the Albany & Susquehanna for the transportation of its coal. At this time, the company purchased $500,000 of the Albany line's second-mortgage bonds as part of an agreement by which the latter agreed to the exclusive distribution of Delaware & Hudson anthracite.[23] In 1869, the Canal company's Board of Managers, in coöperation with Groesbeck and Dabney Morgan & Company, determined to seize possession of the road. On August 5, with eleven small-town businessmen as its agents, the Delaware & Hudson advanced sufficient funds to guarantee a controlling interest in the line.[24] With such strong financial support a Ramsay victory was virtually assured. Upon the completion of this transaction, Ramsay, aided by Phelps, removed the books from the company's vaults and placed them in hiding until the day of the election.[25]

Meanwhile the people of the state were being treated once again to all the familiar features of previous Gould-Fisk raids and fights. There were the adroit, wily Jay Gould with his "trunk full of greenbacks"; Admiral Fisk with his blue coat, brass buttons, and diamond stickpin; and "Erie Judge" Barnard with his numberless injunctions, orders, and receivers. Ramsay centered his attack on the municipal securities purchased on credit. The Erie party, relying on pliant judges and suborned courts, enjoined the Susquehanna faction from voting the forfeited shares purchased by Groesbeck and others and the 9500 shares on which only part payment had been made.[26] In the middle of August, violence broke out along the line between rival groups of the company's employees. After a fierce battle before the long tunnel at Bainbridge, Governor Hoffman seized possession of the road and placed it under military supervision.

On election day, stockholders who favored the Erie interests convened in the company offices and organized a board of directors supporting Fisk and Gould. In the same building, but in a different room, their opponents met and named a board favorable to Ramsay. Many of the towns were represented by two sets of commissioners. Rival officials from Milford and Oneonta, for example, supported opposite sides in the balloting.[27] When the election failed to settle the problem of ownership, Governor Hoffman, acting through his attorney general, instituted proceedings in the state Supreme Court at Rochester to determine which board had been legally elected. The decision handed down on November 29 sustained the Ramsay interests on every important point, but the court ruled that 11 of the 21 municipalities that sold their stock during the raid made unlawful transfers.[28] A few weeks after this decision the Delaware & Hudson leased the Albany & Susquehanna line for 150 years from April 1851. By the terms of this contract, the Delaware & Hudson assumed all of the Susquehanna line's outstanding indebtedness and agreed to pay 7 per cent on the company's capital stock.

This alliance with a rich and powerful anthracite company caused the stock of the Albany & Susquehanna to soar once again and many communities were able to sell at prices equal to those offered during the Erie raid. Of the 22 towns that purchased stock in the road, 17 sold their securities at par or better.[29] Only Cobleskill and Colesville retained their stock beyond the life of the bonds issued to buy it. These municipalities subsequently sold their securities at more than double par value after receiving dividends ranging from 7 to 12 per cent for nearly three-quarters of a century.

In general, leases negotiated by large railroad corporations with municipally aided lines proved highly advantageous to the latter companies. Seldom did the earnings of these lesser roads exceed the consideration in the lease. Only a few communities, however, that owned debenture or guaranteed stock retained it long enough to realize any substantial profit. In their anxiety to reduce their bonded indebtedness most of them disposed of their investment almost as soon as it acquired a market value.

The General Bonding Act of 1869 required municipal officials to set up a sinking fund within three years after the sale of the town's railroad-aid bonds and to pay into the fund annually at least 1 per cent of the total issue. Despite this statutory requirement, scarcely a municipality in the state made any provision for the redemption of its securities. Consequently, as their bonds matured, local authorities were compelled either to refund them or, if the town held railroad stock of market value, to sell it to liquidate the indebtedness. The vast majority of communities preferred to dispose of their holdings even though their bonds might be refunded on very favorable terms. The philosophy that a public debt is a public blessing had few advocates among town officials in the years following the panic of 1873.

The city of Utica, for example, invested $500,000 in the Utica, Chenango & Susquehanna Valley, a 100-mile line extending from Utica to Greene. Upon its completion in 1870, the property was leased to the Delaware, Lackawanna & Western, which agreed to pay dividends equal to 6 per cent on its capital stock. For the next ten years the city annually received a dividend of $30,000, but paid out $35,000 in interest on its bonds. Shortly before these obligations matured, the relation of the city's investment to its bonded indebtedness came up for public discussion. What should the community do about the redemption of these securities, which would fall due at the rate of $100,000 a year after 1882? [30]

In his inaugural address of 1878, Mayor Daniel Griffin urged the city council to dispose of its securities at any price it could get. A fixed debt of $200,000 or $300,000, he argued, would be far better for the community than a contingent liability of $500,000.[31] By 1881, Chenango stock was selling at a premium of $10 to $15 a share and those who advocated retaining the stock as an investment demanded that the city refinance its railroad-aid bonds at 3 or 3½ per cent. In this way, they pointed out, the annual deficit of $5,000 would be converted into a profit of $12,000 or $15,000.[32] This refunding scheme was roundly condemned by both the administration and the press. Mayor George A. Miller protested that the municipality had no moral right to speculate in railroad or other stocks and that the voters would not sustain those who attempted such an experiment.[33] The *Morning Herald* conceded that the city could refund its debt at 4 per cent or better but it doubted the wisdom of such a policy. If the city were a banking house, the paper argued, it should not fail to seize such an opportunity for profit. But, the *Herald* reasoned, it is not a banking house nor properly a railroad stockholder and, therefore, should not enter into this kind of speculation.[34]

When the refunding movement collapsed, some councilmen urged that the entire investment be sold while the market value of the securities was still high. This plan of action had few supporters. Since only $100,000 of the bonds were maturing, what, it was asked, would the city do with the balance from the sale of $440,000 or $450,000? The law which permitted the city to aid construction of the road required that any money obtained from the sale of stock be placed in a sinking fund for redemption of the bonds as they fell due.[35] Since bank interest did not exceed 2 or 2½ per cent, this procedure would have reduced the city's income by $14,000 to $16,000 a year. Moreover, many felt that the sale of such a large block of securities would precipitate a sharp drop in the price of the stock with a resulting loss to the city of several thousand dollars.[36] After several months of debate, the Common Council decided to sell its stock only in amounts sufficient to retire maturing bonds. These sales were conducted with such success that Utica obtained a premium of nearly $50,000 on the transactions.[37] Nine other municipalities held guaranteed 6 per cent stock in the Chenango Valley road. Like Utica, none of them retained its securities after its bonds matured. Most of these communities used their annual dividends to pay the interest on their obligations and then auctioned off their stock when the principal came due.[38]

Virtually every town that invested in the Whitehall & Plattsburg and the New York & Canada disposed of its holdings within a year after the road's completion. In the fall of 1875 the Delaware & Hudson purchased the securities of a number of these towns at $50 a share. Payment for the stock was made in the bonds of the town presenting its securities for sale.[39] In Plattsburg, this exchange was effected only after a bitter factional dispute. Some thought that the price was too low. Others argued that retention of the stock would foster better relations between the company and the town, since, by keeping its investment, the community would be assured of at least one seat on the board of directors. But the taxpayers of the town were anxious to secure immediate relief from the burdens of the depression, so they voted to make the transfer.[40]

There is no record of any company that leased a publicly subsidized line defaulting on its obligations. In two instances, however, the rights of stockholders in the lessor company were so poorly defined in the contract that the municipal shareholders were seriously handicapped in selling their stock. In 1871 the city of Utica subscribed $200,000 to the Utica, Clinton & Binghamton, a line that had been leased upon completion to the New York & Oswego Midland. The loss of a quarter of a million dollars only a decade before in the ill-fated Black River & Utica road prompted the city to proceed with caution in this new venture. In an effort to obtain the utmost protection for its investment, the city retained one of the foremost jurists of the state, Hiram Denio, to negotiate with the company and to draw up the final agreement. Under the terms of the contract, the city sold $200,000 in 7 per cent 30-year bonds and turned the proceeds over to the railroad. In consideration of this aid, the company transferred to the city 2000 shares of its capital stock and agreed to pay upon it, forever, $10,000 annually in the form of dividends. The payment of these dividends was further guaranteed by the lessee of the road, the New York & Oswego Midland, and by the Delaware & Hudson Canal Company. The guarantee was reaffirmed in 1889 when a new lease was drawn up by the Utica, Clinton & Binghamton, the New York Ontario & Western (the successor of the Midland), and the Delaware & Hudson Canal Company.[41]

Annually for thirty years the city received a $10,000 dividend from the railroad. During this period no sinking fund was created, nor was any attempt made to amortize the debt. In 1901, when its railroad-aid bonds matured, the Common Council of the city voted to auction off its stock in order to obtain sufficient funds to meet the obligation. Shortly before the sale began, an attorney for the Utica, Clinton & Binghamton read a lengthy statement to the effect that the guarantee on the securities was made to the city of Utica only and would not be honored in the event the stock were transferred to another party. With its preferred status the stock was worth $140 a share but without this guarantee its value would not exceed $75. When the call for bids brought in only one offer of 110, the city officials, who had agreed in advance not to sell for less than 125, rejected the bid.[42]

Unable to market its stock at what it considered a fair price, the city appealed to the courts for a clarification of its ownership rights. In a test case in November 1904, it sold five shares to Clifford Marklove. When the certificate of ownership sent to him by the railroad failed to carry the endorsement that it was entitled to 5 per cent dividends, Marklove brought an action against the city and the company to have his stock covered by the guarantee. The suit resulted in a victory for the plaintiff.[43] Despite this favorable decision, the city was never able to sell its holdings at the preferred-stock price. Auctions were widely advertised and pamphlets containing a history of the stock were sent to leading investment houses, but brokers refused to bid on the ground that the Marklove decision was rendered by a lower court and had never been appealed.[44] In September 1912, the city clerk, acting under an authorization to sell below par if necessary, disposed of the stock at 102½. To obtain this price, however, the city was required to deposit $30 per share in a local bank for a period of ten years as a guarantee that the Marklove decision would not be reversed by a higher court.[45]

Rochester, like Utica, was plagued for a number of years by doubts about the validity of the lease which guaranteed dividends on its $300,000 stock in the Rochester & Genesee Valley. The city, which owned a controlling interest in the railroad, leased the line, in 1871, to the New York & Erie, which agreed to maintain the property and to pay 6 per cent dividends on its capital stock. During the panic of 1893 this company passed into receivership, but it was reorganized and emerged soon afterward as the Erie Railroad. While the new corporation honored the old lease, it scrupulously avoided making any official acknowledgment of the obligation.[46]

In the spring of 1904, the Rochester Common Council voted to spend several thousand dollars to erect new police and fire houses. Members of the council agreed that these improvements were needed, but they differed sharply over the best method of financing them. Some, like the city comptroller, wanted to borrow the money. The credit of the city at this time was very high and it would have been relatively easy to obtain funds at a low rate of interest.[47] A majority, however, advocated the sale of the city's railroad stock. This policy was strongly endorsed by the propertied interests of the city. A poll of the 20 largest taxpayers, representing one-tenth of the taxable property of Rochester, revealed almost unanimous support for raising the money by this means.[48] Accordingly, the securities were advertised and bids were solicited from leading banks and brokerage houses. Since the city could give no assurance that a lease existed between the Erie and the Rochester & Genesee Valley, only two of the 250 investment houses invited to bid on the stock submitted an offer.[49] "From what we can learn," wrote one broker, "the Erie railroad can surrender this property at its pleasure and does not in any way guarantee the six per cent dividend." [50] With the guarantee the securities were worth $140 to $150 a share; without it they were worth no more than $60 or $70. Fortunately for the city, the two houses that submitted bids did not share the pessimistic views of the other brokerage firms. On April 17, 1904, the city of Rochester sold its 3000 shares of stock at 140¼, or $420,750.[51]

Most local aid to railroads in New York was granted in the form of a subscription to the company's capital stock. Less than 10 per cent was invested in some other manner. A few municipalities sought to insure the safety of their investments by insisting upon securities of a higher order, particularly bonds. These communities generally suffered less financial hardship than did those that held common stock, but the ownership of railroad bonds proved no guarantee against loss. The city of Albany was quite successful in lending its money. Loans of $1,000,000 each were made without loss to the Albany & West Stockbridge[52] and the Albany & Susquehanna lines.[53] An issue of $100,000 of Mohawk & Hudson first-mortgage bonds guaranteed by the city in 1842 and a loan of $125,000 to the same company the following year were negotiated without expense to the community.[54] Only a $300,000 loan to the Albany Northern turned out badly.[55] On the other hand, the towns of Berlin, Peterburgh, Stephentown, New Lebanon, and Chatham lost their entire investment of $263,500 in the bonds of the Lebanon Springs road.[56] Rochester lost $150,000 in second-mortgage bonds of the Rochester, Nunda & Pennsylvania,[57] while Poughkeepsie lost $274,000 when the Poughkeepsie & Eastern passed into bankruptcy.[59]

Troy had a very unfortunate experience. By 1851 four important railroads, the Rensselaer & Saratoga, the Hudson River, the Schenectady & Troy, and the Troy & Boston, terminated in Troy. To connect these lines and thus facilitate the movement of passengers and freight through the city, the directors of the several companies proposed the construction of a jointly owned and operated Troy Union Railroad. To aid in its financing, the city agreed to borrow $700,000 to build the road. As a protection against loss, the coöperating companies gave the municipality a first mortgage on the property and agreed to pay the principal and interest on the city's bonds.[60] Less than six months after completion of the project, the companies began to quarrel among themselves. The New York Central, apparently irritated because the road proved more advantageous to the Rensselaer company than to itself, repudiated the agreement and refused to pay its share of the interest on the Troy bonds.[61] The Hudson River road and the impecunious Troy & Boston quickly followed suit. For the next three years Troy was compelled to appropriate nearly $100,000 to preserve the credit of the community. During this period city officials pleaded with the railroads to reconsider their action. But committees appointed to discuss the matter were not received and letters of protest went unanswered. On one occasion President Gould refused to reply to a communication from the Common Council on the ground that it was not addressed to him as president of the Troy Union railroad.[62]

During the election campaign of 1857, a citizen's committee was formed to oppose any candidate for public office who favored compromise with the railroad companies. The contest, which the *Daily Whig* described as the most exciting in the city's history, resulted in defeat for the mayoralty candidate who favored negotiation and concessions.[63] A suit against the railroads instituted by the new administration resulted simply in a decision by the court that the city might foreclose on its mortgage if it wished.[64] But who wanted to do this? Foreclosure on the mortgage would avail the city little. The road was only two miles long and possessed no rolling stock. The one company in a financial position to purchase the road was the New York Central and this line was unwilling to offer the city more than a fraction of its cost.[65] In 1856 the Central had secured a charter for an Albany bridge and its connection over the Hudson *via* the Union road was no longer of great importance. Municipal operation of the line was not even considered. The city had just finished a long and costly experience in public ownership of a railroad and no one suggested that it should repeat the experiment.

After months of negotiation and litigation, the city conceded that no amicable settlement could be reached unless it made major financial concessions to the railroad companies.[66] In October 1858, the parties to the dispute reached an agreement that ranks as one of the most dishonorable episodes in the story of municipal aid to railroads in the state of New York. Under the new contract, the city agreed to assume $115,000 of the road's outstanding bonds, pay $64,108.95 in back interest, and grant the Troy & Boston a right of way across its main residential section so that it might secure access to the Hudson River for freight.[67]

The story of the Troy Union line is unique as a case of a railroad company defaulting on bonds guaranteed by a municipality but it is not exceptional as an instance of community intimidation by a powerful railroad corporation. A score or more of localities were practically coerced into selling their securities by companies that were attempting to secure control of the road in which they held stock.

By 1870 two important railroads served the northern area of the state—the Rome, Watertown & Ogdensburg, and the Utica & Black River. To connect these lines and gain entrance into the city of Watertown for the latter company, an enterprising group of Jefferson County businessmen undertook the construction of the Carthage, Watertown & Sacketts Harbor road. Most of the capital stock for this undertaking was subscribed by the towns along the route.[68] Shortly after its completion in 1872, the Rome road leased both the Black River and the Sacketts Harbor companies. The increased business that these leases promised to bring caused a sharp rise in the value of the lines' securities, and a few communities, such as Watertown and Champion, decided to retain their railroad stock as an investment.[69]

In 1891 the New York Central leased the Rome road and its lessor companies. To forestall the payment of large and continuous dividends to the Sacketts Harbor stockholders, the Central decided to buy up that company's outstanding shares. When the towns refused to sell, the Central routed its freight and passengers over other lines. Moreover, it threatened to construct a parallel road, passing through the same points, unless the communities relinquished their securities.[70] Since the Central controlled all the connections of the road and supplied 90 per cent of its traffic, the towns were soon compelled to submit. Watertown was first to capitulate. In 1893 the city exchanged its 3000 shares of stock for $25,000 in cash and $275,000 in 4 per cent notes of the New York Central & Hudson River Company with the understanding that neither the notes nor the money were to be used until the New York Court of Appeals had passed on the validity of the transaction. Four months later, however, the agreement was revised to permit the city to use the securities to retire its railroad-aid bonds.[71]

Since the sale of the Watertown stock deprived the towns of a controlling interest in the line, the remaining municipal stockholders soon disposed of their holdings.[72] The speed and thoroughness with which the Central acted in this affair prompted the retiring president of the Sacketts Harbor road, George A. Bagley, to remark:

I read in the *Times* an account of the cool manner in which the Dalton brothers took possession of a bank in a western town and forced the occupants to deliver up the funds. As I stood here this afternoon and watched the New York Central people ensconced in the bank office chairs, I could not help likening this scene to the other one.[73]

In 1900 the Central threatened to foreclose its mortgage on the Dunkirk, Allegheny Valley & Pittsburgh unless the municipal shareholders gave up their stock.[74] The towns of Charlotte, Pomfret, and Gerry, fearful lest an auction sale deprive them of their equity in the road, agreed to dispose of their holdings to the Central at $30 a share.[75] Dunkirk, which refused to sell, eventually profited heavily from its investment.

As late as 1946, the towns of Greene and Cobleskill were compelled to sell their railroad stock, which they had held for more than three-quarters of a century. The Greene railroad, in which the municipality of Greene had invested $198,700, was a little eight-mile line running from the center of the town to the village of Chenango Forks. The importance of the road lay in the fact that it connected the Utica branch of the Delaware, Lackawanna & Western with the main line. In 1870 the Lackawanna leased the road for a period of 99 years at an annual rental of 6 per cent on the capital stock. To the town this meant a guaranteed yearly income of $11,922 on its investment. When their railroad-aid bonds fell due in 1899, the local authorities sold 1400 shares of stock at $145 a share to liquidate the debt. On its remaining 587 shares the town received, until 1943, an annual dividend of $3522.[76]

Prior to the depression of the 1930's, the payment of these dividends was not a serious problem for the Lackawanna. By 1900 the company's earnings were as high as 50 per cent on its capital stock. Dividends between 1906 and 1930 were paid at an average rate of 21.4 per cent. This was twice as much as any other road paid. Despite lavish dividends and extensive outlays for improvements, the accounting surplus of the company, in 1906, had risen to $34,638,996 or 32 per cent more than its total outstanding stock and bonds. The price of common stock at this time reached $680 a share. In 1909, the directors declared a dividend of stock and cash equal to 187.5 per cent per share. This was followed two years later by a cash dividend of 55 per cent.[77] Prosperity for New York's anthracite coal roads came to an end with the panic of 1929. The Lackawanna, with its heavy fixed charges and dependence on the coal trade, was hard hit by the depression. The system was composed mainly of leased lines on which the parent company paid annual rentals of 4 to 12 per cent on their capital stock.[78] In 1943 this meant a dividend yield on the market value of these securities of 10.4 to 32 per cent.[79]

By the outbreak of World War II, the financial outlook of the road appeared very dark. To aid the company's recovery the management launched a program to reduce its fixed charges by merging its lessor companies into the Lackawanna system. In 1942, negotiations were started with the New York, Lackawanna & Western. By 1945, 13 of the 18 leased lines had been merged and the property of another had been acquired by purchase.[80] For many years the Lackawanna had been trying to buy up the interest of the town of Greene in the Greene railroad at prices as high as $50 a share, but the town officials, anxious to protect this source of revenue, gave scant consideration to the offers.[81] In 1946 the town board reconsidered the matter and voted to sell its stock.

Several factors contributed to this change of heart. One of the most important was the road's seemingly shaky financial condition. Since the Lackawanna owned the entire funded debt of the Greene railroad, some members of the town board believed that, in the event of recapitalization, the common stock would be wiped out while the company would be able to maintain its preferred position through ownership of the bonds.[82] Moreover, the town faced a reduction in its dividends as a result of the federal income-tax law. After the passage of this act in 1913 the annual rentals paid to lessor companies, such as the Greene railroad, were subject to federal taxation. For twenty years these levies were paid by the Lackawanna, but a court decision in 1933 led the company to discontinue the payment of such taxes. In April 1942, the United States Circuit Court of Appeals ruled that income taxes assessed against lessor companies must be collected from stockholders out of the rentals paid to them under the leases. It further ordered that no more dividends should be paid until tax liabilities for the period 1933-1942 were satisfied. Since the town of Greene owed $17,657 in back taxes and interest, no dividends were paid to the municipality after 1943. If the town retained its stock, therefore, it would have to pay a federal levy of approximately $1.50 per share.[83]

Following the income-tax decision, the Lackawanna renewed its efforts to purchase the stock. It bid $40, $45, and finally $50 a share, but the municipal officials still refused to sell.[84] In 1944, the company offered to take the 587 shares of the town stock at 50 in exchange for $38,000 par value 4 or 4½ per cent first-mortgage bonds of the New York, Lackawanna & Western railroad then selling at 78. The interest on these bonds would provide the town with an annual income of $1520. This was the best offer made by the company, and the town board asked the state for permission to accept it.[85] But the state comptroller held that such an agreement was illegal because it violated the constitutional provision which prohibited municipalities from lending their credit to private corporations.[86]

After 1944, the company warned the town's officials repeatedly that, if the municipality insisted on retention of its securities, it would appeal to the Interstate Commerce Commission for permission to merge the road into the Lackawanna system. If such a petition were approved, the railroad officials pointed out, the stock of the Greene railroad would be appraised and the town compelled to accept its valuation. The stock of the Utica, Chenango & Susquehanna Valley, a comparable security, was selling at only 82 and the company intimated that this was the price the municipality would receive under the merger plan.[87] Meanwhile, the town board consulted a New York investment house. After a careful study of the Lackawanna's financial position, the firm advised the town to sell its holdings.[88] In 1946 the company raised its price to $100 per share, and the town board accepted the offer.[89]

The Delaware & Hudson, like the Delaware, Lackawanna & Western, recovered slowly from the depression of the thirties. The dwindling of the anthracite trade, heavy rentals on its leased lines, and a large investment in stock of the New York Central, all contributed to its unfavorable financial structure. After 1938, the company tried to improve its condition by a large-scale program of debt reduction, sale of its Central holdings, and reduction of fixed charges by merging its leased lines.[90] One of the roads involved in the company's merger program was the Albany & Susquehanna, the main line of the system extending from Albany to Binghamton. To aid the construction of this road, the town of Cobleskill bonded itself in 1862 for $60,000. During the Erie raid of 1869, the local authorities made a contingent sale of its securities to Jay Gould, but the treasurer of the road refused to transfer the stock on the company's books.[91] After the raid was over, the town board decided that the Susquehanna investment was a good one and resolved to retain possession of the stock as long as it could. In 1882 the last of the town's railroad-aid bonds fell due and the community sold 250 shares at 128 to meet the obligation.[92] No further stock was sold until 1946. In the interval, the town received an excellent return on its securities. Between 1871 and 1903, this averaged more than 7 per cent. From 1903 to 1945 the rate jumped to 9 per cent plus extra dividends totaling $98.85 per share. Over a period of 75 years the dividends amounted to $700.64 per share, or a total income for the town of $301,798.50.[93]

In 1942, the Interstate Commerce Commission authorized the Delaware & Hudson to merge the Albany & Susquehanna into its system if such a move were approved by two-thirds of Susquehanna stockholders. Under the terms of the proposed agreement, stockholders in the Albany & Susquehanna were to receive one $150 principal amount of that company's 4½ per cent general-mortgage bonds (callable at 174) and one share of Delaware & Hudson common stock (selling at 46⅞) in exchange for each share of stock they held in the Susquehanna road. This was a generous offer and the stockholders quickly accepted.[94] But Cobleskill, like Greene, soon learned that the state constitution limited its freedom as a shareholder in a private corporation. In an opinion almost identical with the one he had written in the Greene case, the state comptroller refused to allow the town to make the exchange.[95] The only alternative was to liquidate the investment. In July 1946, Cobleskill sold its 350 shares of Albany & Susquehanna stock at 230½ or $80,629.[96]

Few locally aided railroads were as profitable to the investing communities as the Greene and the Albany & Susquehanna lines. Indeed, the longest and most heavily subsidized road, the New York & Oswego Midland, was a tragic failure. The reasons for this company's bankruptcy have been explained elsewhere, but the final disposition of the town stock deserves some attention here. In September 1873 the Midland passed into the hands of receivers, who operated the line for the next six years. The task of preserving the property and maintaining the line's going value until the creditors could work out a reorganization plan was enormous. The wages of employees were four months in arrears, the interest on more than $12,000,000 in bonds was long overdue, and almost the entire roadbed from Oswego to Middletown needed thorough reconditioning. Expenditures at this time exceeded receipts by more than $3,000 a day.[97]

During this period several proposals were advocated to enable the company to scale down its debts to allow the road to make a fresh start. Holders of large blocks of bonds, notes, and receivers' certificates circularized the towns seeking the right to represent them on security holders' committees. But differences among the various classes of investors were so great that more than five years elapsed before an agreement was reached on a general reorganization plan.[98] Most of the early schemes provided for a capital stock of $20,000,000 and granted the Midland owners fully paid shares in the reorganized company. In the plan finally adopted, however, the original stockholders were required to pay an assessment of $30 a share to obtain pro rata stock in the new corporation. At a foreclosure sale on November 4, 1879, a committee representing the first-mortgage bondholders and the owners of receivers' certificates purchased the road for $4,600,000. Midland stockholders were given the right to redeem the line within six months by paying the "upset price." [99]

Shortly after the terms of the reorganization were announced, the city of Oswego proposed a meeting of railroad commissioners from all the Midland towns to devise some method of obtaining a voice in the affairs of the new company. On February 18, 1880, representatives from 26 towns attended a convention held at Norwich.[100] Several schemes were advanced to protect the interests of the communities but only one was considered seriously by the delegates. At the suggestion of the·commissioners from Oswego, the towns agreed to put their stock in the hands of a central committee which was authorized to sell it in one block at a minimum price. In this way, it was felt, the towns would obtain much better terms than if they sold their securities a few shares at a time. If a satisfactory price could not be secured, the committee was empowered to negotiate with investment bankers to obtain money for the road's redemption. In exchange for the needed $4,600,000, the towns were prepared to offer a first mortgage on the road. Furthermore, as a bonus for advancing the funds, the committee was authorized to grant an additional $500,000 to be included in the lien. By this arrangement, the Midland communities would own a $20,000,000 railroad encumbered only by a mortgage of $5,100,000.[101] Even if the plan failed, its promoters reasoned, the mere threat of redemption would cause a substantial rise in the value of Midland securities.

A few weeks after the Norwich meeting, the central committee reported that although it had been unable to market the stock at an acceptable price, it had succeeded in making arrangements to obtain funds for purchase of the road. The names of the bankers who would advance the capital, it said, could not be made public at the time, but, it declared, the money would be forthcoming as soon as the contract could be drawn up and all the town securities were placed in its hands. At the committee's request, legal forms giving it power of attorney over the stock were sent to the Midland railroad commissioners for their signature. To negotiate the agreement, the meeting selected James Failing of Oswego, who claimed to be the only one acquainted with the party pledging the money.[102]

In the meantime, Midland stock that had been unsalable at any price the previous fall acquired a market value and virtually every community along the line held a special town meeting to discuss the wisdom of selling its holdings.[103] By the terms of the municipal bonding law, town stock could not be sold below par unless the sale were approved by a majority of the taxpayers representing a majority of the taxable property. Consequently, several municipalities took steps that would enable them to sell at a moment's notice should a favorable opportunity arise. To expedite matters, and at the same time to save the communities the expense of securing the necessary consents, the state legislature amended the law to permit the Midland railroad commissioners to sell their securities without waiting for taxpayers' approval.[104]

Offers of $4, $5, and even $10 a share were reported in towns along the line.[105] At Oswego, the chairman of the Midland stock committee urged the city council to resist all bids and predicted that, if the towns would stand together, the stock would rise to at least $50 a share.[106] The Norwich *Telegraph*, a strong supporter of the redemption scheme, repeatedly cautioned the towns against selling their securities for what it called "a mess of pottage." [107] Plans for redeeming the road were proceeding smoothly when, suddenly, the Oswego newspapers announced that the city had sold its 6000 shares at 5¼.[108] This action by the home city of the redemption committee's chairman caught the other communities completely by surprise. Demoralization reigned all along the line as towns rushed to sell before the market collapsed. With the pool broken, negotiations looking toward redemption of the road were suspended.[109] In May 1880, the Midland passed into the hands of a group of Anglo-American bankers who reorganized the line as the New York, Ontario & Western.

In some respects the most valuable parts of the Midland system were two locally aided branch lines, the Rome & Clinton and the Utica, Clinton & Binghamton. These roads had been leased upon their completion at annual rentals of $25,000 and $70,500, respectively. Payment of the rents was guaranteed by the Delaware & Hudson.[110] Municipal stockholders in these companies did quite well on their investment. The Rome road paid dividends ranging from 3 to 8 per cent for nearly three-quarters of a century. The town of Westmoreland, which owned 400 shares, sold its securities at $85 a share immediately after consummation of the lease,[111] but Rome and Kirkland, and other municipal stockholders in the line, retained their holdings for many years. To obtain funds for construction of a new city hall, the city of Rome disposed of its securities in 1894 at 126.[112] Kirkland kept its investment until 1944, when the New York, Ontario & Western purchased the road's outstanding stock at $52 a share.[113]

The Utica, Clinton & Binghamton, like the Rome & Clinton road, was built chiefly from the proceeds of town subscriptions.[114] After the Midland's failure, the line was operated in turn by that company's receivers, the Delaware, Lackawanna & Western, and the Delaware & Hudson. During this period, the latter company, as guarantor of the Midland lease, paid the annual rental. In 1889 the Delaware & Hudson leased the road in perpetuity. By the terms of the agreement, it pledged, among other things, to pay the principal and interest on the lessor company's bonds, 5 per cent dividends on the 2000 shares of stock issued to the city of Utica, and 1¾ per cent on the remainder of the common stock. The New York, Ontario & Western, successor to the Midland, agreed to operate the property. This arrangement remained in effect until 1942, when the Interstate Commerce Commission authorized the Ontario company to purchase the road's outstanding securities.[115] Only Utica, of the five municipalities that aided the construction of the Binghamton line, disposed of its stock before the liquidation. For more than fifty years, the towns of Kirkland, Madison, and Augusta and the village of Hamilton received annual dividends of 1¾ to 4 per cent on their investment. During the 1930's, the New York, Ontario & Western made several attempts to purchase the towns' securities but the local officials rejected the bids. In 1942 the company raised its price to $40 and the towns accepted the offer.[116]

Of the 297 communities that subscribed to the capital stock of railroads in New York, only Dunkirk and Theresa still retain their holdings. In 1867 the town of Dunkirk bonded itself for $125,000 on behalf of the Dunkirk, Allegany Valley & Pittsburgh. Two years later Theresa subscribed $60,000 to aid in the building of the Black River & Morristown. The latter was by far the better investment. Between 1873 and 1914, Theresa received annual dividends ranging from 7 to 21.5 per cent. The Allegany stock, on the other hand, yielded no return until 1900, when a regular dividend rate of 1½ per cent was established.[117]

In 1914 the Black River and Allegany lines were merged into the New York Central system. Both communities thereafter received the regular Central dividends, which averaged better than 6 per cent from 1914 to 1931. Moreover, at various times, the Central granted its stockholders "subscription rights" or the privilege of purchasing stock in the company at less than market value.[118] Forbidden by constitutional restrictions from taking full advantage of these offers, the towns converted their "rights" into cash. These "subscription rights" gave the communities substantial additions to their regular dividends. In the case of Theresa, the income from these sales amounted to more than $16,000 by 1930.[119] Late in the summer of 1929, when Central stock was selling at more than $250 a share, there was a strong movement in Dunkirk and Theresa to sell their securities. A majority of the people, however, looked on the investment as a perpetual source of income or as a contingent fund to be spent only in a great emergency. Today, there is no talk of selling the stock. On the contrary, many in these towns voice the opinion that somehow or someway shares in the New York Central will rise again to the 1929 level.[120]

From a strictly investment point of view, New York communities suffered heavily by aiding in the construction of railroads. Only 52 of the 297 municipalities that bought stock in a railroad company disposed of their securities at par or better; 162 held stock with no market value. Losses resulting from investment in bonds were almost as great. Of the nine localities that held railroad bonds only one, the city of Albany, received any of the principal or interest on its securities. Public aid, however, cannot be assessed on this narrow basis. Unlike private individuals, municipalities did not subscribe to the stocks and bonds of railroads with the primary purpose of making money. Indeed, the very fact that public money was required to build the lines is proof of the hazardous financial character of the investments. Private capital could be selective in its choice of securities; municipalities could not. While enthusiastic promoters and newspaper editors frequently alluded to the possibility of profits, the underlying motive prompting municipal aid for railroad construction was the development of the community through improved transportation facilities. In New York State this objective was achieved. Approximately 85 per cent of the municipalities that subsidized railroad construction obtained the road they assisted. Although only one municipality in 25 showed a profit on its investment, this unfavorable record must be attributed in part to constitutional restrictions governing local aid and in part to the reluctance of many communities to retain their securities even though their investments were sound ones. Moreover, the incidence of loss experienced by these localities was probably no greater than that suffered by individuals who speculated in railroads or other forms of business enterprise at this time.

The communities' failure to realize substantial financial returns on their investments cannot be ascribed in great measure to fraud. A few railroad schemes, of course, were swindles from the outset, and any expectations of dividends that the subsidizing towns might have entertained were generally dashed soon after their bonds were handed over to the promoters. While a number of locally aided lines did fail, their bankruptcy was due more often to unwarranted optimism, incompetent direction, or unsettled business conditions than to chicanery or fraudulent management. For example, the city of Utica, in 1853, bonded itself for $250,000 to aid in construction of the Black River & Utica, a line projected from Utica to the St. Lawrence River. As in most early railroad ventures, the promoters planned to finance the road wholly through the proceeds of stock subscriptions. But the arrangement was soon abandoned because it tended to postpone, until the line was a demonstrated success, both dividends and sales of the stock at a premium. Moreover, finding it easier to sell bonds than stock, the management resorted to large bond issues in the hope that the borrowed capital would yield a return greater than the interest on the loan.[121] Shortly after the road reached Boonville, 30 miles from Utica, the panic of 1857 struck the country. During the depression the entire income of the company was absorbed in meeting fixed charges. To help pay these expenses and to increase the line's working capital, the directors began to issue bonds at discounts of 30, 40, and even 50 per cent.[122] Such injudicious financing soon precipitated the road into receivership, and in 1860 the line was sold under a mortgage foreclosure.

Buffalo had a comparable experience. Between 1873 and 1875 this city and a number of towns in Erie, Cattaraugus, and Chautauqua Counties contributed more than $1,000,000 to build the Buffalo & Jamestown railroad, now the main line of the Erie entering Buffalo. Like the Black River road, this project was launched on the eve of a disastrous panic, and, as in the Black River case, its directors issued bonds in disproportionate quantities in an effort to complete the undertaking. During the depression years, the fixed charges exceeded the company's earning power and in September 1877 the bondholders took possession of the property.[123] The reorganization agreement gave stockholders the right to redeem the road within six months or to exchange their stock for that of the new company by paying a small assessment.[124] Relieved of some of its bonded debt, the road had excellent prospects, and many stockholders hastened to exchange their securities. The exigencies of the situation demanded that the municipalities should add a little more to what they had invested already, but the constitutional provision prohibiting loans of their credit to private corporations prevented them from taking any part in redeeming the old road or investing further in the new one.

In both the Black River and the Buffalo & Jamestown enterprises, the municipalities involved suffered a heavy financial loss on their investments. A taxpayers' meeting in Buffalo declared: "We might as well give the city's stock in that road to the comptroller to light his cigar with." [125] Yet, if these projects had been undertaken at a more propitious time or had been financed more conservatively, they would have yielded the subsidizing communities substantial dividends on their investment. After 1878 the Buffalo & Jamestown became an important coal and oil carrier and contributed greatly to the industrial growth of Buffalo and the towns along the line. Following its reorganization in 1861, the Black River & Utica, with the aid of additional municipal subscriptions, completed its road to the St. Lawrence. The communities which bought stock in the road at this time were far more fortunate than the city of Utica had been. Between 1875 and 1886, the company paid dividends as high as 19 per cent.[126] Subsequently, annual dividends of 7 per cent were paid out to the stockholders.

Scores of other New York communities that invested in railroad securities suffered financial reverses comparable to those experienced by Utica and Buffalo. Yet, in most instances, these localities were amply compensated for their losses by the expansion of trade, the growth of manufacture, and the increase in the value of their lands. The true criterion of public aid to railroads lies not in the amount of dividends that a municipality received but in the growth and development of the community resulting from its position on a completed line.

NOTES

Notes

I. Sources of Railroad Capital

1. *Hunt's Merchants' Magazine,* XXIX (November 1853) 613. Carter Goodrich, "Local Planning of Internal Improvements," *Political Science Quarterly,* LXVI (September 1951), 431. J. H. Hollander, "The Cincinnati Southern Railway: A Study in Municipal Activity," *Johns Hopkins University Studies in Historical and Political Science,* XII (1894), 1–96.

2. *Niles Register,* XLIV (June 1833), 284.

3. *American Railroad Journal,* VI (July 1837), 481.

4. *Ontario Repository and Freeman,* March 29, 1837.

5. Minutes of the Board of Directors of the New York & Erie Railroad, Feb. 6, 1849. Records of the Erie Railroad (Midland Building, Cleveland, Ohio).

6. *Report of the Board of Directors of the New York & Erie Railroad for 1849* (New York, 1850).

7. Minutes of the Board of Directors of the Albany & Susquehanna Railroad, Dec. 25, 1852. Records of the Delaware & Hudson Company (230 Park Ave., New York City). Two years later the contractors complained that the company's securities were so "tainted as to be wholly unavailable for sale or as collateral for loans." *Ibid.,* June 7, 1854.

8. Minutes of the Board of Directors of the New York & Oswego Midland Railroad, May 31, 1871. Records of the New York, Ontario & Western Railroad (29 Broadway, New York City).

9. Estimated from the annual reports to the Legislature by the State Engineer and Surveyor. Hereafter cited as *A.R.S.E.S.*

10. B. H. Meyer and C. E. MacGill, eds., *History of Transportation in United States Before 1860* (Washington, 1917), 368.

11. L. H. Haney, *Congressional History of Railways,* I, 119, 150–151.

12. Benjamin Tibbits to Edward Ellice, April 11, 1852. Tibbits Letterbooks.

13. *Sen. Ex. Doc. No. 42,* 33 Cong., 1 Sess. (1853–1854), 38.

14. *Ibid.* Archibald Gilkins to James Wadsworth, June 7, 1852. Wadsworth Papers. *The Times* (London), May 18, 1852.

15. *Sen. Ex. Doc. No. 42,* 33 Cong., 1 Sess. (1853–1854), 48.

16. Minutes of the Board of Directors of the Utica & Schenectady Railroad, Oct. 15, 1850. Records of the New York Central Railroad (230 Park Ave., New York City).

17. Schuyler Livingston to Erastus Corning, March 2, 1860. Corning

Papers. Livingston handled Ingham's financial investments in the United States.

18. Minutes of the Board of Directors of the New York Central Railroad, July 17, 1853; Jan. 23, 1857. Records of the New York Central Railroad (230 Park Ave., New York City). *American Railroad Journal*, Nov. 1, 1856.

19. Stock Ledger of the New York Central Railroad, London Agency, 1857–1863. Records of the New York Central Railroad (466 Lexington Ave., New York City).

20. *The House of Baring*, p. 430.

21. *Commercial & Financial Chronicle*, Jan. 29, 1870.

22. *Sen. Ex. Doc. No. 42*, 33 Cong., 1 Sess. (1853–1854), 38. The initial capital of the Erie was furnished by the government. As late as 1842, nearly seven years after construction began, more than two-thirds of the money invested in the line was furnished by the state. New York (state) *Messages from the Governors*, III, 965.

23. *Railroad Gazette*, Sept. 4, 1875.

24. *Annual Report of the Comptroller of the State of New York, Ass. Doc. 10* (1843).

25. Professor Schumpeter, *Business Cycles*, I, 335, argues that the construction of American railroads, 1866–1873, was financed almost entirely by approximately $2,000,000,000 of foreign capital imported during these years. This is probably an exaggeration. It is certainly not true of New York State. Railroad construction in New York at this time was confined almost exclusively to short, parochially built lines. Scarcely any of the securities issued for the building of these roads were sold abroad.

26. *Railroad Gazette*, Feb. 21, 1874; *Commercial & Financial Chronicle*, Feb. 21, 1874.

27. Minutes of the Board of Directors of the New York, Ontario & Western Railroad, Oct. 1, 1884. Records of the New York, Ontario & Western Railroad (29 Broadway, New York City). *The Statist*, Jan. 12, 1884.

28. Minutes of the Board of Directors of the Delaware & Hudson Company, July 24, 1872. Records of the Delaware & Hudson Company (230 Park Ave., New York City).

29. Minutes of the Board of Directors of the New York & Canada Railroad, June 16, 1874. Records of the Delaware & Hudson Company (Albany, New York).

30. Henry Clews, *Twenty-eight Years in Wall Street* (New York, 1888), 369; *Commercial & Financial Chronicle* (Investors' Supplement), Jan. 1889, 45.

31. Dividend Book of the New York Central & Hudson River Railroad (London Agency), Oct. 15, 1880. Foreign holdings were listed as follows: Oct. 15, 1880, 94,974; July 15, 1881, 218,355; Dec. 31, 1885, 240,206; Sept. 30, 1886, 317,296; March 15, 1888, 289,486; Dec. 31, 1902, 120,980.

32. Bond records of New York Central & Hudson River Railroad Co. Records of the New York Central Railroad (466 Lexington Ave., New York City).

33. Directors' Minutes (New York & Oswego Midland), Aug. 19, 1873; Directors' Minutes (New York & Erie), Feb. 21, 1849; Jan. 11, 1850; Aug.

9, 1854. See also Document Book, 1844–1855 (Records of the New York & Erie Railroad).

34. Stock Record Book of the Auburn & Rochester Rail Road, Records of the New York Central Railroad (466 Lexington Avenue, New York City).

35. Stock Transfer Books of the Albany & Susquehanna Railroad, 1852–1870. Records of the Delaware & Hudson Co. (Albany, New York).

36. John B. Edwards to Gerrit Smith, March 12, July 13, 1868. Smith Papers.

37. Directors' Minutes (Utica & Schenectady), July 10, 1833; Oct. 15, 1850.

38. Annual Report of the Board of Directors of the Watertown & Rome Railroad for 1849. Cited in Harlow, *The Road of the Century*, p. 550.

39. Dividend Book of the Rome, Watertown & Ogdensburg Railroad, July 6, 1855. Records of the New York Central Railroad (466 Lexington Ave., New York City).

40. Minutes of the Board of Directors of the Buffalo & State Line Railroad (1849–1867). Records of the New York Central Railroad (230 Park Ave., New York City).

41. Dividend Books of the Dunkirk, Allegany Valley & Pittsburgh Railroad, 1871–1880, Records of the New York Central Railroad (466 Lexington Ave., New York City). Minutes of the Board of Directors of the Clayton & Theresa Railroad, 1871–1873, Records of the New York Central Railroad (230 Park Ave., New York City). Stock Record Book of the Utica, Clinton & Binghamton Railroad 1866–1872, Records of the New York, Ontario & Western Railroad (First Citizens Bank & Trust Company, Utica, New York). Records of the New York, Ontario & Western Railroad (Hayes National Bank, Clinton, New York).

42. *American Railroad Journal*, Nov. 25, 1854, 746.

43. Report of the Special Committee of Stockholders of the Buffalo, Corning & New York Railroad, Sept. 11, 1854. Wadsworth Papers.

44. Ira Davenport to Charles Davenport, Oct. 19, 1853. Davenport Papers.

45. Scoville, *The Old Merchants of New York City*, I, 362.

46. Malone, *Dictionary of American Biography*, XIII, 168. Morgan, who was president of the Hudson River Railroad in 1853, held only five shares of stock in the company.

47. Rogers Papers.

48. New York (state) *Messages from the Governors*, III, 120.

49. *Stillwell Report*, Ass. Doc. 68 (1832).

50. *Ass. Doc.* 296 (1836).

51. N. Y. *Laws*, Ch. 253 (1826).

52. *Ibid.*, Ch. 294 (1833).

53. *Ibid.*, Ch. 349 (1836).

54. *Ibid.*, Ch. 228 (1834); Ch. 292 (1836); Ch. 335 (1844).

55. *Ibid.*, Ch. 335 (1844). On July 10, 1851, the legislature abolished the payment of all canal tolls by railroads, *ibid.*, Ch. 497 (1851).

56. *Ibid.*, Ch. 294 (1833).

57. *Ibid.*, Ch. 292 (1836).

58. *Ibid.*, Ch. 26 (1790).

59. *Ibid.*, Ch. 24 (1797).

60. Lincoln, *Constitutional History of New York*, II, 94.

61. *Ass. Doc.* 70 (1826), 17.

62. For examples see N. Y. *Laws*, Ch. 178 (1807); Ch. 148 (1808).

63. N. Y. *Laws*, 1790–1846. Lincoln, *Constitutional History*, II, 92.

64. N. Y. *Laws*, Ch. 62 (1827); Ch. 346 (1829).

65. Directors' Minutes (New York & Erie), Oct. 2, 1835.

66. *Report of the Board of Directors of the New York & Erie Railroad to the Stockholders for 1853* (New York, 1854), 4.

67. *Ibid.*, Ch. 70 (1836).

68. Directors' Minutes (New York & Erie), April 6, 1837.

69. *Ibid.*, Ch. 226 (1838); Ch. 196 (1839). Directors' Minutes (New York & Erie Railroad), Dec. 5, 1838; Dec. 27, 1839.

70. New York (state) *Messages from the Governors*, III, 999–1000.

71. *Annual Report of the State Comptroller*, Ass. Doc. 10 (1843). The legislature did, however, direct the state comptroller to postpone any action against the company until the spring of 1843.

72. N. Y. *Laws*, Ch. 325 (1845). This law also required the shareholders to exchange their securities for new stock on the basis of one share for each two surrendered. As a result of this reorganization the liabilities of the company were reduced by $3,740,730. *Report of the Board of Directors of the New York & Erie Railroad for 1849*. These bonds were not paid off until 1944. *New York Times*, Sept. 1, 1944.

73. See Table 2.

74. *Annual Report of the State Comptroller*, Ass. Doc. 10 (1843); *Troy Daily Whig*, May 23, 1842.

75. *Troy Daily Whig*, Nov. 16, 1852. *Annual Report of the State Comptroller*, Ass. Doc. 4 (1855).

76. State comptrollers protested vigorously against this practice and repeatedly pointed out that the laws covering aid to railroads were "mere shadows of security." *Ass. Doc.* 10 (1843).

77. *The Debt of the State of New York Past, Present, and Future; A Report by the Special Joint Committee on Taxation and Retrenchment, Leg. Doc. No. 70* (1926), 37.

78. Decisions of the Interstate Commerce Commission of the United States, Valuation Reports (Washington, 1926–1931), XXVII, 601–602; 603–605. Hereinafter cited *V.R.I.C.C.*

79. Directors' Minutes (New York & Erie), Sept. 24, 1839; Feb. 8, 1844.

80. *Annual Report of the State Comptroller*, Ass. Doc. 10 (1843), 22–23.

81. Hammond, *The History of Political Parties in New York State*, III, 287.

82. *Annual Report of the State Comptroller*, Ass. Doc. 10 (1843), 22–23.

83. Lincoln, *The Constitutional History of New York*, II, 180.

84. 116 *V.R.I.C.C.*, 727–728. N. Y. *Laws*, Ch. 70 (1863); Ch. 164 (1867). Governor Morgan (1859–1863) repeatedly vetoed bills offering aid to the Albany & Susquehanna on the ground that such assistance was a deliberate evasion of the state constitution.

85. New York (state) *Messages from the Governors*, VI, 70–71.

86. N. Y. *Laws*, Ch. 103 (1867); Ch. 169 (1872).

87. *Ibid.*, Ch. 118 (1824).

88. Ringwalt, *Development of Transportation Systems in the United States*, 81. Federal Coördinator of Transportation, *Public Aids to Transportation, Aids to Railroads and Related Subjects* (Washington, 1938), II, 64.

89. 116 *V.R.I.C.C.* 611. These so-called "wild lands" were sold in 1887 and 1889 for $145,250 cash, and the balance, $1,338,395.20, was written off to profit and loss. Donaldson, *History of the Adirondacks*, II, 135–136.

90. N. Y. *Laws*, Ch. 546 (1866); Ch. 398 (1866).

91. *Annual Report of the Board of Railroad Commissioners for 1883, Ass. Doc.* 25 (1884), 160.

92. N. Y. *Laws*, Ch. 398 (1866); Ch. 433 (1866).

93. *Proceedings of the Buffalo Common Council*, March 25, 1872. Hereinafter cited as *P.C.C.*

94. Town Minute Book (Theresa), 186.

95. *P.C.C.*, Utica, July 19, 1871.

96. See Table 1. See also pp. 115–117.

97. *P.C.C.*, Troy, December 16, 1852.

98. N. Y. *Laws*, Ch. 160 (1866).

99. 141 *V.R.I.C.C.*, 162.

100. 19 Wall (U. S.) 83.

101. 70 N. Y. 29.

102. 116 *V.R.I.C.C.*, 275.

103. Albany donated land valued at $25,000 to the Mohawk & Hudson. *P.C.C.*, Albany, July 11, 1843. The village of Bath donated $300 to the Bath & Hammondsport road. 130 *V.R.I.C.C.*, 761. The village of Sacketts Harbor gave $6,000 to the Carthage, Watertown & Sacketts Harbor line. Town Minute Book (Sacketts Harbor), 1870. Center Village contributed $1,450 to the Delaware & Hudson toward the construction of a new station at that point. 116 *V.R.I.C.C.*, 712.

104. *P.C.C.*, Albany, Aug. 15, 1842.

105. 141 *V.R.I.C.C.*, 12.

106. 34 *V.R.I.C.C.*, 10–11

107. *Carrier's Protest* (New York Central) *Before the Interstate Commerce Commission, Valuation Docket No. 1022* (New York, 1927), 343–346, 350–351.

108. *Public Aids to Transportation*, II, 65–66.

109. Letter, A. V. Vallandingham to W. E. Eppler, Jan. 19, 1921, Records of the Delaware & Hudson Company (230 Park Ave., New York City).

110. Directors' Minutes (Albany & Susquehanna), May 12, 1854; Nov. 18, 1857; June 12, 1862; July 14, 1868.

111. *Address by the Directors of the Albany & Susquehanna Railroad Together with Laws Authorizing Town Subscriptions* (Albany, 1856).

112. *I.C.C.* Accountant's Field Schedule of the Albany & Susquehanna Railroad. Records of the Delaware & Hudson Railroad (230 Park Ave., New York City).

113. *A.R.S.E.S.* (1870). The minute books of the Susquehanna line

reveal that scores of persons were unwilling to pay more than 10 per cent of their subscription unless sued. As late as July of 1868, nearly 8,000 shares of partly paid-up stock were forfeited through the refusal of the owners to complete their subscription. Directors' Minutes (Albany & Susquehanna), July 14, 1868.

114. *Proceedings and Debates of the Constitutional Convention of the State of New York, Held in 1867 and 1868 in the City of Albany* (Albany, 1868), II, 1140.

115. Directors' Minutes (New York & Oswego Midland), Aug. 19, 1873.

116. *A.R.S.E.S.* (1872); (1874).

117. *Oneonta Herald*, Nov. 23, 1871.

118. *Annual Report of the Delaware & Hudson for 1827.*

119. Directors' Minutes (New York & Erie), Oct. 2, 1835. When private capital refused to invest in even a preliminary survey of the route the state legislature appropriated $15,000 to aid in locating the proposed line. N. Y. *Laws*, Ch. 247 (1834).

120. Directors' Minutes (New York & Erie), Dec. 16, 1846. *Report of the Directors of the New York & Erie Railroad to the Stockholders for 1849. Niles Register*, LXIX (Oct. 4–18, 1845).

121. *Hunt's Merchants' Magazine*, XXV (July 1851).

122. Directors' Minutes (New York & Erie), Feb. 8, 1844.

123. For the terms of the contracts and the amount of the discount on securities that were hypothecated for the purchase of supplies see the Document Book of the New York & Erie Railroad, 1844–1855 (Records of the Erie Railroad, Cleveland). See also, Directors' Minutes (New York & Erie), Feb. 21, 1849; Jan. 11, 1850; Aug. 9, Oct. 13, 1854. The directors reported in 1845 that the bonds of the company could not be sold and that its stock had only a "fictitious value."

124. *DeBow's Review* reported that, in June 1856, a $100 New York State bond was worth $45 more than a $100 first-mortgage bond of the New York & Harlem, $31 more than one of the Buffalo & State Line's, $30 more than one of the New York Central's, $27.50 more than one of the Hudson River's, and $23.50 more than one of the New York & Erie's. Since municipal credit at this time was as high as, or perhaps higher than, that of the state, the differential would have been at least as great where municipal bonds were involved. XXI (Oct. 1856), 433.

125. Stevens, *Beginnings of the New York Central*, 174–175.

126. Thomas Y. How to John Delafield, April 7, 1837. How Letterbooks.

127. How to Delafield, March 7, 25, May 11, September 19, 1837. How Letterbooks.

128. How to James L. Graham, January 4, 1838. How Letterbooks.

129. N. Y. *Laws*, Ch. 293 (1838). *Annual Report of the State Comptroller, Ass. Doc.* 10 (1843). By 1840 the Auburn & Rochester was in a similar financial condition when the state came to its assistance with a loan of $200,000. Charles Seymour, an official of the company, wrote to a director, "Our stock can not be sold." Charles Seymour to William Mercer, March 26, 1841. Seymour Letterbooks.

130. *New York Tribune*, Nov. 18, 1842. Minutes of the Board of

Directors of the Mohawk & Hudson Railroad, March 11, 1842. Records of the New York Central Railroad (230 Park Ave., New York City).

131. See Chapter IV.

132. To carry out these projects, the city of Albany, of its own volition, purchased lands valued at $25,000 and leased them to the Mohawk & Hudson for one cent. *P.C.C.*, Albany, July 11, 1843.

133. The Auburn & Syracuse, which faced ruin in 1838, paid dividends ranging from 8 to 57.5 per cent from 1844 to 1850; the Auburn & Rochester averaged 10.6 per cent during this same period.

134. Excluding land grants.

II. The Law of Municipal Bonding

1. N. Y. *Laws,* Ch. 321 (1837).
2. *Ibid.,* Ch. 412 (1837).
3. *Ibid.,* Ch. 389 (1851).
4. *Ibid.,* Ch. 283 (1853).
5. *Ibid.,* Ch. 484 (1851); Chs. 134, 375 (1852).
6. *Utica Morning Herald,* April 29, 1871.
7. *Rome Sentinel,* June 17, 1853.
8. *Albany Argus,* May 18, 1852. Utica bonded in favor of the Black River & Utica at this time by a vote of 791 to 19. *Utica Daily Gazette,* June 14, 1853.
9. *P.C.C.,* Albany, Aug. 14, 1840.
10. *Rochester Daily Democrat,* March 18, 1851.
11. N. Y. *Laws,* Ch. 389 (1851).
12. Azariah Boody to Erastus Corning, May 21, 1853. Corning Papers. Boody, who was a director of the road, reported that, if friends of the narrow gauge could control about $75,000 more stock, they could rescind a resolution adopting the wide gauge and thus develop the line for the benefit of the New York Central instead of the Erie.
13. *P.C.C.,* Rochester (1853), 520–532.
14. *Ibid.* (1856), 371–375.
15. *Freeman Clarke v. City of Rochester,* 13 How. Prac. 204.
16. *Albany Argus,* April 22, 1857.
17. *Starin v. Town of Genoa,* 23 N. Y. 439; *Gould v. Town of Sterling,* 23 N. Y. 439; *Murdock v. Town of Venice,* 92 U. S. 498.
18. *Bank of Rome v. Village of Rome,* 18 N. Y. 38.
19. Rome: *Bank of Rome v. Village of Rome,* 18 N. Y. 38. Rochester: *Freeman Clarke v. City of Rochester,* 28 N. Y. 605. Summit: *People v. Mitchell,* 35 N. Y. 551. Duanesburg: *Town of Duanesburg v. Jenkins,* 57 N. Y. 194.
20. Communities may aid the construction of a railroad even though the line is outside the municipality or even the state. Buffalo, for example, invested $150,000 in the Buffalo, Brantford & Goderich, a road built in the province of Ontario, Canada. The town of Ellicott was permitted to

subscribe $200,000 to the stock of the Buffalo & Jamestown, which was projected mainly within the state of Pennsylvania. *Falconer v. Buffalo & Jamestown Railroad,* 69 N. Y. 491; 103 U. S. 821. On the other hand, the courts have held that a statute which authorized an issue of bonds to aid certain individuals, classes, or private enterprises, such as a manufacturing plant, is void even though the public is remotely or indirectly benefited by such action. *Weismer v. the Village of Douglas,* 64 N. Y. 91. *Ottawa v. Carey,* 108 N. S. 110.

21. As early as 1837, the courts ruled that lands taken for the construction of a railroad were for the public use. Judge Southerland in *Bloodgood v. Mohawk & Hudson Railroad* (14 Wend 57) declared: "Railroads, though made by private corporations, when designed for travelling and transportation, are great public improvements. They can be made profitable to corporations only by affording the most liberal accommodations to the public. They are from their very nature devoted and exclusively devoted to the public use, upon such terms and conditions as the Legislature, in their wisdom, think reasonable and proper, in order to insure the owners of the stock an adequate remuneration for the hazard and expense incurred in their construction."

22. *Bank of Rome v. Village of Rome,* 18 N. Y. 38.

23. *Olcott v. the Supervisors,* 16 Wall. 695 (1872). Also *Railroad Co. v. Otoe County,* 16 Wall. 667; *St. Joseph Township v. Rogers,* 16 Wall. 644; *Rogers v. Burlington,* 3 Wall. 654; *Mitchell v. Burlington,* 4 Wall. 270.

24. *Queensbury v. Culver,* 19 Wall. 83; 22 L. ed., 100.

25. *N. Y. Laws,* Ch. 907 (1869).

26. The bonding law was amended in 1871 (Ch. 925) to define the persons who were taxpayers and who had the right to sign petitions. The revised act required the statement that the petitioners comprise a majority of the taxpayers of the municipality "not including those taxed for dogs or highway tax only."

27. *Utica Morning Herald,* May 9, 18; June 1, 13; July 12, 1871.

28. Town of Varick, *People ex. rel. Sayre v. Franklin,* 5 Lans. 129.

29. *Chenango American,* Dec. 2, 1869; Feb. 10, 1870. *In re the Taxpayers of the Town of Greene,* 38 How. Prac. 515.

30. *The People v. Sawyer,* 52 N. Y. 299. The court took a similar position in the bonding of the towns of Pavilion, *People v. Henshaw,* 61 Barb. 409; Belport, *People v. Hatch,* 65 Barb. 430; Rochester, *People ex. rel. Rochester v. Deyoe,* 2 Thomp. & Co., 142.

31. *P.C.C.,* Auburn, Dec. 30, 1942; *Auburn Citizen-Advertiser,* April 23, 1943.

32. Town Minute Book (Moravia), March 16, 1943.

33. Town Minute Book (Owego), May 6, 1922.

34. The records of most of these towns are in a wretched condition. There are no records of the Southern Central Railroad. D. J. Mullane (Secretary and Treasurer of the Lehigh Valley Railroad) to the author, March 2, 1948.

35. *Report of the Investigating Committee appointed by the Town Board of Seneca Falls to examine into the affairs of the Pennsylvania & Sodus Bay Railroad* (Seneca Falls, 1874).

36. *P.C.C.*, Rochester, July 23, 1875; *Rochester Union & Advertiser*, July 24, 1875.

37. *Report of the Special Committee to the Common Council of the Meeting of Railroad Directors and Town Commissioners at Mt. Morris. P.C.C.*, Rochester, July 27, 1875.

38. *Chenango Telegraph*, June 16, 1869.

39. A few towns such as Kirkland, Utica, and Greene were aided in paying the interest on their bonds by regular stock dividends.

40. *Clark v. Sheldon*, 106 N. Y. 104; 12 N.E. 341; *Vinton v. Board of Supervisors*, 50 Hun. 600; 2 N. Y. S. 367.

41. N. Y. *Laws*, Ch. 336 (1899). *Ulster County v. State*, 79 A. D. 277; 177 N. Y. 189. *Annual Report of the Comptroller of the State of New York*, Ass. Doc. 3 (1905); Ass. Doc. 37 (1906); Ass. Doc. 1 (1907).

42. *The Bond Buyer*, June 17, 1893.

43. Minute Book (Andes), 1893–1897.

44. *The Daily Bond Buyer*, July 11, 1918.

45. *Annual Report of the City Comptroller of Rochester* (1914). The interest on these loans up to 1904 amounted to $1,324,973.67. *Ibid.*, 1904.

46. *Special Report on Municipal Accounts by the State Comptroller*, Leg. Doc. 13 (1930). At this time 20 towns and cities had railroad-aid bonds outstanding.

47. *Joslyn v. Dow*, 19 Hun. 494.

48. *Town of Wayne v. Sherwood*, 21 Hun. 423; N. Y. 599.

49. *Gould v. Town of Oneonta*, 3 Hun. 401.

50. *P.C.C.*, Oswego, Feb. 4, 1880; *Oswego Daily Times*, Jan. 21, 1880.

51. *Chenango Semi-Weekly Telegraph*, Dec. 17, 1879. N. Y. *Laws*, Ch. 21 (1880).

52. *P.C.C.*, *Watertown*, Aug. 29; Dec. 19, 1893.

53. Frank Moore to Willard Knickerbocker, Nov. 22, 1944. Letter in town clerk's office in Greene.

54. C. L. Chamberlain to G. R. Selkirk, March 23, 1945. Letter in town clerk's office in Cobleskill. The opposition of the comptroller was based on the premise that the exchange by a municipality of one kind of a security for another was illegal because it violated the constitutional provision forbidding a community from lending its credit to a private corporation. See *Wheatland v. Taylor*, 29 Hun. 70.

55. Town Minute Book (Colesville), July 12, 1945; Jan. 17, 1946.

56. Town Minute Book (Dunkirk), July 6, 1914.

57. Town Minute Book (Theresa), Aug. 21, 1914.

58. Town Minute Book (Alexandria), Jan. 8, 1916; Nov. 25, 1925; Jan. 31, 1934; Dec. 10, 1938; May 7, 1940; Sept. 19, 1942. *Thousand Islands Sun*, Oct. 29, 1942.

59. *Empire v. Darlington*, 101 U. S. 87.

60. *Rochester, Nunda & Pennsylvania Railroad v. Cuyler*, 7 Lans. 431.

61. Stockton, *People ex. rel. Dunkirk, Warren & Pittsburgh Railroad v. Batchellor*, 53 N. Y. 128; Dresden, *People ex. rel. New York & Canada Railroad v. Barrett*, 19 Hun. 206; Summit, *People ex. rel. Albany & Susquehanna Railroad v. Mitchell*, 35 N. Y. 55.

62. Town of Shawangunk, *Hardenbergh v. Van Keuren*, 16 Hun. 17;

Town of Stockton, *The People ex. rel., The Dunkirk, Warren & Pittsburgh Railroad v. Batchellor*, 53 N. Y. 128; *Town of Thompson, Horton v. Thompson*, 71 N. Y. 513. This decision was later overruled by the U. S. Supreme Court in *Thompson v. Perrine*, 103 U. S. 813.

63. *Town of Guilford v. Supervisors of Chenango County*, 13 N. Y. 143. In *People v. Flagg* (46 N. Y. 401), it was held that an act compelling the town of Yonkers to issue bonds for the construction of highways was constitutional.

64. *Dunkirk Railroad v. Batchellor*, 53 N. Y. 128.

65. Town of Duanesburg, N. Y. *Laws*, Ch. 402 (1864), *Duanesburg v. Jenkins*, 57 N. Y. 194. Towns of Greenwood, West Union, and Hornellsville, N. Y. *Laws*, Ch. 638 (1874); *People ex. rel. Rogers v. Spencer*, 55 N. Y. 1. Town of Lebanon, N. Y. *Laws*, Ch. 61 (1868); *People v. Clark*, 53 Barb. 171. Towns of Deerpark and Forestburg, N. Y. *Laws*, Ch. 809 (1871). Town of Summit, N. Y. *Laws*, Ch. 402 (1864); *People ex. rel. Albany & Susquehanna Railroad v. Mitchell*, 35 N. Y. 550.

66. Broadside in the William L. Marcy Phelps Papers.

67. N. Y. *Laws*, Ch. 402 (1864).

68. *Duanesburg v. Jenkins*, 40 Barb, 574; 57 N. Y. 177; 66 N. Y. 129.

69. *Falconer v. Buffalo & Jamestown Railroad*, 69 N. Y. 491; 103 U. S. 821.

III. The Period of Promotion

1. *Albany Argus*, May 15, 1852.

2. E. M. Ruttenber, *A History of the Town of Newburg* (Newburg, 1859), p. 147.

3. John B. Edwards to Gerrit Smith, Feb. 27, 1868. Smith Papers.

4. *Ontario County Times*, Jan. 20, 1873.

5. *Ithaca Journal*, June 22, 1869.

6. Lyman Murdock to Ezra Cornell, Nov. 27, 1866. Cornell Papers.

7. James J. Crofts to his nephew, Nov. 15, 1865. Crofts Papers.

8. Clark, *History of Manufactures*, 355.

9. *Buffalo Commercial-Advertiser*, July 28, 1866. P.C.C., Buffalo, May 4, 1868.

10. *Rochester Express*, Oct.–Nov. 1865, April 3, 1866, *Rochester Democrat*, April 16, May 12, 1868; P.C.C., Rochester (1869–1870), 153, 209–210.

11. *Rochester Chronicle*, Aug. 18, 1869.

12. P.C.C., Rochester, Aug. 10, 1869.

13. *The Commerce, Manufacturers & Resources of Rochester, New York* (Rochester, 1881).

14. *Roman Citizen*, June 23, 1870.

15. *Utica Morning Herald*, Feb. 1, 1871.

16. *Seneca Falls Reveille*, March 4, 1870.

17. *Chenango Telegraph*, Jan. 4, 1871.

18. *Oneonta Herald*, Aug. 25, 1869.

19. *Ontario County Times,* Jan. 15, 1873.

20. *Ithaca Democrat,* Oct. 20, 1870.

21. *Proceedings and Debates of the Constitutional Convention,* 1867–1868, II, 1154–1155.

22. Prospectus of the Albany & Susquehanna Railroad Co., Feb. 26, 1855. Records of the Delaware & Hudson Co. (Albany, New York).

23. Durant and Peirce, *History of Jefferson County,* 119.

24. *American Agriculturalist,* April, 1871, 128.

25. *Schoharie Republican,* Oct. 15, 1856.

26. *Ithaca Journal,* Oct. 18, 1870.

27. *Geneva Gazette,* Feb. 18, 1870.

28. *Chenango Telegraph,* May 9, 1866.

29. Town Minute Book (Greene), 1870.

30. *Rome Sentinel,* Aug. 16, 1870. *Clinton Courier,* April 14, 1870.

31. *P.C.C.,* Utica, July 19, 1871.

32. *Railroad Gazette,* Aug. 16, 1873.

33. *Rochester Union & Advertiser,* Feb. 4, 1873.

34. Ezra P. Prentice to Edward Tompkins, Feb. 19, 1858. Prentice Papers.

35. *Utica Daily Gazette,* March 11, Aug. 12, 1853.

36. Directors' Minutes (New York & Oswego Midland), Oct. 4, 1865; *Chenango Telegraph,* Nov. 1, 1865.

37. *P.C.C.,* Buffalo, July 19, 1866.

38. *American Railroad Journal,* May 28, 1853.

39. Charles Courter to Ezra Prentice, July 15, 1856. Phelps Papers.

40. *Rochester Union & Advertiser,* April 29, 1870; June 9, 1871.

41. Edward Tompkins to Prentice, April 9, 1856. Phelps Papers.

42. Tompkins to H. A. Hickcox, Aug. 18, 1856. Hickcox Papers.

43. 116 *V.R.I.C.C.,* 727–728; *Albany Evening Journal,* Aug. 9, 1869. Ramsay's commission on $900,000 worth of town bonds amounted to $18,000. Ramsay, who was a comparatively poor man when he began his railroad career, owned 1581 shares of Delaware & Hudson stock in 1870. Record of Delaware & Hudson Co. Stockholders for 1870 (Records of the Delaware & Hudson Co., Albany).

44. *Report of the Investigating Committee Appointed by the Town Board of Seneca Falls to Examine into the Affairs of the Pennsylvania & Sodus Bay Railroad* (Seneca Falls, 1874).

45. Quoted by Mott, *Between the Ocean and the Lakes,* 9; from the *Independent Republican* (Goshen), Dec. 26, 1831.

46. *Chenango Telegraph,* Dec. 20, 1865.

47. *Some Considerations Respecting the Proposed Construction of the Albany & Susquehanna R. R.* (Albany, 1852).

48. Jervis Papers. The collection has considerable material on this convention.

49. *Utica Daily Gazette,* Aug. 17, 1853.

50. *Chenango Telegraph,* Oct. 11, 1865.

51. *Ibid.*

52. *Utica Daily Gazette,* June 18, 1853.

53. Edwards to Smith, Jan. 29, 1868. Smith Papers.

54. Leslie, *Skaneateles*, p. 275.

55. Quoted in the *Ithaca Journal*, July 5, 1870.

56. *Utica Daily Gazette*, March 30, 1853.

57. *Geneva Gazette*, Feb. 18, 1870.

58. *Oswego Daily Palladium*, Dec. 1, 1866.

59. Edwards to Smith, Feb. 24, 1868. Smith Papers.

60. Towns that had already invested in the enterprise strongly supported this procedure in locating the road. A Norwich paper asserted: "The route has been finally located *via* Eaton summit, which is very proper, considering the inactivity of opposing interests. The friends in Eaton have worked early and late to forward the interests of the company and now the town makes a subscription of $50,000 in addition to that already made to secure the location. Their perseverance had entitled them to their success." *Chenango Semi-Weekly Telegraph*, May 28, 1868.

61. William Kessler, "Railroads in Madison County," *New York History*, XXII (Jan. 1941). Before Eaton would turn over its bonds, the company had to promise that it would neither build nor operate (if built by others) a line through Hamilton. Directors' Minutes (New York & Oswego Midland), June 3, 1868.

62. *Clinton Courier*, Nov. 25, 1869. *Hamilton Republican*, Nov. 18, 1869. The citizens of Hamilton and Clinton arranged to boycott the city if it did not contribute.

63. Town Minute Book (Phelps), 1872–1875. *Bond Buyer*, Nov. 4, 1895.

64. Robert Hood to Col. Edward Silvernail, Aug. 26, 1870. Silvernail Papers.

65. *Ithaca Democrat*, May 31, 1870.

66. *Geneva Gazette*, April 7, 1871.

67. *Ithaca Daily Journal*, June 7, 1873.

68. Edwards to Smith, Sept. 5, 1867. Smith Papers.

69. Edwards to Smith, June 12, 1873. Smith Papers.

70. John Cook to E. P. Prentice, June 16, 1856. Phelps Papers.

71. Edwards to Smith, March 30, 1868. Smith Papers.

72. *Ithaca Journal*, Feb. 1, 1870.

73. *Albany Evening Journal*, Aug. 9, 1869.

74. *Oswego Palladium*, Aug. 25, 1866, Jan. 25, 1867.

75. *Chenango Telegraph*, June 21, 1871.

76. *Proceedings and Debates of the Constitutional Convention*, 1867–1868, II, 1137–1139.

77. *Ibid.*, 1142.

78. Edwards to Smith, March 12, 1868; Feb. 22, 1868. Smith Papers.

79. Edwards to Smith, March 23, 1868. Smith Papers.

80. *Geneva Gazette*, May 27, 1870.

81. E. R. Ford to Ezra Prentice, June 6, 1856. Prentice Papers.

82. *Seneca Falls Reveille*, July 22, 1870.

83. *Oswego Palladium*, Aug. 27, 1866.

84. None of these companies ever had any track. The route planned by the promoters of the Utica, Ogdensburg & New York was so crooked that townspeople nicknamed the line the Ramshorn.

85. *Cooperstown Glimmerglass,* August 1938.

86. *Troy Daily Whig,* May 28, 1852. Commenting on the failure of the road, the *Whig* declared: "The iron was bought before the company owned a rod of land or had any actual basis for the mortgage. But it all went for the good in England. The trick could not be played there again." *Troy Daily Whig,* Sept. 10, 1853.

87. *New York Times,* April 10, 1875 (8, 7).

88. Minute Book of the Executive Committee of the New York & Oswego Midland, Oct. 12, 1871. Records of the New York, Ontario & Western Railroad (29 Broadway, New York City).

89. Directors' Minutes (New York & Oswego Midland), Jan. 30, 1873.

90. *Ontario County Times,* Aug. 10, 1870; Oct. 9, 1872: P.B.S. (Ontario), Oct. 3, 1872.

91. *New York Laws,* Ch. 185 (1872).

92. *P.C.C.,* Buffalo, March 25, 1872; *Buffalo Courier,* April 19, 1872.

93. *Geneva Gazette,* Jan. 20, 1871.

94. *Journal of the Constitutional Commission of 1872, Document No. 1.* Frank B. Hough, *History of Lewis County* (Syracuse, 1883), 126.

95. See Chart No. 2.

96. *Journal of the First Annual Session of the New York State Grange of the Patrons of Husbandry* (Elmira, 1874), 37.

97. Despite this seemingly airtight provision, the legislature in 1878 leased the state-owned Plattsburg & Dannemora line, which had been constructed at a cost of $178,000, to the Delaware & Hudson at an annual rental of one cent. 116 *V.R.I.C.C.* 784.

IV. A Municipally Owned Railroad

1. Ellis, "Albany and Troy — Commercial Rivals," 484–516.

2. *Troy Daily Whig,* April 18, 1850.

3. *Laws of New York,* Ch. 427 (1836).

4. *P.C.C.,* Troy, May 21, 1840. *Troy Daily Whig,* May 29, 1840.

5. *Ibid.,* Dec. 16, 1841. *Troy Daily Budget,* May 19, 1840.

6. *Laws of New York,* Chs. 134, 135 (1843). Surprisingly enough, Schenectady showed little interest in the construction of the Troy road.

7. *Troy Daily Whig,* July 10, 1841. *American Railroad Journal,* XVIII (1845), 19.

8. *Troy Daily Whig,* Nov. 21, 1840.

9. *Ibid.,* July 10, 1841.

10. Minutes of the Board of Directors of the Mohawk & Hudson Railroad, Feb. 19, 1840. Records of the New York Central Railroad (230 Park Ave., New York). The cost of operating these planes amounted to $22,011.50 in 1838 and $24,329.77 in 1839.

11. *Ibid.,* June 1, 1842.

12. *Ibid.,* Aug. 22, 1842.

13. *Ibid.,* Sept. 3, 1841. Stevens, *Beginnings of the New York Central,* 69–70. In December 1841, an issue of $35,000 in 7 per cent first-mortgage

bonds brought only $25,375 into the Treasury. Directors' Minutes (Mohawk & Hudson), March 11, 1842.

14. Minutes of the Board of Directors of the Utica & Schenectady Railroad, July 26, 1838.

15. *Assembly Journal* (1839), 308, 1340. Senate Journal (1839), 556. Directors' Minutes (Mohawk & Hudson), Feb. 2, 1839.

16. *Ibid.*, May 24, 1839.

17. To carry out the latter project, the city of Albany purchased additional lands costing $25,000 and leased them to the company for one cent. *P.C.C.*, Albany, Aug. 15, 1842; July 11, 1843; Nov. 27, 1843. Directors' Minutes (Mohawk & Hudson), Aug. 22, 1842; July 13, 1843; Aug. 12, 1843.

A resolution of the Albany Common Council stated that the purpose of the loans was "to enable the said company so to terminate and arrange their road as to enable it to enter into a successful competition with the Troy & Schenectady and induce the transit of travelers through the city of Albany." *P.C.C.*, Albany, July 24, 1843.

18. *The Schenectady & Troy Railroad Company, A Statement* (Troy, 1846), 1.

19. John B. LaSala to Corning, Sept. 7, 1842; Thomas Y. How, Jr., to Corning, Dec. 24, 1842; Theodore Sedgewick to Corning, Dec. 7, 1843. Corning Papers. Directors' Minutes (Mohawk & Hudson), Aug. 28, 1843; April 27, 1844.

20. *New York Herald*, April 10, 1872.

21. LaSala to Corning, Oct. 3, 1842. Corning Papers.

22. 27 *V.R.I.C.C.* 593. Directors' Minutes (Mohawk & Hudson), July 15, 1851; Jan. 19, 1852.

23. *Sen. Docs.* 83, 84, 85 (1847). Directors' Minutes (Mohawk & Hudson), Feb. 22, 1847.

24. Directors' Minutes (Mohawk & Hudson), Oct. 24, 1839.

25. *Annual Report of the Mohawk & Hudson Railroad for 1840.*

26. Troy papers frequently appealed for the lifting of this restriction and referred to the line as the "law-locked road." *Troy Daily Whig*, Dec. 26, 1842.

27. Wittke, *We Who Built America*, 119–120. Railroads took the passenger traffic away from the canals almost immediately. The Canal commissioners reported that after the coming of railroads "canal boats were constructed . . . in reference to freight alone." *Annual Report of the Canal Commissioners, Ass. Doc.* 15 (1852), 144. Immigrants were usually carried in inferior coaches for half fare.

28. The bulk of immigrant traffic over the Central lines was handled by Harnden & Co., Wolf & Rischmiller Co., and Livingston & Wells Co. For proposed contracts, see Harnden & Co. to Isaac Newton, May 23, 1846; Wolf & Rischmiller Co. to Corning, Nov. 8, 1847; Livingston & Wells to Corning, Oct. 17, 1846. This traffic is analyzed in detail in Wolf & Rischmiller's *Statement of Emigrant Passenger Business for 1847*. Corning Papers.

29. *The Schenectady & Troy Railroad Company, A Statement*, 13.

30. Immigrant companies frequently complained that under contracts proposed by Corning they would be compelled to operate at a loss. J. T.

Marshall to Corning, June 11, 1845. Corning to Isaac Newton, April 4, 1850. Corning Papers.

31. These loans are discussed at some length in Directors' Minutes (Albany & Schenectady), July 15, 1851; Jan. 19, 1852. See also 27 V.R.I.C.C., 582–618.

32. *The Schenectady & Troy Railroad Company, A Statement.*

33. Isaac Newton to Corning, Feb. 24, 1845. Corning Papers. The Central lines got $250 a mile for carrying the mail. This was the highest rate paid to any road save those between New York and Washington. John Wilkinson to Corning, April 30, 1852. Corning Papers.

34. James Wasson to Corning, April 21, 1845; Livingston to Corning, April 30, 1852. Corning Papers.

35. Young to Corning, June 22, 1843. Corning Papers.

36. William Kittle to Corning, Aug. 8 and Sept. 7, 1843. Corning Papers.

37. *Ibid.*, Aug. 10, 1843.

38. J. D. to Corning, July 17, 1843; Newton to Corning, Sept. 15, 1845; C. Livingston to Corning, Dec. 22, 1845; John Wilkinson to Corning, April 5, 1844. Corning Papers.

39. Marshall to Corning, Jan. 19, June 20, 1843, April 15, 1844. Corning Papers.

40. Joseph Warren (Mayor of Troy) to Alonzo C. Paige, June 16, 1843. Young to Warren, June 16, 1843. John Paine (Pres. of the S. & T. R. R.) to Corning, July 31, 1846. Corning Papers.

41. Directors' Minutes (Utica & Schenectady), Nov. 24, 1846.

42. *Annual Report of the Albany & Schenectady Railroad to Its Stockholders* (Albany, 1848). See Table 5.

43. *Award of the Commissioners Under the Act in Relation to Rail-Road Corporations in the Matter Between the Schenectady & Troy Rail-Road Company and the Utica & Schenectady Rail-Road Company and the Albany & Schenectady Rail-Road Company* (Troy, 1847), 9.

44. *Ibid.*, 11. A proposal by Alonzo Paige to make the Troy line a party to an agreement then being worked out among the roads from Albany to Rochester was defeated 9 to 4. Directors' Minutes (Utica & Schenectady), Aug. 7, 1846.

45. *Laws of New York*, Ch. 222 (1847). Paine to Corning, May 18, 1847. Corning Papers.

46. John Pruyn to Corning, June 22, 1847. Corning Papers.

47. *Award of the Commissioners*, 3–6. *Ass. Doc.* 159 (1849).

48. How to Corning, Dec. 22, 1847. How, who was secretary and treasurer of the Auburn & Syracuse, characterized Wilkinson as "unscrupulous" and desirous of seeing the Central lines disorganized. How to Corning, January 3, 1848. Corning Papers.

49. Contract in *Ass. Doc.* 92 (1850). In 1847, the name of the Mohawk & Hudson was changed to the Albany & Schenectady.

50. Wolf & Rischmiller Co. to Corning, April 1, 1848. Corning Papers.

51. *Troy Daily Budget*, Jan. 4, 1842.

52. *Troy Daily Whig*, Sept. 28, 1841.

53. *Ibid.*, June 12, 1849. The *Whig* predicted that the line would be

the salvation of the Schenectady & Troy; ". . . you thereby remove an onerous and burdensome tax, which now rests like an incubus upon Troy, while you make her the great point of conveyance and divergence for the immense travel from east to west, north and south."

54. Newton to Corning, March 7, 1845. Corning Papers.

55. *Ass. Doc.* 51 (1846). Parker Hall to Corning, January 23, 1846. Corning Papers.

56. George E. Pomeroy to Corning, Jan. 21, 1846. Corning Papers.

57. *Ibid.*

58. *A Communication to the Legislature by the Utica & Schenectady Railroad, in reply to a Statement of the Schenectady & Troy* (Albany, 1846), 2.

59. The *Utica Daily Gazette* urged the line "as a means of reducing exorbitant charges demanded on the present railroad." Nov. 24, 1845. Nicholas Devereux to Corning, July 20, 1846. Pomeroy to Corning, Jan. 18, 1845. Corning Papers.

60. Watkinson to Corning, Dec. 4, 1845; Howland to Corning, March 16, 1846. Corning Papers.

61. *Troy Daily Whig,* April 16, 1846. The fare was reduced from three dollars to two. The stock dropped from 126 to 115. Directors' Minutes (Utica & Schenectady), May 25, 1847.

62. Livingston to Corning, Dec. 2, 1845. Corning Papers.

63. Pomeroy to Corning, Nov. 16, 1846. Corning Papers.

64. D. Francis Bacon to Corning, Aug. 17, 1847. Corning Papers. *Sen. Doc.* 122 (1846).

65. Devereux to Corning, July 20, 1850. Corning Papers.

66. *Troy Daily Whig,* Aug. 9, 1851.

67. By the end of September 30, 1852, $1,131,500 had been subscribed. *Ass. Doc.* 10 (1853).

68. Pruyn to Corning, July 21, 1852. Paige to Corning, July 16, 1852. Corning Papers.

69. Pruyn to Corning, July 21, 1852. Corning Papers.

70. Minutes of the Board of Directors of the Mohawk Valley Railroad, July 28, 1852. Records of the New York Central Railroad (230 Park Ave., New York).

71. Francis B. Spinner to Corning, Aug. 21, 1852. Corning Papers.

72. *Private Ledger No. 1,* 172. Pruyn Papers.

73. *Stock Ledger of the Mohawk Valley Rail Road for 1853.* Records of the New York Central Railroad (466 Lexington Ave., New York).

74. *P.C.C.,* Troy, May 4, 1843. *Laws of New York,* Ch. 299 (1840).

75. *Laws of New York,* Ch. 61 (1842). *P.C.C.,* Troy, June 11, 1840.

76. *Annual Report of the Chamberlain of the City of Troy for 1849,* p. 6.

77. *P.C.C.,* Troy, March 13, 1850. *Troy Daily Whig,* March 15, 1850.

78. *P.C.C.,* Troy, March 26, 1850. The city had been authorized to borrow only $650,000 and permission to raise additional funds had to be obtained from the legislature. *Laws of New York,* Ch. 224 (1850).

79. *Troy Daily Budget,* March 14, 1850.

80. *Troy Daily Whig,* March 15, 1850.

81. *Annual Report of the Chamberlain of the City of Troy* (Troy, 1850).

82. *Troy Daily Whig*, January 23, 1850.

83. *Ass. Doc.* 8 (1850). *Troy Daily Whig*, March 27, 1850.

84. *Troy Daily Budget*, January 8, 1850.

85. *Troy Daily Whig*, March 25, 27, 28, 1850.

86. *P.C.C.*, Troy, March 23, 1850. The protest charged that passage of the bill would leave the city with a large debt for the railroad but without any control over its operations. *Senate Journal* (1850), 443.

87. James Boorman to Corning, Feb. 10, 1851. Corning Papers.

88. Boorman to Corning, March 10, 1851. Corning Papers.

89. *P.C.C.*, Troy, Feb. 19, 1852. Edwin D. Morgan to James Boorman, Jan. 22, 1852. Morgan Papers.

90. Construction of the line was finally authorized in December, 1852, with the Hudson River road replacing the Harlem in the agreement. *P.C.C.*, Troy, Dec. 2, 1852.

91. Morgan to Joseph Warren (Mayor of Troy), Jan. 22, 1852; Morgan to Boorman, Jan. 24, Feb. 11, 22, 1852. Morgan Papers.

92. Morgan to Boorman, Feb. 28, 1852. Morgan Papers.

93. *P.C.C.*, Troy, July 1, 1852.

94. Ezekiel C. McIntosh to Corning, c. Dec. 1851. Corning Papers. This was not the first proposal to consolidate the two roads. See Directors' Minutes (Albany & Schenectady), June 20, 1842; Oct. 15, 1842; Feb. 22, 1847.

95. McIntosh to Corning, June 3, 1852. Corning Papers.

96. Russell Sage to Morgan, July 31, 1852. Morgan Papers. Note the willingness of Wilkinson to disrupt the Central lines on the eve of consolidation.

97. *P.C.C.*, Troy, Jan. 6, 21, 1853.

98. *Ibid.*, Jan. 24, 1853. The agreement is printed in the proceedings of the council. Morgan to Boorman, Jan. 19, 1853, Morgan Papers.

99. Morgan to Boorman, Jan. 24, 1853. Morgan Papers.

100. *Troy Daily Times*, Jan. 28, 1853.

101. *Troy Daily Whig*, Jan. 24, 1853.

102. *Troy Daily Budget*, Jan. 29, 1853.

103. *Schenectady Reflector*, Feb. 4, 1853.

104. *New York Tribune*, Jan. 27, 1853. The *New York Times*, Jan. 28, 1853, *Troy Daily Whig*, Feb. 1, 1853.

105. Daniel Gardner to Corning, Aug. 17, 1850. Corning Papers.

106. Gardner to Corning, Oct. 25, 1851; July 6, 1852. Corning Papers.

107. Dean Richmond to Corning, Dec. 14, 1852. Horace White to Corning, Jan. 11, 1853. John H. Chedell to Corning, Dec. 22, 1852. Corning Papers.

108. *Troy Daily Budget*, Feb. 3, 1853. *Troy Daily Whig*, Feb. 2, 1853. *P.C.C.*, Troy, May 5, 1853. To facilitate matters, the council waived the requirement that five directors of the road should be from Troy. See also Morgan Papers, Memorandum on the sale of the Schenectady & Troy Railroad (n.d.), *P.C.C.*, Troy, May 7, 1853.

109. Corning owned 1537 shares, Hamilton White 813 shares, Dean Richmond 650 shares, and Morgan 3500 shares. Morgan to Corning, July

29, 1853. Morgan to White, Aug. 1, 1853; Morgan to Richmond, July 29, 1853; Morgan to Pruyn, Aug. 11, 1853. Morgan Papers.

Corning subsequently turned over 337 shares to Pruyn. *Private Ledger No. 1*, 337. Pruyn Papers.

In a memorandum in the Morgan Papers (n.d.), Morgan recorded that he informed the Troy committee that "Mr. Boorman, and perhaps some others . . . would be interested with me in the road."

Shortly after the line was purchased, Wilkinson wrote to Corning: "I suppose Mr. Morgan will arrange as to the interests in the road he has purchased." Wilkinson to Corning, Jan. 30, 1853. Corning Papers.

Russell Sage was identified with all aspects of the sale, and it is possible that Morgan passed some part of his stock on to him.

110. McIntosh to Corning, Dec. 18, 1852. Corning Papers.

111. Robert B. Doxtater to Corning, Oct. 9, 1852. Corning Papers.

112. Morgan to Corning, May 14, 1853. Morgan Papers. Pruyn to Corning, May 13, 1853. Corning Papers. At the organization of the new company, Pruyn recorded that Corning held a "large majority of the proxies" and practically dictated all procedure. *Personal Journal, No. 1*, p. 37. Pruyn Papers.

113. *Troy Daily Times*, May 10, 1853.

114. Horace White to Corning, April 27, 1853.

115. *Troy Daily Budget*, April 8, 9, 1856.

116. *P.C.C.*, Troy, March 13, 14, 18, 1856. Sen. Doc. 55 (1856).

V. Repudiation of Railroad-Aid Bonds

1. Scott, *Repudiation of State Debts;* McGrane, *Foreign Bondholders and American State Debts.*

2. Prior to 1850, only Detroit and Mobile, Alabama, are known to have defaulted on their bonds. In 1839, the city of Mobile, hard hit by two disastrous fires and a serious yellow-fever epidemic, found itself unable to meet its obligations. Two years later Detroit defaulted on an issue of public-improvement bonds. Hillhouse, *Municipal Bonds*, 88–89.

3. Adams, *Public Debts*, 343. The first official statistics, published in 1843, revealed that the total municipal debt at this time was approximately $27,500,000. *The United States Magazine and Democratic Review*, XII (Feb. 1843), 212.

4. Studenski, *Public Borrowing*, 20. Hillhouse, Municipal Bonds, 31.

5. *Report on the Valuation, Taxation, and Public Indebtedness in the United States as Returned at the Tenth Census, June 1, 1880* (Washington, 1884), 281–294.

6. See Chart No. 1.

7. *Census of the State of New York for 1875* (Albany, 1877), 470.

8. *Hall's Investors Guide to United States Municipal Bonds; Proving that these Bonds Constitute an Exceptionally Safe and Remunerative Investment* (London, 1874).

9. *P.C.C.* (Rochester), July 11, 1853.

10. N. Y. *Laws*, Ch. 147 (1852); Ch. 278 (1853).

11. Accounting Schedule of the Interstate Commerce Commission for the Albany & Susquehanna Railroad (Records of the Delaware & Hudson Company, New York City).

12. 27 *V.R.I.C.C.*, 363.

13. N. Y. *Laws*, Ch. 907 (1869).

14. The defaulting towns were Venice, Sterling, Rome, Genoa, and Duanesburg. See Table 3.

15. See Table 3. The village of Douglas bonded itself for $10,000 to aid in the construction of a manufacturing plant. *Weismer v. the Village of Douglas*, 64 N. Y. 91.

16. Buck, *The Granger Movement*, 200.

17. Scores of communities in the state sought to shift their heavy tax burden onto the railroads that they aided by levying exorbitant assessments on company property. Oxford raised the valuation of the New York & Oswego Midland within the town from $4,000 to $8,500 per mile. *De Ruyter Gleaner*, Jan. 8, 1879. Rosendale jumped the assessment of the Walkill Valley road from $62,000 to $152,000. *New York Times*, Aug. 29, 1878 (5,2). Local officials in Oswego, Middletown, Delhi, and Paris seized and threatened to auction off passenger stations and rolling stock unless the companies paid their revised tax bills. *Railroad Gazette*, Dec. 19, 1874; Feb. 6, 1875; Feb. 23, 1877. *Clinton Courier*, Feb. 17, 1870.

18. *Oswego Daily Palladium*, May 5, 1866. *Report to the First Mortgage Bondholders of the New York & Oswego Midland Rail Road* (New York, 1874).

19. *Railroad Gazette*, Sept. 27, 1873. *American Railroad Manual for the United States & Dominion for 1873* (New York, 1874), 134–35.

20. *Oswego Daily Times*, April 10, 1880.

21. *American Railroad Manual* (1874), 96. *The Bond Buyer*, Feb. 24, 1896. *Farnham v. Benedict*, 107 N. Y. 165.

22. *Report of the Investigating Committee Appointed by the Town Board of Seneca Falls to Examine into the Affairs of the Pennsylvania & Sodus Bay Railroad.*

23. *Geneva Gazette*, Aug. 19, 1870.

24. *Haines v. Smith*, 45 N. Y. 772.

25. *Ibid.*

26. Mentz: *Town of Mentz v. Cook*, 108 N. Y. 504; Caneadea: *Wilson v. Town of Caneadea*, 15 Hun. 218; Potter: *Whiting v. Town of Potter*, 2 Fed. 517; Northampton: *Clarke v. Town of Northampton*, 120 Fed. 661.

27. *Angel v. Town of Hume*, 17 Hun. 274.

28. Greenwich: *Potter v. Town of Greenwich*, 92 N. Y. 662.

29. Seneca Falls: *Syracuse Savings Bank v. Town of Seneca Falls*, 86 N. Y. 317.

30. Ft. Edward: *Culver v. Village Fort Edward*, 8 Hun. 340.

31. Thompson: *Horton v. Town of Thompson*, 71 N. Y. 513.

32. Lansing: *People v. Van Valkenberg*, 63 Barb. 105. *Ithaca Journal*, Dec. 3, 1872.

33. Yates: *Phelps v. Town of Yates*, 16 Blatchf. 192; Solon: *Town of Solon v. Williamsburg Savings Bank*, 35 Hun. 1; Taylor: *Chapman v. Town*

of Taylor, 64 Hun. 633; Springport: *Avery v. Town of Springport,* 14 Blatchf. 272.

34. This case is unusual in the respect that private property was taken for the payment of a debt of a municipal corporation. In the enforcement of a judgment against a town the usual remedy is by writ of mandamus where the money is available and in the absence of such funds to force a tax sufficient to discharge the debt. Only in New England may private property be seized for municipal debts. McQuillan, *Law of Municipal Corporations,* VI, sec. 2670.

35. *Steuben Advocate* (Bath), Feb. 22, 1882. *Rogers v. Spencer,* 55 N. Y. 1.

36. N. Y. *Laws,* Ch. 638 (1874).

37. *Rogers v. Smith,* 5 Hun. 475.

38. *P.B.S.,* Steuben (1873–1881).

39. *Steuben Advocate,* Feb. 22, 1882. *Canisteo Times,* Feb. 16, 1882.

40. *Hornell Daily Times,* Feb. 11, 1882.

41. *Ibid.,* March 21, 1882.

42. *Ibid.,* Feb. 20, 1882.

43. *Ibid.,* Feb. 16, 1882; *New York Tribune,* Feb. 15, 1882.

44. *Elmira Advertiser,* March 14, 1882.

45. After raising the necessary funds, the tax collector tried to use them for the payment of state and county charges against the town. Served with a court order by the bondholders, the collector hanged himself rather than turn over the money. *Steuben Advocate,* Sept. 6, 1882.

46. *Ibid.,* Dec. 13, 1882. *P.B.S.,* Steuben (1883).

47. Town Minute Book (Hancock), Feb. 11, 1873.

48. *De Ruyter Weekly Gleaner,* Nov. 20, 1878.

49. Town Minute Book (Seneca Falls), Nov. 9, 1876.

50. Town Minute Book (Delhi), Nov. 23, 1872.

51. *Chenango Semi-Weekly Telegraph,* Nov. 23, 1878. Within two weeks De Ruyter bonds dropped to 20 per cent of their par value. *De Ruyter Weekly Gleaner,* Dec. 4, 1878.

52. *New York Times,* Dec. 6, 1878.

53. *De Ruyter Weekly Gleaner,* Dec. 4, 1878.

54. *Chenango Semi-Weekly Telegraph,* Sept. 2, 1868. Women were especially invited to put their savings in municipal bonds. *Ithaca Journal,* April 12, 1870; Jan. 24, 1871.

55. *Chenango Semi-Weekly Telegraph,* April 6, 1881.

56. *Ibid.,* March 13, 1873.

57. *Hancock Herald,* March 9, 1882; March 10, 1887.

58. *New York Times,* Jan. 16, 1879.

59. *Ibid.,* March 29, 1879. *The Times* claimed that not less than 40 per cent of the cases appealed from the courts of first resort were overruled by the higher courts, and that more than 25 per cent of the decisions rendered by the general terms of the several appellate courts were reversed when carried to the Court of Appeals.

60. The towns of Forestburg and Deerpark, which bonded in behalf of the Monticello & Port Jervis, voted to await the outcome of the *Perrine v. Town of Thompson* (106 U. S. 589) litigation before repudiating them-

selves. *Chenango Evening Telegraph,* May 7, 1881. A decision of the New York Court of Appeals holding the bonds of the town of Scipio invalid induced the people of De Ruyter to continue to resist payment on their obligations. *De Ruyter Gleaner,* April 29, 1880.

61. *Chenango Semi-Weekly Telegraph,* March 13, 1873. The people of Hancock were not particularly concerned over cost of litigation. When the bonds fell due, the local newspaper explained, 60 per cent of the town's taxes would be paid by the Erie railroad, the Standard Oil Company, and the New York, Ontario & Western railroad. *Hancock Herald,* April 27, 1882.

62. *Cagwin v. Town of Hancock,* 84 N. Y. 532. *Hancock Herald,* March 17, 1881. *New York Daily Tribune,* March 24, 1881.

63. A Norwich editor wrote: "Perhaps the courts are entering upon a crusade against bonds, and will come to the relief in a summary way of all debt-ridden towns. If so what a panic there will be among the 'bloated bondholders.' Blessed is Nothing." *Chenango Semi-Weekly Telegraph,* April 7, 1881.

64. *Ibid.,* April 6, 1881. *De Ruyter Weekly Gleaner,* April 7, 1881.

65. *Chenango Semi-Weekly Telegraph,* April 9, 1881.

66. *Hancock Herald,* March 9, 1882.

67. *De Ruyter Weekly Gleaner,* Jan. 15, 1879. *Merrill v. Town of Monticello,* 138 U. S. 673. The owners of Genoa's Midland bonds banded together and kept their case alive in the courts for over 16 years. *Oswego Times,* Nov. 20, 1901. *Bond Buyer,* Dec. 7, 1901; Nov. 22, 1902. Before 1887, in cases involving diversity of citizenship, the matter in controversy had to exceed $500. By Act of March 3, 1887, the amount was raised to $2,000.

68. In the *Town of Lansing v. Lytle,* 38 Fed. 204, the court refused to recognize the bondholders as bona fide purchasers for value. The real owners, it declared, feigned the transfers in order to put them in the hands of persons who might pose as innocent purchasers.

A comparable situation arose in the town of Shawangunk. This time, however, the bondholders were successful in prosecuting their case. After their defeat before the New York Court of Appeals the creditors of the town, which were principally savings banks, made a pretended sale of their holdings to one Henry Daboll, of Philadelphia. In payment, Daboll gave his note but left the bonds with the bank as collateral security. The federal courts after some hesitation upheld the validity of the transaction. *Carrier v. Town of Shawangunk,* 20 Batchf. 307. *New York Times,* Jan. 22, 1878. (2,1); Dec. 13, 1879. (3,1). *Thompson v. Perrine,* 106 U. S. 589, 592.

69. *Mercer County v. Hackett,* I Wall. (U. S.) 83. *Rich v. Town of Mentz,* 132 U. S. 632.

Section 32 of the Judiciary Code of 1789 (Revised Statutes, sec. 721) provides that "the laws of the several states, except where the Constitution, treaties, or statutes of the United States shall otherwise require or provide, shall be regarded as rules of decisions in trials at common law in the courts of the United States, in cases where they apply."

Until the decision of Justice Story in *Swift v. Tyson,* 16 Pet 1 (1842), the United States Supreme Court generally conceded that decisions of state courts were binding upon federal courts in matters not involving the constitution, statutes, or treaties of the United States even though they did not involve the construction of state statutes. The ruling in *Swift v. Tyson* marks the turning point of opinion as to the obligation of the federal courts to follow state-court decisions in matters of general commercial law. Justice Story held that in contracts and other instruments of a commercial nature the true interpretation is to be found not in the decisions of the local tribunals but in the general principles and doctrine of commercial jurisprudence. "Undoubtedly," he declared, "the decisions of the local tribunals upon these subjects are entitled to, and will receive, the most deliberate attention and respect of this court; but they cannot furnish positive rules, or conclusive authority, by which our own judgments are to be bound up and governed." For a criticism of Story's position see Charles Warren, "New Light on the History of the Federal Judiciary Act of 1789," 37 *Harvard Law Review* 49.

The rule established in *Swift v. Tyson* was reversed by the decision of the United States Supreme Court in *Erie Railroad Company v. Tompkins,* 304 U. S. 64 (1938). Mr. Justice Brandeis delivered the opinion of the court: "Diversity of citizenship jurisdiction was conferred in order to prevent apprehended discrimination in state courts against those not citizens of the state. *Swift v. Tyson* introduced grave discrimination by non-citizens against citizens. It made rights enjoyed under the unwritten 'general law' vary according to whether enforcement was sought in the state or in the federal court; and the privilege of selecting the court in which the right should be determined was conferred on the non-citizen. Thus the doctrine rendered impossible equal protection of the law." Harry Shulman, "The Demise of Swift v. Tyson," 47 *Yale Law Journal* 1336.

70. *Third National Bank of Syracuse v. Town of Seneca Falls,* 15 Fed. 783.

71. *Murdock v. Town of Venice,* 92 U. S. 498.

72. N. Y. *Laws,* Ch. 298 (1871).

73. P.B.S., Tompkins, 1876. *Thomas v. Town of Lansing,* 14 Fed. 618. *Purdy v. Town of Lansing,* 128 U. S. 557.

74. *Oswego County Savings Bank v. Town of Genoa,* 172 N. Y. 635. Genoa considered defaulting as early as 1879, but the proposal was voted down at a special town meeting. *De Ruyter Gleaner* Jan. 1, 1879. *Bond Buyer,* Oct. 1, 1898; July 1, 1899; Dec. 7, 1901; Nov. 22, 1902.

75. N. Y. *Laws,* Ch. 925 (1871).

76. *Town of Mentz v. Cook,* 38 Hun. 637; *Strang v. Cook,* 47 Hun. 46; *Town of Mentz v. Cook,* 108 N. Y. 504.

77. *Rich v. Town of Mentz,* 18 Fed. 54.

78. 134 U. S. 632.

79. *Bond Buyer,* May 16, 1903.

80. *Clarke v. Town of Northampton,* 189 U. S. 513. On the other hand, in *Whiting v. Town of Potter* (2 Fed. 517) the court held that a municipality might not question the validity of securities on which it had paid interest over a period of years. "Such conduct," it declared, "was a direct ratification of the acts of those who issued the bonds. It was ratification made with full knowledge on the part of the town of the defect now alleged to have existed."

81. Fairman, *Mr. Justice Miller*, 232.

82. *Ibid.*

83. *McClure v. Town of Oxford*, 94 U. S. 429.

84. *Railroad Company v. Cowdrey*, 11 Wall. 459. Moreover, the courts have ruled that, if any previous owner of a bond was a bona fide holder, the plaintiff could avail himself of his predecessor's position without showing that he himself was an innocent purchaser. *Montclair v. Ramsdell*, 107 U. S. 147.

85. N. Y. *Laws*, Chs. 134, 375 (1852).

86. Genoa: *Starin v. Town of Genoa*, 23 N. Y. 439; *Fiedler v. Mead*, 36 N. Y. 224; Venice: *Town of Venice v. Woodruff*, 62 N. Y. 462; Scipio: *People v. Morgan*, 55 N. Y. 587; Sterling: *Gould v. Town of Sterling*, 53 N. Y. 128.

87. Genoa: *Town of Genoa v. Woodruff*, 92 U. S. 502; Venice: *Town of Venice v. Murdock*, 92 U. S. 502; Scipio: *Town of Scipio v. Wright*, 101 U. S. 665. This decision invalidated 17 of the municipality's bonds. On the balance of its railroad-aid debt or $8,000 the town agreed to settle with the bondholders at 80 cents on the dollar. *Seneca Falls Reveille*, October 2, 1874. *P.B.S.*, Cayuga, 1875–1882. Sterling. *P.B.S.*, Cayuga, 1877.

88. *Town of Venice v. Murdock*, 92 U. S. 502.

89. Hancock: *Cagwin v. Town of Hancock*, 84 N. Y. 532; *Foote v. Town of Hancock*, Fed. Cas. No. 4911; Andes: *Craig v. Town of Andes*, 93 N. Y. 405; *Town of Andes v. Ely*, 158 U. S. 312; Lyons: *Town of Lyons v. Chamberlain*, 89 N. Y. 478; *Town of Lyons v. Munson*, 99 U. S. 684; Orleans: *Irwin v. Sawyer*, 52 N. Y. 296; *Town of Orleans v. Platt*, 99 U. S. 676.

90. See Table 3.

91. *Congressional Record*, 45 Cong., 3 sess., Vol. 8, p. 29.

92. *Ibid.*, 2 sess., Appendix, 387.

93. "The Federal Judiciary and Repudiation," *Nation*, XVIII (Jan. 2, 1879), 5.

94. *New York Times*, Jan. 16, 1879. (4,2).

95. *New York Daily Tribune*, April 13, 1882.

96. *New York Times*, Sept. 10, 1874; Feb. 6, 1878; Dec. 6, 1878. *Assembly Journal* (1878), 161, 759. *Senate Journal* (1880), 331, 488, 1037.

97. *New York Times*, Feb. 6, 1878 (4,1).

98. *Ibid.*, Dec. 24, 1878 (4,2). *Railroad Gazette*, June 13, 1878.

99. N. Y. *Laws*, Ch. 522 (1881).

100. *Ibid.*, Ch. 538 (1879).

101. Town Minute Book (Seneca Falls), 1873–1887. *Seneca Falls Reveille*, Nov. 14, 1874; June 22, Oct. 26, 1883; July 2, 1887. *Seneca County News*, April 10, 1883.

102. Town Minute Book (Phelps), 1872–1896. *Phelps Citizen*, Dec. 10, 1896. *Bond Buyer*, Nov. 4, 1895; April 12, 1897.

103. *P.B.S.*, Alleghany, 1884–1887.

104. *Rochester Democrat & Chronicle*, Nov. 5, 1897. *Bond Buyer*, Sept. 24, 1898. *P.B.S.*, Wayne, 1900.

105. *P.B.S.*, Jefferson, 1884.

106. Town Minute Book (Andes), Nov. 29, 1892.

107. Town Minute Book (Hancock), 1872–1889. *P.B.S.*, Delaware, 1876–1887. *Hancock Herald*, Aug. 11, 1887. In 1884, the town voted 151 to 29 against compromising the debt at 50 cents on the dollar. *Ibid.*, Dec. 4, 1884.

108. *Troy Times*, Dec. 22, 1900.

109. *De Ruyter Gleaner*, Sept. 29, 1887; Feb. 16, 1888.

110. *Ibid.*, Feb. 21, 1889.

111. *Ibid.*, Feb. 20, 1890.

112. Town Minute Book (De Ruyter), 1882–1895. The village of De Ruyter compromised its bonds at same rate as the township. *De Ruyter Gleaner*, May 4, 1882.

113. Although no bonds had been issued since 1875, municipal indebtedness for railroad construction in 1901 was greater in New York than in any state in the union save Kansas. *Bond Buyer*, August 3, 1901.

114. See Tables 3 and 6.

115. See Table 4.

VI. The Sale of Stock

1. One month before the road opened, the total paid-in capital stock amounted to only $1,861,393.13, of which $950,000 was owned by the towns. The city of Albany lent the road $1,000,000. *Annual Report of the Albany and Susquehanna Railroad for 1868.*

2. Adams, "A Chapter of Erie," *North American Review*, CXII (April 1871), 245.

3. *Albany Evening Journal*, Aug. 6, 1869.

4. Jay Gould to Thomas Dickson, Oct. 1, 1870; Dickson to Gould, Oct. 8, 1870. Minutes of the Board of Directors of the Delaware & Hudson Canal Company. Records of the Delaware & Hudson Canal Company (230 Park Ave., New York).

5. Stock Transfer Books of the Albany & Susquehanna Railroad for 1869. Records of the Albany & Susquehanna Railroad Company (Albany, New York).

6. Phelps Papers. The correspondence of the company's treasurer reveals that hundreds of subscribers were reluctant to pay more than their 10 per cent down unless sued.

7. Directors' Minutes (Albany & Susquehanna), July 14, 1868.

8. *Ibid.*, April 7, 1868; June 3, 1868; Dabney Morgan to Joseph Ramsay, April 29, 1868. Ramsay Papers. David Groesbeck to W. L. M. Phelps, Aug. 5, 1869. Phelps Papers. *Rochester Daily Democrat*, Dec. 10, 1869.

9. *An Appeal from the Town Commissioners of Railroads in behalf of the Albany & Susquehanna Railroad* (1866). Broadside in the Phelps Papers. Directors' Minutes (Albany & Susquehanna), July 14, 1868.

10. *Laws of New York*, Ch. 195 (1852); Ch. 64 (1856).

11. Memorandum of W. L. M. Phelps, July 30, 1869. Phelps Papers.

12. *Oneonta Herald*, Aug. 4, 1869.

13. Milford, Unadilla, Davenport, Scrap Book No. 3, Phelps Papers; Colesville, *Binghamton Daily Democrat*, Aug. 9, 1869; Maryland, *Albany Argus*, Aug. 5, 1869; Westford, *Freeman's Journal* (Cooperstown), May 5, 1870.

14. *Ibid.*, July 30, 1869.

15. *Albany Daily Knickerbocker*, Jan. 1, 1870.

16. *Oneonta Herald*, Aug. 18, 1869.

17. *Home and Abroad* (Unadilla), Sept. 4, 18, 1869.

18. *Albany Evening Journal*, Aug. 24, 1869.

19. Telegrams, Ramsay to Phelps, July 31, 1869; Case to Phelps, July 31, 1869. Phelps Papers.

20. Memorandum of W. L. M. Phelps, Aug. 3, 1869. Phelps Papers. Oneonta sued Gould to make good on his contract but the courts held the agreement void. Minute Book (Oneonta), Nov. 8, 1878; *Gould v. Town of Oneonta*, 3 Hun. 401.

21. *Rochester Daily Democrat*, Dec. 4, 1869.

22. *Ibid.*

23. Directors' Minutes (Albany & Susquehanna), March 7, 1866.

24. Jay Gould to Thomas Dickson, Oct. 1, 1870. Directors' Minutes (Delaware & Hudson). The stock was purchased on Aug. 5, 1869, and transferred to the Delaware & Hudson Co. during the week of March 17, 1870 (Albany & Susquehanna).

25. Memorandum of W. L. M. Phelps, Aug. 14, 1869. Phelps Papers.

26. *Rochester Daily Democrat*, Dec. 11, 1869. Within a month, 22 law suits were instituted and 20 injunctions were issued.

27. *Oneonta Herald*, Nov. 24, 1869; *Freeman's Journal*, Sept. 24, 1869.

28. *People v. Albany & Susquehanna Railroad Co.*, How. Prac. 228. The complete testimony of the trial was carried in the *Rochester Daily Democrat*, Dec. 2–20, 1869. While waiting for the court to hand down its decision, Gould and Fisk were not idle. On September 24, they conducted their famous gold corner.

29. See Table 1. Duanesburg, which had been challenging since 1862 the procedure under which it had subscribed to the road's stock, now dropped all litigation and disposed of its securities at par. *P.B.S.* (Schoharie), Oct. 31, 1879.

30. *P.C.C.*, Utica, March 12, 1878; Jan.–Feb. 1881. *Utica Morning Herald & Daily Gazette,* Jan. 11, 1881.

31. *P.C.C.*, Utica, March 12, 1878.

32. *Utica Morning Herald & Daily Gazette,* Jan. 11, 12, 1881.

33. *Ibid.*, March 9, 1881.

34. *Ibid.*, Jan. 11, 1881.

35. N. Y. *Laws*, Ch. 50 (1866).

36. *Utica Morning Herald & Daily Gazette,* Jan. 12, 1881.

37. *P.C.C.*, Utica, March 11, 1881. *Utica Morning Herald and Daily Gazette,* Oct. 5, 1885.

38. Sangerfield, whose bonds matured annually between 1875 and 1890, sold a small number of shares each year until the debt was paid. *P.B.S.* (Oneida), 1875–1890. Paris disposed of its stock in ten separate auctions. Minute Book (Paris), 1870–1891.

39. *Plattsburg Republican,* Nov. 6, 1875.

40. *Ibid., P.B.S.* Clinton, 1876.

41. *P.C.C.,* Utica, July 19, 1871. *Utica Morning Herald,* July 22, 1871. Agreements dated June 14, 28, and July 5, 1871 are in the city clerk's office in Utica. Franchise Book No. 339, p. 316; the contract of Dec. 4, 1889 is in the Oneida County Clerk's Office. Book of Deeds, No. 478, p. 441.

42. *Utica Daily Press,* June 26, 1901. *P.C.C.* Utica, June 25, 1901.

43. *Ibid.,* Jan. 3, Sept. 19, 1905. *Utica Herald-Dispatch,* March 18, Sept. 16, 1905. 48 Misc. Rep. 258.

44. *P.C.C.,* Utica, Jan. 8, Feb. 5, 1909. *Utica Herald-Dispatch,* Jan. 25, 1909.

45. *Utica Daily Press,* Sept. 7, 1912.

46. *Utica Daily Press,* Sept. 7, 1912.

47. *Rochester Union & Advertiser,* April 15, 1904.

48. *Ibid.*

49. *P.C.C.,* Rochester, April 12, 1904. *Rochester Union & Advertiser,* April 11, 1904. In its circulars to brokerage houses, the city insisted that the lease was binding on the Erie company. *Bond Buyer,* April 2, 1904. Circulars in the Pliny Fisk Papers.

50. Sykes & Company to the city comptroller of Rochester, cited in the *Rochester Union & Advertiser,* April 11, 1904.

51. *Ibid.,* April 18, 1904. Bids were received from Vermilye & Company for $140.25 and Keen, Van Cortlandt & Company for $138.25. *Bond Buyer,* April 16, 1904.

52. *V.R.I.C.C.,* 111. These were redeemed (1866–1876), $250,000 by the Western Railway of Massachusetts and $750,000 by its successor, the Boston & Albany.

53. *P.C.C.,* Albany, March 26, 1852. These were redeemed by the Delaware & Hudson in 1902.

54. *Ibid.,* Aug. 15, 1842; July 11, Nov. 27, 1843. These were redeemed by the New York Central.

55. *P.C.C.,* Albany, April 14, 1856.

56. 130 *V.R.I.C.C.,* 205.

57. *Rochester Union,* April 20, 1874.

58. *Troy Daily Whig,* Nov. 16, 1852.

59. *Poughkeepsie Eagle,* June 12, 1875.

60. *P.C.C.,* Troy, Dec. 16, 1852. The Edwin D. Morgan Papers contain much material on the importance of this line to the Hudson River Railroad. See especially Morgan to James Boorman, Feb. 19, 1852; Morgan to Russell Sage, August 27, 1852.

61. *P.C.C.,* Troy, Nov. 2, 1854. *Troy Daily Whig,* March 24, 1858. The Schenectady & Troy was consolidated into the Central in 1853.

62. *P.C.C.,* Troy, Dec. 7, 1854.

63. *Troy Daily Whig,* Feb. 27, 1857; March 4, 1857.

64. *P.C.C.,* Troy, May 21, 1857.

65. *Troy Daily Whig,* April 10, 1855.

66. *P.C.C.,* Troy, Oct. 7, 1858.

67. *Ibid.,* Nov. 5, 1858; Dec. 2, 1858; 108 *Troy Book of Deeds,* 279. *Troy Daily Budget,* Oct. 8, 1858. The Troy Union Railroad is still in opera-

tion, with the New York Central paying 50 per cent, the Delaware & Hudson 25 per cent, and the Boston & Maine 25 per cent of its operating costs.

68. Upon the completion of the road, the towns owned $401,000 of the $464,700 paid in capital stock. *A.R.S.E.S.* (1873).

69. *Lowville Journal and Republican,* April 10, 1884.

70. *Watertown Daily Times,* Oct. 28; Nov. 1, 1893.

71. *P.C.C.,* Watertown, Aug. 29; Dec. 19, 1893. The sale of the stock touched off a dispute over distribution of the proceeds of the money. Since the township in 1893 was somewhat larger than the one which bonded for the road in 1872, many argued that only that part of the town which subscribed for the stock and paid for the bonds should benefit from the sale. In a special election, the voters decided to use the money to reduce taxes in the area of the old town only. *P.C.C.,* Watertown, Feb. 6, March 26, May 18, 1894. *Watertown Daily Times,* March 30, May 4, 1894.

72. Both Hounsfield and Champion sold to the Central at par. In Hounsfield this meant a reduction in the town tax rate of more than 40 per cent. *Watertown Daily Times,* Dec. 8, 1893.

73. *Ibid.,* Nov. 1, 1893.

74. *Dunkirk Evening Observer,* April 4, May 26, and June 2, 1900.

75. *Fredonia Censor,* June 19, 1901. Minute Book (Pomfret), Oct. 29, 1900.

76. Minute Book (Greene) June 22, 1899; Feb. 1, 1900. Up to this time, the town had paid nothing on its bonded indebtedness. *Greene American,* Jan. 5, 1899.

77. Ripley, *Railroads, Finance & Organization,* 231. Condensed financial statements, dividend rates, and stock prices are printed in *Poor's Manual of Railroads* for these years.

78. *Remarks by William White, President, the Delaware, Lackawanna & Western Company at Annual Meeting of Stockholders,* May 9, 1944.

79. Paine, Webber, Jackson & Curtis to the First National Bank of Greene, Sept. 1, 1943. Letter file, town clerk's office in Greene.

80. *Remarks by President White,* May 9, 1944.

81. *Chenango-American* (Greene), Sept. 26, 1946.

82. Willard Knickerbocker to the author, Feb. 28, 1948.

83. *Moody's Manual of Railroads* (1942). *Remarks of President White,* May 9, 1944. Paine, Webber, Jackson & Curtis to the First National Bank of Greene, Sept. 1, 1943. Letter file in town clerk's office in Greene.

84. Wood, Struthers' Co. to Knickerbocker, July 2, 1943. Adams & Peck to Knickerbocker, March 9, 1944. R. L. Enderlin to Knickerbocker, May 8, Dec. 28, 1943; Nov. 9, 1944; July 16, 1946. *Ibid.* Minute Book (Greene), Sept. 11, 1943.

85. *Ibid.,* Nov. 9, 1944. Enderlin explained the proposition before a meeting of the town board. Enderlin to Knickerbocker, Sept. 16, 1944. Letter file in town clerk's office in Greene. The New York, Lackawanna & Western was the main line of the Lackawanna between Binghamton and Buffalo.

86. The comptroller declared in part: "At the present time the town owns stock. If it exchanges the same for bonds it will become the owner of bonds in a private corporation. Incidentally it will become the owner

of bonds in a different corporation than that in which it now owns stock acquired prior to constitutional prohibition." Frank C. Moore to Knicker-bocker, Nov. 22, 1944. Minute Book (Greene), Dec. 2, 1944.

87. *Ibid.*, Aug. 10, 1946. Enderlin to Knickerbocker, July 16, 1946. Letter file in town clerk's office in Greene.

88. Paine, Webber, Jackson & Curtis to the First National Bank of Greene, Oct. 1, 1945. *Ibid.*

89. Minute Book (Greene), Aug. 10, 1948.

90. *Moody's Manual of Investments* (Railroads), 1947. The D. & H. held more than 300,000 shares of New York Central. This stock yielded no returns until 1943, when a dividend of $1.50 per share was declared. These holdings were completely sold by May 1946.

91. *Cobleskill Index*, Sept. 9, 1869.

92. Minute Book (Cobleskill), Feb. 17, 1883. In May 1882, the town sold 100 shares at 132; in June it sold nine shares at 133⅞ and 141 shares at 124⅞.

93. Dividend Record of the Albany & Susquehanna Railroad; Records of the Delaware & Hudson Co. (230 Park Ave., New York).

94. *Agreement of Merger Between the Delaware & Hudson Co. and the Albany and Susquehanna Railroad. Ibid.* This was approved by the Albany & Susquehanna stockholders on May 2, 1945.

95. C. L. Chamberlain (chief municipal accountant in the state comp-troller's office) to C. R. Selkirk (Cobleskill supervisor). Minute Book (Cobleskill), March 23, 1945.

96. Minute Book (Cobleskill), Aug. 8, 1946. *Cobleskill Times*, July 11, 1946.

For nearly 50 years the towns of Otsego and Middlefield held a con-trolling interest in the Cooperstown & Susquehanna Valley, a branch line operated under lease by the Delaware & Hudson. Unable to purchase the road at a price it considered reasonable, the company set out to coerce these communities into selling their stock by establishing exorbitant rates on freight delivered over the line. In 1913, Otsego reached an understanding with the railroad company whereby the town agreed to sell its $200,000 par value stock for $7,500 in return for the discontinuance of all arbitrary freight rates and the construction by the D. & H. of a new passenger sta-tion in the village of Cooperstown. In a special election the voters approved of the contract 302 to 74. A short time later, the company made a com-parable agreement with Middlefield. *Otsego Farmer*, July 4–Nov. 21, 1913.

97. *Railroad Gazette*, Sept. 27; Nov. 15, 1873. *Oswego Daily Palladium*, Nov. 17, 1873.

98. *Railroad Gazette*, Feb. 28, March 21, 1874. The foreign bondholders were particularly difficult to satisfy. *Chenango Semi-Weekly Telegraph*, April 10, 1880.

99. *Railroad Gazette*, Nov. 21, 1879. *New York Daily Tribune*, Jan. 23, 1880. A number of newspapers in the state opposed reorganization of the line on any basis. *The Buffalo Courier* urged abandonment of the road "as a perpetual monument of the occasional foolishness of capital and a warn-ing against the evils of town bonding." Nov. 17, 1879. The *Utica Morning Herald* conceded that construction of the line was a terrible blunder but

pointed out that scores of communities were dependent upon it for transportation and that the company should be given another opportunity to prove itself. Nov. 20, 1879.

100. *Oswego Daily Times,* Feb. 10, 1880.

101. Chenango Semi-Weekly Telegraph, Feb. 21, 1880.

102. *Ibid.,* March 24, April 3, 1880. The identity of the party in New York who promised to advance the money was never made public. No one questioned, however, that such an agreement had been made. See *New York Financial Reporter,* March 3, 1880; *Railroad Gazette,* April 9, 1880. The announcement that the road would be redeemed caused the stock of the reorganized company to drop from 32 to 25. Midland stock rose from 2 to 10. *Chenango Semi-Weekly Telegraph,* March 24, 1880.

103. *Ibid.,* Dec. 17, 1879. *P.C.C.* (Oswego), Dec. 9, 1879. *Oswego Daily Times,* Jan. 21, 1880.

104. *New York Laws,* Ch. 21 (1880).

105. *Oswego Daily Times,* March 4, 1880.

106. *P.C.C.,* Oswego, March 4, 1880. *Oswego Daily Times,* March 5, 1880.

107. *Chenango Semi-Weekly Telegraph,* Feb. 21, 1880.

108. *Oswego Daily Times,* March 5, 1880.

109. *Chenango Semi-Weekly Telegraph,* April 17, May 5, 1880. *Delaware Republican* (Delhi), May 1, 1880.

110. The details of these leases and the negotiations leading up to them are in the Minutes of the Board of Directors of the Rome & Clinton Railroad (1870). Records of the Rome & Clinton Railroad (Hayes National Bank, Clinton); Minutes of the Board of Directors of Utica, Clinton & Binghamton Railroad (1870–1871). Records of the New York, Ontario & Western Railroad (First Citizens Bank & Trust Company, Utica).

111. *P.B.S.* Oneida, 1872. This action reduced the town debt from $40,000 to $6,216.46.

112. *Annual Report of the Chamberlain of the City of Rome for 1894* (Rome, 1895). *Rome Sentinel,* Feb. 14, 1895.

113. Directors' Minutes (Rome & Clinton), Dec. 1944. *Clinton Courier,* Dec. 21, 1944; Jan. 4, 1945.

114. Upon completion, the paid-in capital stock of the Rome & Clinton amounted to $172,000, of which $140,000 was owned by the towns. The paid-in stock of the Utica, Clinton & Binghamton amounted to $640,325, of which $464,000 was municipally owned.

115. Records of the New York, Ontario & Western Railroad (New York City).

116. Town Minute Book (Kirkland), 1934–1941. *Clinton Courier,* Dec. 17, 1942. In Kirkland, the receipt of $11,800, representing one-half the sale price, caused the tax rate for 1943 to drop from $13.20 to $10.20 in the village and from $17 to $13.45 in the rest of the township.

117. The Black River & Morristown was leased in 1873 by the Utica & Black River. In 1902 Theresa sold 162 shares of stock at 160. Dividend Record Book of the Utica & Black River Railroad. (Records of the New York Central Railroad, 466 Lexington Ave., New York.) Dunkirk has never sold any of its stock. In a reorganization of the Dunkirk line in 1872,

the town was forced to give up two shares of stock in the old company for one in the new. Under the terms of the consolidation agreement of 1914, the town relinquished eight shares of its stock for three in the New York Central. The stock of Theresa, on the other hand, was taken into the consolidation at a premium of 80 per cent.

Today Dunkirk holds 235 shares and Theresa 790. Two other municipalities hold New York Central stock: Groton (Mass.) has 43 shares and West Brookfield (Mass.), 50 shares. Record of New York Central stockholders for 1948, *Ibid.*

118. Subscription rights were offered on Jan. 2, 1917; Jan. 2, 1924; Aug. 10, 1927; June 15, 1928; Nov. 15, 1929.

119. Dunkirk received $5170. Town Minute Book (Dunkirk), 1917–1930.

120. A. D. Houland (Railroad Commissioner of Theresa) to author, Jan. 24, 1948; Jacob Ludes (supervisor of Dunkirk) to author, March 6, 1948.

121. *Utica Morning Herald & Daily Gazette*, May 30, 1856.

122. *Ibid.*, Jan. 23, 1857; Nov. 25, 1858.

123. *Buffalo Commercial-Advertiser*, Sept. 12, 1877. *P.C.C.*, Buffalo, Jan. 1, 1877.

124. *Ibid.*, Jan. 8, 1878. *Jamestown Journal*, Feb. 23, 1877.

125. *Buffalo Commercial-Advertiser*, April 14, 1877.

126. *Annual Report of the Board of Railroad Commissioners* (1883). In addition to regular dividend of 7 per cent, the road paid a special dividend in 1883 of 12 per cent.

APPENDIX: MAPS, CHARTS, AND TABLES

BIBLIOGRAPHY

INDEX

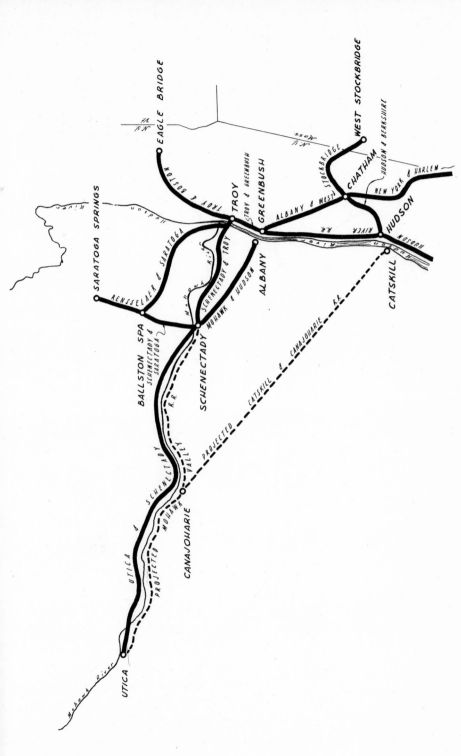

Map 1. Albany and Troy railroads, 1852.

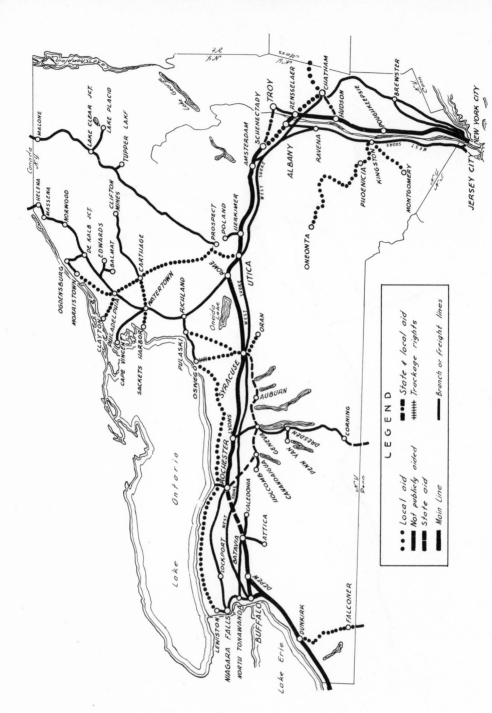

Map 2. New York Central System in New York State.

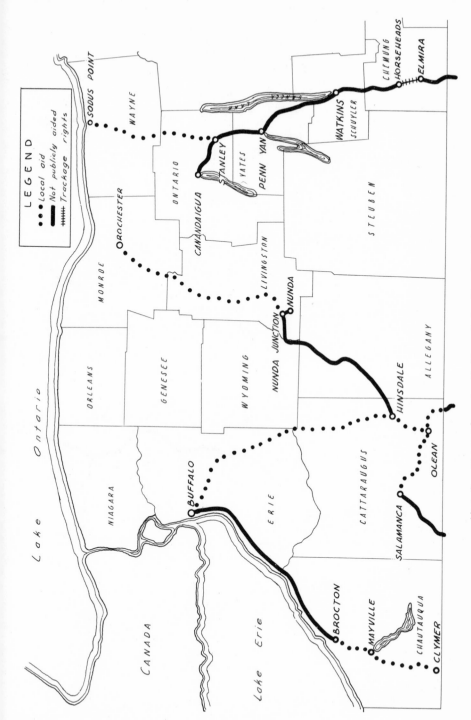

Map 3. Pennsylvania Railroad in New York State.

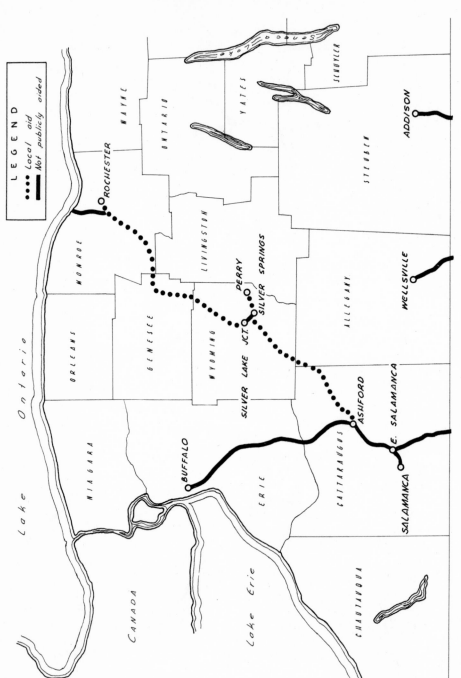

Map 4.   Baltimore & Ohio Railroad in New York State.

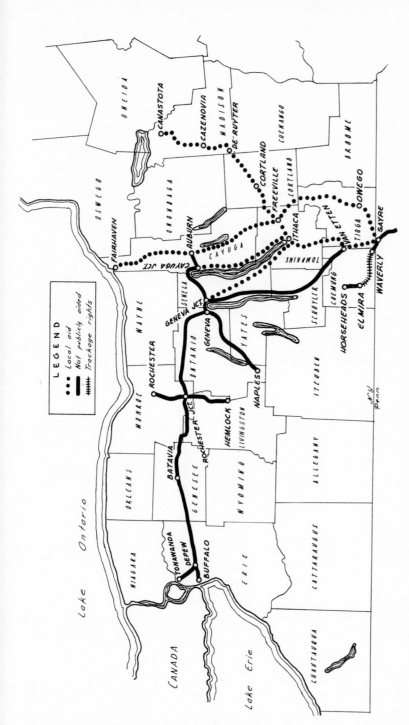

LEGEND
•••• Local aid
—— Not publicly aided
++++ Trackage rights

Map 5. Lehigh Railroad in New York State.

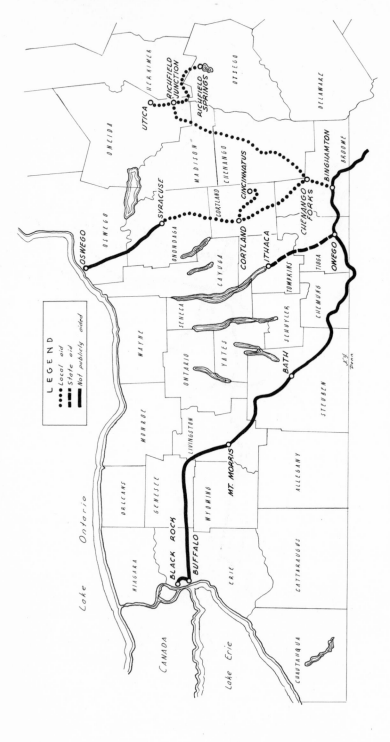

Map 8.   Delaware, Lackawanna & Western Railroad in New York State.

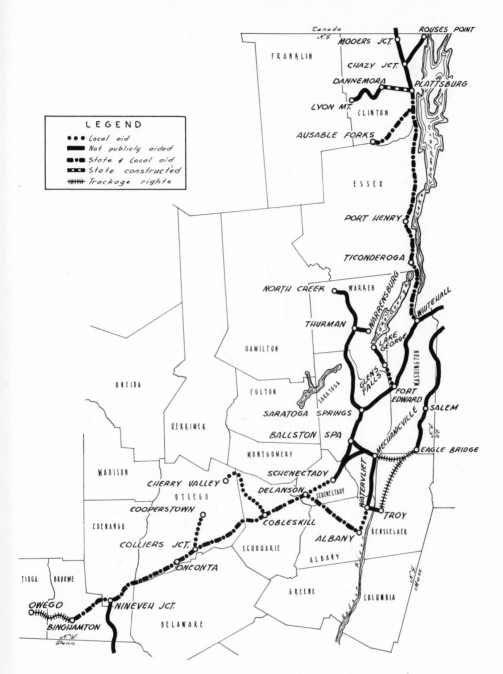

Map 7.   Delaware & Hudson Railroad in New York State.

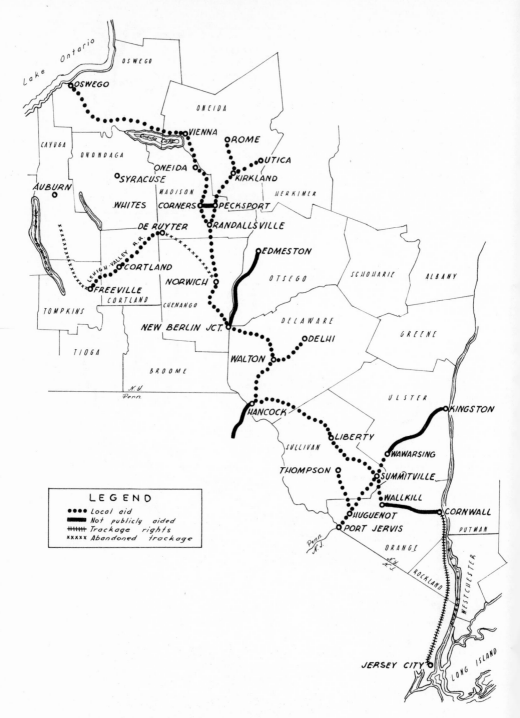

Map 8. New York, Ontário & Western Railroad in New York State.

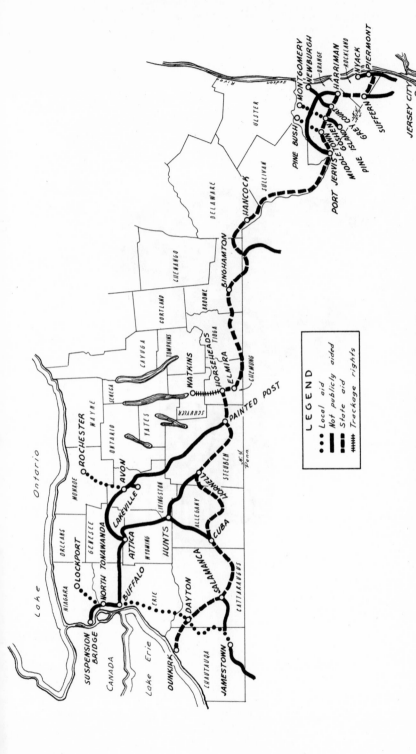

Map 9. Erie Railroad in New York State.

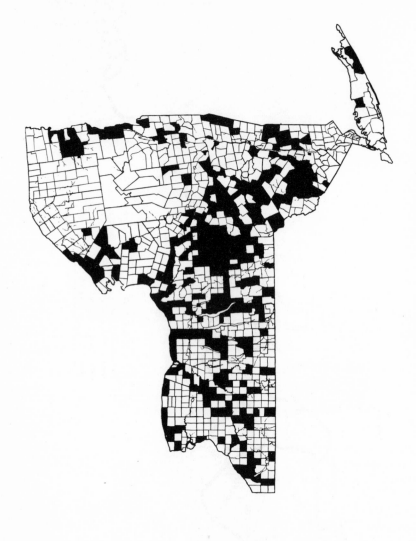

Map 10. Municipal aid to railroads, 1837–1875.

Chart 1. Public debt of municipalities aiding in the construction of railroads on January 1, 1875.

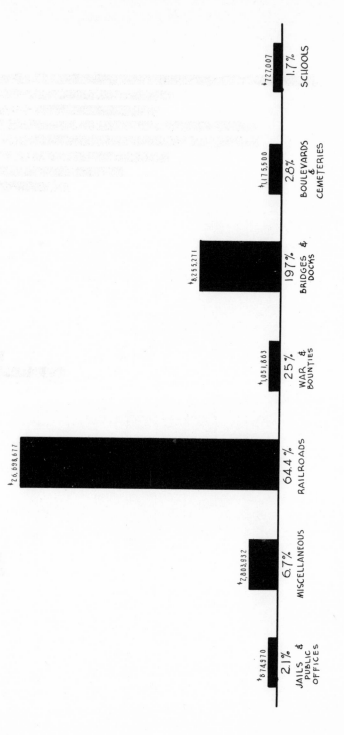

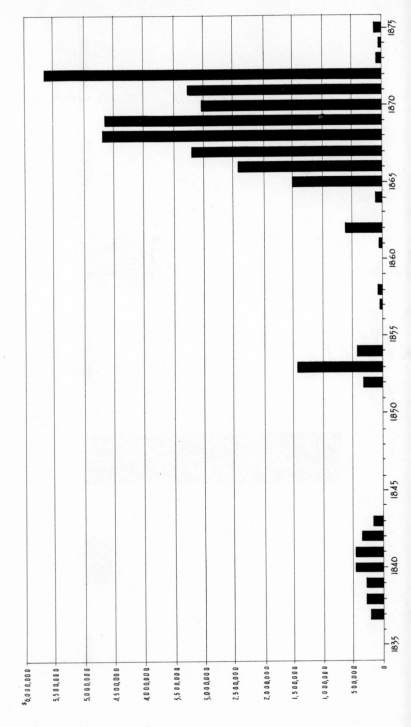

Chart 2. Municipal aid to railroads in New York State, 1835–1875.

Chart 3. Railroad construction in New York State, 1830–1875.

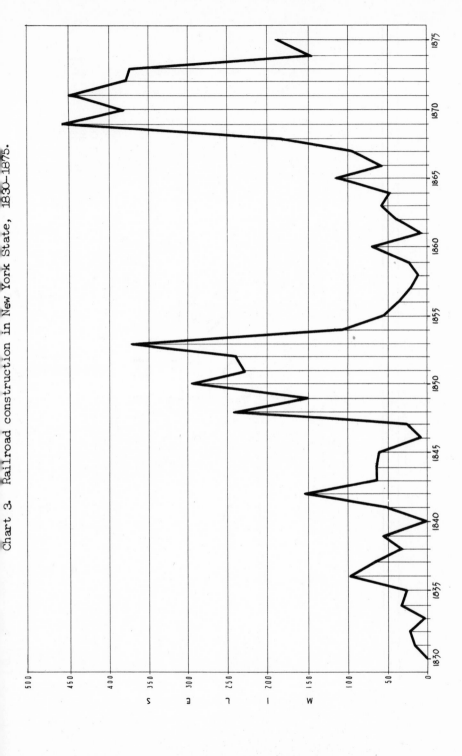

Table 1. MUNICIPAL AID TO RAILROADS (1837-1875).

Municipality	Date	Amount	Railroad	Present System	Date of Sale	Price per Share
Albany County						
Albany	1842-43	$ 250,000	Mohawk & Hudson	New York Central	a	
"	1838-41	1,000,000	Albany & West Stockbridge	" " "	b	
"	1865	1,000,000	Albany & Susquehanna	Delaware & Hudson	b	
"	1854	300,000	Albany & Northern	"	c	
Allegany County						
Amity	1872	40,000	Buffalo & Belmont	Extinct	d	
Angelica	1872	65,000	Rochester, Nunda & Pennsylvania	"	d	
Birdsall	1872	20,000	" " " "	"	d	
Caneadea	1871	40,000	Buffalo & Belmont	"	e	
Hume	1871	50,000	" "	"	e	
Broome County						
Binghamton	1852	50,000	Syracuse & Binghamton	Delaware, Lackawanna & Western	d	
"	1867	50,000	Albany & Susquehanna	Delaware & Hudson	1873	88
Colesville	1858	50,000	" "	"	1946	230
Cattaraugus County						
Dayton	1872	10,000	Buffalo & Jamestown	Erie	d	
Ellicottville	1868	40,000	Cattaraugus	Extinct	d	
Farmersville	1872	10,000	Buffalo, New York & Philadelphia	Pennsylvania	1881	100
Franklinville	1872	30,000	" " " "	"	1881	100
Ischua	1872	15,000	" " " "	"	1881	100
Machias	1872	15,000	" " " "	"	1881	100
"	1968	8,000	Cattaraugus	Extinct	d	
Olean	1872	20,000	Buffalo, New York & Philadelphia	Pennsylvania	1881	100
Persia	1872	30,000	Buffalo & Jamestown	Erie	d	
Postville	1872	30,000	Buffalo, New York & Philadelphia	Pennsylvania	1881	100
Yorkshire	1872	20,000	" " " "	"	1881	100

178

Municipality	Date	Amount	Railroad	Present System	Date of Sale	Price per Share
			Cayuga County			
Auburn	1853	100,000	Lake Ontario, Auburn & New York	Extinct	d	
"	1867	500,000	Southern Central	Lehigh Valley	1943	1½
Brutus	1869	50,000	" "	" "	f	
Cato	1871	30,000	" "	" "	g	
Genoa	1852	50,000	Lake Ontario, Auburn & New York	Extinct	d	
"	1872	75,000	New York & Oswego Midland	"	e	
Ira	1871	40,000	Southern Central	Lehigh Valley	f	
Ledyard	1870	100,000	Cayuga Lake	" "	e	
Locke	1867	49,400	Southern Central	" "	f	
Mentz	1872	30,000	Cayuga Northern	Extinct	e	
Montezuma	1872	20,000	"	"	d	
Moravia	1868	84,000	Southern Central	Lehigh Valley	1943	1½
Scipio	1853	25,000	Lake Ontario, Auburn & New York	Extinct	e	
"	1872	100,000	New York & Oswego Midland	"	d	
Springport	1870	100,000	Cayuga Lake	Lehigh Valley	d	
Sterling	1853	25,000	Lake Ontario, Auburn & New York	Extinct	d	
"	1867	30,000	Southern Central	Lehigh Valley	e	
Venice	1872	75,000	New York & Oswego Midland	Extinct	d	
"	1852	25,000	Lake Ontario, Auburn & New York	"	d	
			Chautauqua County			
Carroll	1868	20,000	Dunkirk, Warren & Pittsburg	New York Central	1901	31
Charlotte	1867	34,000	" " "	" " "	1901	31
Chautauqua	1867	100,000	Buffalo & Oil Creek Cross Cut	Pennsylvania	d	
Cherry Creek	1872	44,000	Buffalo & Jamestown	Erie	d	
Clymer	1866	20,000	Buffalo & Oil Creek Cross Cut	Pennsylvania	d	
Dunkirk	1867	125,000	Dunkirk, Warren & Pittsburg	New York Central	g	
Gerry	1867	34,000	" " "	" " "	1901	31
Pomfret	1867	50,000	" " "	" " "	1901	31
Portland	1866	20,000	Buffalo & Oil Creek Cross Cut	Pennsylvania	d	
Sherman	1866	30,000	" " "	"	d	
Stockton	1861	34,000	Dunkirk, Warren & Pittsburg	New York Central	e	

Municipality	Date	Amount	Railroad	Present System	Date of Sale	Price per Share
			Chemung County			
Erin	1870	30,000	Utica, Ithaca & Elmira	Lehigh Valley	d	94½
Horseheads	1870	125,000	" " "	"	d	130
Van Etten	1869	25,437	Ithaca & Towanda	"	d	5¼
			Chenango County			
Afton	1864	30,000	Albany & Susquehanna	Delaware & Hudson	1871,1874	131⅛
Bainbridge	1865	30,000	"	"	1871,1882	
Columbus	1868	40,000	New York & Oswego Midland	New York, Ontario & Western	1880	5
Greene	1870	198,700	Greene	Delaware, Lackawanna & "	1899,1946	5¼
Guilford	1868	180,000	New York & Oswego Midland	New York, Ontario & Western	1880	5
Lincklaen	1868	20,000	"	"	1880	5¼
McDonough	1868	20,000	"	"	1880	5
New Berlin	1868	150,000	"	"	1880	5
Norwich	1869	371,000	"	"	1880	5¼
North Norwich	1868	100,000	"	"	1880	5¼
Norwich (Vil.)	1869	75,000	"	"	1880	5¼
Otselic	1868	83,700	"	Extinct	d	
Oxford	1868	200,000	"	New York, Ontario & Western	1880	5¼
Pharsalia	1870	24,000	"	Extinct	d	
Pitcher	1870	5,000	"	"	d	
Plymouth	1865	100,000	"	"	d	
Preston	1868	20,000	"	"	d	
Sherburne	1871	145,000	Utica, Chenango & Susquehanna Valley	Delaware, Lackawanna & " "	1871,1880	100
Smithville	1871	128,000	Central Valley	Extinct	d	
Smyrna	1868	120,000	New York & Oswego Midland	New York, Ontario &	1880	5
			Clinton County			
Black Brook	1867	20,000	Whitehall & Plattsburg	Delaware & Hudson	1873	2
Peru	1868	30,000	" "	"	1873	2
Plattsburg	1867	100,000	" "	" "	1875	50
Plattsburg	1875	100,000	New York & Canada	" "	1881	100

Municipality	Date	Amount	Railroad	Present System	Date of Sale	Price per Share
Columbia County						
Ancram	1870	30,875	Poughkeepsie & Eastern	New York, New Haven & Hartford	d	
Chatham	1867	53,500	Lebanon Springs	Rutland	c	
Gallatin	1874	27,000	Rhinebeck & Connecticut	New York, New Haven & Hartford	d	
Hudson	1837	50,000	Hudson & Berkshire	New York Central	c	
New Lebanon	1867	100,000	Lebanon Springs	Rutland	c	
Courtland County						
Cincinnatus	1870	44,500	Utica, Chenango & Cortland	Delaware, Lackawanna & Western	d	
Cortland	1870	150,000	"	" "	d	
"	1870	100,000	Utica, Ithaca & Elmira	Lehigh Valley	d	
Cuyler	1870	64,000	New York & Oswego Midland	" "	d	
Harford	1869	40,000	Southern Central	" "	f	
Solon	1870	44,800	Utica, Chenango & Cortland	Extinct	d	
Taylor	1870	20,000	"	"	d	
Truxton	1870	124,000	New York & Oswego Midland	Lehigh Valley	d	
Willet	1872	20,000	Utica, Chenango & Cortland	Delaware, Lackawanna & Western	d	
Delaware County						
Andes	1872	98,000	Delhi & Middletown	Extinct	d	
Davenport	1865	100,000	Albany & Susquehanna	Delaware & Hudson	1869	100
Delhi	1867	245,000	New York & Oswego Midland	New York, Ontario & Western	1880	5½
"	1872	30,000	Delhi & Middletown	Extinct	d	
Hamden	1870	100,000	New York & Oswego Midland	New York, Ontario & Western	1880	5
Hancock	1871	100,000	" " "	" " "	d	
Harpersfield	1870	100,000	Albany & Susquehanna	Delaware & Hudson	1869	100
Middletown	1867	100,000	New York & Oswego Midland	New York, Ontario & Western	1867	5
Roxbury	1869	132,000	Rondout & Oswego	New York Central	d	
Sidney	1869	50,000	Albany & Susquehanna	Delaware & Hudson	1869	100
Stamford	1869	100,000	Rondout & Oswego	New York Central	d	
Walton	1868	165,000	New York & Oswego Midland	New York, Ontario & Western	1880	5

Municipality	Date	Amount	Railroad	Present System	Date of Sale	Price per Share
			Dutchess County			
Clinton	1870	5,000	Poughkeepsie & Eastern	Extinct	d	
East Fishkill	1868	25,000	Dutchess & Columbia	New York, New Haven & Hartford	d	
LaGrange	1868	25,000	"	Extinct	d	
North East	1868	30,000	"	"	d	
Pine Plains	1868	20,000	"	"	d	
Pleasant Valley	1866	25,000	Poughkeepsie & Eastern	"	d	
Poughkeepsie	1869	600,000	"	New York, New Haven & Hartford	i	
Rhinebeck	1870	100,000	Rhinebeck & Connecticut	Extinct	d	
Stanford	1868	25,000	Dutchess & Columbia	"	d	
"	1870	15,000	Poughkeepsie & Eastern	"	d	
Washington	1863	33,700	Dutchess & Columbia	"	d	
			Erie County			
Buffalo	1852	150,000	Buffalo, Brantford & Goderich	Extinct	(1856)	48
"	1866	700,000	Buffalo, New York & Philadelphia	Pennsylvania	(1861)	100
"	1872	1,000,000	Buffalo & Jamestown	Erie	d	
Collins	1872	5,000	"	"	d	
Eden	1872	40,000	"	"	d	
Gowanda (Vil.)	1872	15,000	"	"	d	
			Essex County			
Chesterfield	1872	25,000	New York & Canada	Delaware & Hudson	1086	100
Crown Point	1868	50,000	Whitehall & Plattsburg	"	1873	2
Jay	1867	25,000	"	"	1873	2
Moriah	1867	100,000	"	"	1873	2
Ticonderoga	1867	40,000	New York & Canadian	"	1873	2
Westport	1872	40,000	"	"	1876	50
Wilmington	1867	4,000	Whitehall & Plattsburg	"	1873	2
			Fulton County			
Johnstown	1868	175,800	Fonda, Johnstown & Gloversville	Fonda, Johnstown & Gloversville	h	
Northampton	1872	30,000	Gloversville & Northville	"	e	

Municipality	Date	Amount	Railroad	Present System	Date of Sale	Price per Share
			Genesee County			
Le Roy	1872	100,000	Rochester & State Line	Baltimore & Ohio	d	
Le Roy (Vil.)	1872	15,437	" " "	" "	d	
Pavilion	1872	40,000	" "	" "	d	
			Green County			
Catskill (Vil.)	1837	100,000	Canajoharie & Catskill	Extinct	d	
Halcott	1869	10,700	Rondout & Oswego	New York Central	d	
			Hamilton County			
Hope	1868	10,000	Gloversville & Northville	Fonda, Johnstown & Gloversville	e	
			Herkimer County			
Columbia	1868	50,000	Utica, Chenango & Susquehanna Valley	Delaware, Lackawanna & Western	1875	75
Frankfort (Vil.)	1871	10,000	Frankfort & Ilion	Extinct	h	
German Flats	1870	32,000	New York, Utica & Ogdensburg	"	d	
Herkimer (Vil.)	1871	12,000	Herkimer & Mohawk Street	"	h	
Winfield	1869	75,000	Utica, Chenango & Susquehanna Valley	Delaware, Lackawanna & Western	1874,1875,1876	75
			Jefferson County			
Alexandria	1870	60,000	Black River & Morristown	New York Central	1912	183½
Carthage (Vil.)	1870	10,000	Carthage, Watertown & Sacketts Harbor	"	1884	100
Champion	1870	10,000	" " " "	"	1893	100
"	1870	25,000	Utica & Black River	"	1884	100
Clayton	1871	100,000	Clayton & Theresa	"	1893	100
Hounsfield	1871	75,000	Carthage, Watertown & Sacketts Harbor	"	1893	100
Orleans	1872	80,000	Clayton & Theresa	"	1885	100
Philadelphia	1871	15,000	Black River & Morristown	"	1912	180
"	1871	15,000	Utica & Black River	"	1912	180
Sacketts Harbor(Vil)	1870	6,000	Carthage, Watertown & Sacketts Harbor	"	h	
Theresa	1869	60,000	Black River & Morristown	"	g	
Watertown	1871	300,000	Carthage, Watertown & Sacketts Harbor	"	1893	100
Wilna	1868	56,000	Black River & St. Lawrence	"	d	
"	1870	50,000	Utica & Black River	"	1884	50

183

Municipality	Date	Amount	Railroad	Present System	Date of Sale	Price per Share
			Lewis County			
Diana	1869	50,000	Black River & St. Lawrence	Extinct	d	
Lowville	1867	100,000	Utica & Black River	New York Central	1884	100
Martinsburg	1867	30,000	" "	" "	1884	100
			Livingston County			
Groveland	1869	10,000	Erie & Genesee Valley	Erie	d	
Mt. Morris	1871	73,700	Rochester, Nunda & Pennsylvania	Pennsylvania	d	
"	1871	25,700	Avon, Geneseo & Mt. Morris	Erie	f	
North Dansville	1869	100,000	Erie & Genesee Valley	"	d	
Nunda	1871	75,000	Rochester, Nunda & Pennsylvania	Pennsylvania	d	
West Sparta	1872	7,500	Erie & Genesee Valley	Erie	d	
York	1872	100,000	Rochester, Nunda & Pennsylvania	Pennsylvania	d	
			Madison County			
Brookfield	1867	60,000	Utica,Chenango & Susquehanna Valley	Delaware, Lackawanna & Western	1871,72	76 3/8
Canastota (Vil)	1869	60,000	Cazenovia & Canastota	Lehigh Valley	d	
Cazenovia	1869	150,000	" "	"	d	
De Ruyter	1869	100,000	New York & Oswego Midland	"	d	
De Ruyter(Vil.)	1869	20,000	" " "	"	d	
Eaton	1868	150,000	" " "	New York, Ontario & Western	d	
Fenner	1869	20,000	Cazenovia & Canastota	Lehigh Valley	d	
Georgetown	1870	30,000	Syracuse & Chenango Valley	New York Central	d	
Hamilton (Vil)	1869	60,000	Utica, Clinton & Binghamton	New York, Ontario & Western	1942	40
Lebanon	1868	125,000	New York & Oswego Midland	" " "	1880	5
Madison	1869	100,000	Utica, Clinton & Binghamton	" " "	1942	40
Nelson	1870	50,000	Syracuse & Chenango Valley	New York Central	d	
Oneida (Vil.)	1869	40,000	New York & Oswego Midland	New York, Ontario & Western	1880	5
Stockbridge	1868	143,000	" " "	" " "	1860	5

Municipality	Date	Amount	Railroad	Present System	Date of Sale	Price per Share
			Monroe County			
Chili	1872	20,000	Rochester, Nunda & Pennsylvania	Extinct	d	
Greece	1872	10,000	Lake Ontario Shore	New York Central	d	
Hamlin	1872	80,000	" " "	" " "	d	
Rochester	1853	300,000	Rochester & Genesee Valley	Erie	1904	$140\frac{1}{4}$
"	1872	150,000	Rochester, Nunda & Pennsylvania	Pennsylvania	d	
"	1872	600,000	Rochester & State Line	Baltimore & Ohio	d	
Webster	1872	30,000	Lake Ontario Shore	New York Central	d	
Wheatland	1872	70,000	Rochester & State Line	Baltimore & Ohio	d	
			New York City			
		3,197,033.78				
			Niagara County			
Lewiston	1872	231,500	Lake Ontario Shore	New York Central	d	
Newfane	1872	125,000	" " "	" " "	d	
Somerset	1872	90,000	" " "	" " "	d	
Wilson	1872	165,000	" " "	" " "	d	

185

Municipality	Date	Amount	Railroad	Present System	Date of Sale	Price per Share
			Oneida County			
Augusta	1869	44,000	Utica, Clinton & Binghamton	New York, Ontario & Western	1942	40
Bridgewater	1868	50,000	Utica, Chenango & Susquehanna Valley	Delaware, Lackawanna & Western	1869	75
Kirkland	1867	40,000	Utica, Clinton & Binghamton	New York, Ontario & Western	1942	40
"	1869	40,000	Rome & Clinton	"	1944	52
Paris	1866	150,000	Utica, Chenango & Susquehanna Valley	Delaware, Lackawanna & Western	1871-92	105
Rome (Vil.)	1854	150,000	Ogdensburg, Clayton & Rome	Extinct	d	
"	1870	60,000	Rome & Clinton	New York, Ontario & Western	1894	125½
Sangerfield	1868	100,000	Utica, Chenango & Susquehanna Valley	Delaware, Lackawanna & Western	1870-89	106
Utica	1853	250,000	Black River & Utica	New York Central	d	
"	1871	200,000	Utica, Clinton & Binghamton	New York, Ontario & Western	1912	102½
"	1866	500,000	Utica, Chenango & Susquehanna Valley	Delaware, Lackawanna & Western	1861-85	110
Vienna	1868	68,500	New York & Oswego Midland	New York, Ontario & Western	1880	5
Westmoreland	1870	40,000	Rome & Clinton	" " "	1872	80
			Onondaga County			
Manlius	1870	100,000	Syracuse & Chenango Valley	New York Central	d	
Salina	1870	120,000	Syracuse Northern	" "	d	
Skaneateles	1867	30,000	Skaneateles	Skaneateles	1899	100
Syracuse	1869	500,000	Syracuse Northern	New York Central	d	
"	1869	500,000	Syracuse & Chenango Valley	" " "	d	
			Ontario County			
Geneva	1871	99,904.77	Geneva & Ithaca	Lehigh Valley	d	
" (Vil.)	1872	64,625.00	"	" "	d	
Gorham	1871	50,000	Geneva & Southwestern	Extinct	e	
Naples	1872	50,000	"	"	d	
Phelps	1871	33,000	Sodus Point & Southern	Pennsylvania	d	
Seneca	1871	50,095.23	Geneva & Ithaca	Lehigh Valley	d	

Municipality	Date	Amount	Railroad	Present System	Date of Sale	Price per Share
			Orange County			
Crawford	1870	80,000	Middletown & Crawford	Erie	d	
Deer Park	1868	200,000	Monticello & Port Jervis	New York, Ontario & Western	d	
Minisink	1869	75,000	New York & Oswego Midland	" " "	1880	5
Montgomery	1867	47,900	Montgomery & Erie	Erie	d	
"	1872	60,000	Wallkill Valley	New York Central	d	
Wallkill	1872	300,000	New York & Oswego Midland	New York, Ontario & Western	1880	5
			Orleans County			
Kendall	1872	60,000	Lake Ontario Shore	New York Central	d	
Yates	1872	100,000	" " "	" " "	d	
			Oswego County			
Constantia	1868	87,500	New York & Oswego Midland	New York, Ontario & Western	1880	5
Hannibal	1871	60,000	Lake Ontario Shore	New York Central	d	
Hannibal (Vil.)	1871	6,000	" " "	" " "	d	
Hastings	1868	80,000	New York, Oswego Midland	New York, Ontario & Western	1880	5
"	1870	25,000	Syracuse Northern	New York Central	d	
Oswego	1868	600,000	New York, Oswego Midland	New York, Ontario & Western	1880	$5\frac{1}{4}$
"	1871	530,000	Lake Ontario Shore	New York Central	d	
Parish	1871	35,000	Syracuse Northern	" " "	d	
Phoenix (Vil.)	1870	20,000	Syracuse, Phoenix & Oswego	" " "	d	
Richland	1869	60,000	" " "	" " "	d	
Sandy Creek	1870	80,000	" " "	" " "	d	
Scriba	1869	20,000	New York & Oswego Midland	New York, Ontario & Western	1880	5
Schroeppel	1873	50,000	Syracuse, Phoenix & Oswego	New York Central	d	
Volney	1868	300,000	New York & Oswego Midland	New York, Ontario & Western	1880	5
West Monroe	1867	40,000	" " "	" " "	1880	5

Municipality	Date	Amount	Railroad	Present System	Date of Sale	Price per Share
			Otsego County			
Cherry Valley	1869	150,000	Cherry Valley & Mohawk River	Delaware & Hudson	J 1869	100
Decatur	1857	20,000	Albany & Susquehanna	"	d	
Edmeston	1868	40,000	New York & Oswego Midland	New York, Ontario & Western		
Maryland	1862	70,000	Albany & Susquehanna	Delaware & Hudson	1872, 1878, 1881	115½
Middlefield	1866	50,000	Cooperstown & Susquehanna Valley	"	1913	4
Milford	1862	60,000	Albany & Susquehanna	"	1871- 81	121
Oneonta	1862	70,000	"	"	1871	92
Otego	1862	70,000	"	"	1871	92
Otsego	1865	200,000	Cooperstown & Susquehanna Valley	"	1913	3¾
Pittsfield	1868	40,000	New York & Oswego Midland	New York, Ontario & Western	1880	5
Plainfield	1868	25,000	Utica, Chenango & Susquehanna Valley	Delaware, Lackawanna & Western	1883	110
Richfield	1868	100,000	" " "	" "	1874-83	105
Richfield Springs (Vil.)	1870	30,000	" " "	" "	1872-83	100
Unadilla	1862	70,000	Albany & Susquehanna	Delaware & Hudson	1874	95
Westford	1862	30,000	"	"	1869	100
Worcester	1862	65,000	"	"	1869	100
			Rensselaer County			
Berlin	1868	60,000	Lebanon Springs	Rutland	c	
Petersburg	1864	20,000	"	"	c	
Stephentown	1868	30,000	"	"	c	
Troy	1840-42	700,000	Schenectady & Troy	New York Central	k	
"	1853	680,000	Troy Union	Troy Union	m	
			St. Lawrence County			
Edwards	1868	35,000	Black River & St. Lawrence	Extinct	d	
Hammond	1870	60,000	Black River & Morristown	New York Central	1884	85
Morristown	1870	20,000	" " "	" " "	1884	85
			Saratoga County			
Saratoga Springs	1871	100,000	Saratoga, Schuylerville & Hoosac Tunnel	Extinct	e	

Municipality	Date	Amount	Railroad	Present System	Date of Sale	Price per Share
Schenectady County						
Duanesburg	1862	30,000	Albany & Susquehanna	Delaware & Hudson	1879	100
Princetown	1870	10,000	Schenectady & Susquehanna	" "	d	
Schenectady	1870	100,000	" "	" "	d	
Schoharie County						
Cobleskill	1862	60,000	Albany & Susquehanna	Delaware & Hudson	1882,1946	188
Esperance	1862	30,000	" "	" "	1869	100
Gilboa	1869	20,000	Rondout & Oswego	New York Central	d	
Middleburg	1867	50,000	Middleburgh & Schoharie	Extinct	f	
Richmondville	1862	50,000	Albany & Susquehanna	Delaware & Hudson	1869	100
Schoharie	1864	30,000	" "	" "	1869	100
"	1865	20,000	Schoharie Valley Railroad	Extinct	h	
Seward	1864	30,000	Albany & Susquehanna	Delaware & Hudson	1869	100
"	1869	25,000	Cherry Valley & Mohawk River	" "	j	
Sharon	1868	100,000	" "	" "	j	
Summit	1862	25,000	Albany & Susquehanna	" "	1869	100
Seneca County						
Covert	1871	50,000	Pennsylvania & Sodus Bay	Extinct	d	
Ovid	1871	60,000	" "	"	d	
Seneca Falls	1871	200,000	" "	"	d	
Steuben County						
Bath (Vil.)	1871	40,000	Bath & Hammondsport	Bath & Hammondsport	f	
Bradford	1872	25,000	Sodus Bay, Corning & New York	Extinct	d	
Corning	1867	150,000	" "	"	d	
Greenwood	1872	30,000	Rochester, Hornellsville & Pine Creek	"	d	
Hornellsville	1872	70,000	" "	"	d	
Hornellsville(Vil)	1872	10,000	" "	"	d	
Urbana	1872	40,000	Bath & Hammondsport	Bath & Hammondsport	f	
Wayne	1872	30,000	Sodus Bay, Corning & New York	Extinct	d	
West Union	1872	14,000	Rochester, Hornellsville & Pine Creek	"	d	

189

Municipality	Date	Amount	Railroad	Present System	Date of Sale	Price per Share
			Suffolk County			
Smithtown	1872	70,000	Smithtown & Port Jefferson	Long Island	1891	10n
Southhampton	1870	115,000	Manor & Sag Harbor	"	h	
			Sullivan County			
Fallsburgh	1866	99,507	New York & Oswego Midland	New York, Ontario & Western	d	
Forrestburgh	1869	23,000	Monticello & Port Jervis	" "	d	
Liberty	1869	108,500	New York & Oswego Midland	" "	1880	5
Mamakating	1869	175,000	" "	" "	1880	5
Rockland	1868	34,200	" "	" "	1880	5
Thompson	1869	148,000	Monticello & Port Jervis	" "	d	
			Tioga County			
Berkshire	1867	37,000	Southern Central	Lehigh Valley	f	
Newark Valley	1867	45,600	"	" "	f	
Owego	1867	290,000	"	" "	1922	1
Richford	1867	45,000	"	" "	f	
Spencer	1869	25,000	Ithaca & Towanda	" "	d	
			Tompkins County			
Enfield	1871	25,000	Pennsylvania & Sodus Bay	Extinct	d	
Groton	1867	50,000	Southern Central	Lehigh Valley	f	
"	1871	15,000	Utica, Ithaca & Elmire	" "	d	
Ithaca	1869	300,000	Ithaca & Athens	" "	d	
"	1871	100,000	Geneva & Ithaca	" "	d	
Lansing	1871	75,000	Cayuga Lake	" "	e	
"	1872	75,000	New York & Oswego Midland	Extinct	e	
Newfield	1871	52,000	Pennsylvania & Sodus Bay	"	d	
Ulysses	1870	75,000	" " "	"	d	

Municipality	Date	Amount	Railroad	Present System	Date of Sale	Price per Share
			Ulster County			
Gardiner	1866	82,790	Wallkill Valley	New York Central	d	
Kingston	1866	600,000	Rondout & Oswego	" "	d	
"	1867	200,000	Wallkill Valley	" "	d	
New Paltz	1868	124,000	"	" "	d	
Olive	1867	87,480.92	Rondout & Oswego	" "	d	
Rosendale	1868	92,800	Wallkill Valley	" "	d	
Standaken	1868	40,000	Rondout & Oswego	" "	d	
Shawangunk	1866	116,000	Wallkill Valley	" "	d	
Warwarsing	1868	259,000	New York & Oswego Midland	New York, Ontario & Western	1880	5
			Warren County			
Queensbury	1867	100,000	Glens Fall Railroad	Delaware & Hudson	h	
			Washington County			
Fort Edward	1867	20,000	Glens Falls Railroad	Delaware & Hudson	h	
Greenwich	1869	60,000	Greenwich & Johnsonville	Greenwich & Johnsonville	p	
Kingsbury	1872	25,000	Whitehall & Plattsburgh	Delaware & Hudson	1873	2
Putnam	1872	12,000	" "	" "	1873	2
Sandy Hill	1867	25,000	Glens Falls Railroad	" "	h	
Whitehall	1872	10,000	Whitehall & Plattsburgh	" "	1873	2
			Wayne County			
Arcadia	1870	122,000	Sodus Point & Southern	Pennsylvania	d	
Lyons	1872	150,000	Sodus Bay & Corning	Extinct	d	
Ontario	1871	85,000	Lake Ontario Shore	New York Central	d	
Red Creek(Vil.)	1871	2,000	" "	" "	d	
Sodus	1870	102,000	" "	" "	d	
"	1871	88,600	Sodus Point & Southern	Pennsylvania	d	
Williamson	1871	60,000	Lake Ontario Shore	New York Central	d	
Wolcott	1870	128,000	" "	" "	d	

191

Municipality	Date	Amount	Railroad	Present System	Date of Sale	Price per Share
			Wyoming County			
Arcade	1870	22,000	Attica & Arcade	Attica & Arcade	d	
"	1872	100,000	Buffalo, New York & Philadelphia	Pennsylvania	f	
Attica	1870	27,500	Attica & Arcade	Attica & Arcade	d	
Covington	1872	45,000	Rochester & State Line	Baltimore & Ohio	d	
Eagle	1872	30,000	" " "	" "	d	
Gainesville	1872	50,000	" " "	" "	d	
Java	1873	20,000	Attica & Arcade	Attica & Arcade	d	
Middlebury	1872	50,000	Rochester & State Line	Baltimore & Ohio	d	
Perry	1870	100,000	Silver Lake	" "	1910	128
Sheldon	1873	20,000	Attica & Arcade	Attica & Arcade	d	
Warsaw	1872	120,800	Rochester & State Line	Baltimore & Ohio	d	
			Yates County			
Italy	1872	15,000	Geneva & Southwestern	Extinct	d	
Jerusalem	1872	75,000	" " "	"	d	
Middlesex	1872	50,000	" " "	"	d	
Potter	1872	34,000	" " "	"	d	

a City endorsed $100,000 of the company's bonds without loss; $25,000 donated; $125,000 loan repaid.
b Loan repaid.
c Road bankrupt, bonds worthless.
d Road bankrupt, stock worthless.
e Town bonds held void; town stock destroyed.
f No record of sale.
g Retains stock. In 1902, Theresa sold 162 shares at 120.
h Donation.
i Road bankrupt, $274,000 in second mortgage bonds and $328,000 in common stock worthless.
j Stock transferred (1879) to the D. & H. Co. which agreed to operate the road and to pay its bonded indebtedness.
k See Chap. 4.
m See pp. 116-117.
n $20,000 of this amount donated.
p Town bonds held void, railroad bonds destroyed.

Table 2. STATE AID TO RAILROADS

Original Company	Present System	Date	Amount	Interest Paid by State	Paid Back	Total State Aid
Albany & Susquehanna	Delaware & Hudson	1863-67	$750,000	---	Donation	$750,000.00
Auburn & Rochester	New York Central	1841	200,000	---	$200,000	200,000.00
Auburn & Syracuse	" " "	1840	200,000	---	200,000	200,000.00
Catskill & Canajoharie	Extinct	1838	200,000	$180,000	11,600	368,400.00
Delaware & Hudson	Delaware & Hudson	1827-29	800,000	---	800,000	800,000.00
Hudson & Berkshire	New York Central	1840	150,000	153,797.28	---	303,797.28
Ithaca & Owego	Delaware, Lackawanna & Western	1838	315,700	338,114.67	4,500	647,314.67
Long Island	Pennsylvania	1841	100,000	---	100,000	100,000.00
New York & Canada	Delaware & Hudson	1872	179,610	---	Donation	179,610.00
New York & Erie	Erie	1834-42	3,015,000	3,217,096.86	---	6,232,096.86
Ogdensburg & Lake Champlain	Rutland	1840	4,000	---	Donation	4,000.00
Plattsburgh & Dannemora	Delaware & Hudson	1878	183,035.98	---	Donation	183,035.98
Schenectady & Troy	New York Central	1841	100,000	---	100,000	100,000.00
Tioga Iron, Mining & Manufacturing	" " "	1840	70,000	---	70,000	70,000.00
Tonawanda	" " "	1840	100,000	---	100,000	100,000.00
Whitehall & Plattsburg	Delaware & Hudson	1867	70,390	---	Donation	70,390.00

Table 3. DEFAULTED RAILROAD-AID BONDS.

Municipality	Amount	Railroad	Case Reference
Ancram	$30,875	Poughkeepsie & Eastern	62 Barb. 545; 4 Lans. 529; 42 How. Prac. 425;
Andes	98,000	Delhi & Middletown	28 Hun. 441; 93 N. Y. 405; 121 N. Y. 69; 158 U.S. 312
Angelica	65,000	Rochester, Nunda & Pennsylvania	21 Blatchf. 448; Proceedings of the Alleghany County Board of Supervisors (1887)
Attica	27,500	Attica & Arcade	21 Blatchf. 499; 23 Blatchf. 68; 107 N.Y. 159; Bond Buyer, Feb. 24, 1896
Berlin	60,000	Lebanon Springs	Fed. Cas. No. 9562
Cherry Creek	44,000	Buffalo & Jamestown	2 N.Y.S. 514; 50 Hun. 601; 25 N.E. 389; 123 N.Y. 161
Delhi	30,000	Delhi & Middletown	Delhi Republican, Aug. 12, 1872; Minute Book (Delhi), Nov. 4, 1880
De Ruyter	102,000	New York & Oswego Midland	De Ruyter Weekly Gleaner, Nov. 13, 1878; Town Minute Book (De Ruyter), 1882-1889
De Ruyter (Vil.)	20,000	New York & Oswego Midland	De Ruyter Weekly Gleaner, May 4, 1882
Duanesburg	30,000	Albany & Susquehanna	40 Barb. 574; 57 N.Y. 177; N.Y. Laws, Ch. 402 (1864); 66 N.Y. 129
Edwards	25,000	Black River & St. Lawrence	N.Y. State Census Report (1875), 459
Fallsburg	99,507	New York & Oswego Midland	25 Hun. 152
Genoa	25,000	Lake Ontario, Auburn & New York	1 Thomp. & Co. 130; 29 Barb. 442; 65 Barb. 597; 23 N.Y. 439; 24 N.Y. 114; 36 N.Y. 224; 92 U.S. 502
Greenwood	30,000	Rochester, Hornellsville & Pine Creek	55 N.Y. 1; N.Y. Laws, Ch. 638 (1874)
Hancock	100,000	New York & Oswego Midland	84 N.Y. 532; 16 Blatchf. 343; Fed. Cas. No. 4911; 20 Blatchf. 344
Lebanon	125,000	New York & Oswego Midland	53 Barb. 171
Lewiston	231,500	Lake Ontario Shore	15 Blatchf. 131; Fed. Cas. No. 11,078; 21 Blatchf. 336
Lyons	150,000	Sodus Bay & Corning	25 Hun. 49; 89 N.Y. 578; 99 U.S. 684
Newfane	125,000	Lake Ontario Shore	New York Times, April 7, 1879, New York State Census Report (1875), 454
Ontario	85,000	Lake Ontario Shore	Fed. Cas. No. 13,085; 18 Blatchf. 454; 99 N.Y. 324; 4 Fed. 396
Orleans	80,000	Clayton & Theresa	13 Hun. 582; 35 Hun. 83; 50 Hun. 54; 62 How. Prac. 201; 52 N.Y. 296; 99 U.S. 676
Potter	30,000	Geneva & Southwestern	2 Fed. 518; 18 Blatchf. 185
Phelps	33,000	Sodus Point & Southern	45 N.Y. 772; 70 Fed. 29; 79 Fed. 1003

Municipality	Amount	Railroad	Case Reference
Queensbury	$100,000	Glens Falls	19 Wall. 83; 22 L. ed. 100
Rome	150,000	Ogdensburg, Clayton & Rome	18 N.Y. 38
Salina	120,000	Syracuse Northern	34 Hun. 143; 98 N.Y. 599
Seneca Falls	200,000	Pennsylvania & Sodus Bay	21 Hun. 304; 86 N.Y. 317
Shawangunk	116,000	Wallkill Valley	16 Hun. 17; 10 Fed. 220; 20 Blatchf. 307; N.Y. Laws, Ch. 90 (1882)
Sodus	102,000	Lake Ontario Shore	Oswego Daily Times, March 17, 1880
Solon	44,000	Utica, Chenango & Cortland	19 N.Y.S. 44; 32 N.E. 1083; 64 Hun. 633; 136 N.Y. 663
Somerset	90,000	Lake Ontario Shore	New York Times, April 7, 1879; New York State Census Report (1875), 454
Springport	100,000	Cayuga Lake	75 N.Y. 397; Fed. Cas. No. 676; 104 U.S. 501
Sterling	25,000	Lake Ontario, Auburn & New York	53 N.Y. 128; Proceedings of the Cayuga County Board of Supervisors (1877)
Taylor	20,000	Utica, Chenango & Cortland	19 N.Y.S. 44; 64 Hun. 633; 136 N.Y. 663; 33 N.E. 645
Thompson	148,000	Monticello & Port Jervis	7 Hun. 452; 71 N.Y. 513; 137 N.Y. 179; 103 U.S. 806; 106 U.S. 589; 154 U.S. 677
Venice	25,000	Lake Ontario, Auburn & New York	1 Thomp. & Co. 130; 29 Barb. 442; 62 N.Y. 482; 92 U.S. 494
Wolcott	128,000	Lake Ontario Shore	7 Fed. 892
Wayne	30,000	Sodus Bay & Corning	21 Hun. 423; 76 N.Y. 599
Webster	30,000	Lake Ontario Shore	New York State Census Report (1875), 454
Wilson	183,000	Lake Ontario Shore	Oswego Daily Times, April 4, 1879; New York Times, April 7, 1879; New York State Census Report (1875), 454
Yates	100,000	Lake Ontario Shore	16 Blatchf. 192; Fed. Cas. No. 11,076
York	100,000	Rochester, Nunda & Pennsylvania	Proceedings of the Livingston County Board of Supervisors (1879)

Table 4. DEFAULTED MUNICIPAL BONDS (1850-1950)

Municipality	Amount	Purpose	Case Reference
Amherst	$239,000	General	Daily Bond Buyer, March 3, 1932; 258 N.Y. 76
Brighton	4,000	Highway	143 Misc. 21
Cheektowaga	232,000	General	Daily Bond Buyer, July 23, 1932
Clarendon	40,000	Drainage	Daily Bond Buyer, July 11, 1933; June 17,1933
Cohoes	1,439,000	General	New York Herald Tribune, March 17, 1930; Bond Buyer, July 27, 1929; October 5, 1929; October 12, 1929; October 26, 1929
Dolgeville	4,000	School district	Bond Buyer, April 5, 1902
Greenburgh	149,000	Bridge	31 Misc. 428; 65 N. Y. S. 554; 173 N.Y. 215
Hudson	5,000	Street improvement	Daily Bond Buyer, February 24, 1938; Hudson Register, February 5, 1938
Irondequoit & Brighton	2,000,000	Public improvement	Rochester Times-Union, December 3, 1932; Wall Street Journal, July 2, 26, 1934
New York City (Jamaica)	40,000	Town hall	70 N.Y.S. 987; 61 A.D. 464
New York City (Jamaica)	15,000	School	Bond Buyer, Sept. 10, 1898; Dec. 17, 1898
New York City (Jamaica)	20,000	Park	Bond Buyer, June 2, 1900
Richmond (County)	18,000	General	Bond Buyer, Dec. 21, 1896; June 2, 1900
Steuben (County)	12,000	Armory	Bond Buyer, April 15, 1895
Tonawanda	232,000	Street improvement	Bond Buyer, March 26, 1898

Table 5. COMPARISON OF INCOME AND DEBTS, SCHENECTADY & TROY AND MOHAWK & HUDSON

| Year | No. Passengers | Income | | Debt |
		Passengers	Freight	
		Schenectady & Troy		
1843	71,044	$26,159.00	$ 839.00	$ 2,823.32
1844	66,096	31,067.25	1,578.39	8,770.00
1845	58,316	28,243.70	3,070.34	7,435.81
1846	62,782	29,497.15	7,280.00	7,421.81
1847	68,878	33,232.88	12,319.00	14,003.97
1848	65,714	31,826.49	14,280.94	17,133.64
1849	55,836	26,693.02	19,610.60	39,004.69
1850 (30 Sept.)	56,812	26,539.80	14,926.89	78,454.98
1851 (30 Sept.)	70,473	28,652.01	16,263.89	93,778.70
1852 (30 Sept.)	87,566	34,364.01	25,741.48	59,000.00 (3 Feb.)
1853 (1 Aug.)	70,602	27,816.54	46,385.05	
		Mohawk & Hudson		
1843	115,290	49,782.77	9,215.01	None
1844	132,685	66,293.81	10,059.79	None
1845	158,541	79,644.85	14,781.08	None
1846	174,853	92,194.87	18,321.59	None
1847	229,401	110,051.67	46,591.67	25,000.00
1848	—	113,741.88	57,139.61	70,000.00
1849	249,810	115,717.59	62,550.02	70,000.00
1850	284,279	132,207.69	70,242.69	70,000.00
1851	303,045	146,649.61	87,432.64	70,000.00
1852	413,154	171,752.74	117,859.94	81,616.80
1853 (1 Aug.)	324,315	208,043.54	261,109.61	49,692.00

197

Table 6. RAILROAD-AID BONDS HELD VOID.

Municipality	Amount	Railroad	Case Reference
Belport	$ 30,000	Buffalo & Belmont	65 Barb. 430; 1 Thomp. & Co. 113
Caneadea	40,000	Buffalo & Belmont	15 Hun. 218; 16 Fed. 532; 21 Blatchf. 351
Fort Edward	20,000	Glens Falls	8 Hun. 430; 70 N.Y. 29; 156 N.Y. 363
Genoa	75,000	New York & Oswego Midland	28 Misc. 71; 66 App. Dev. 330; 65 N.E. 1120; 59 N.Y.S. 829; 172 N.Y. 635; Bond Buyer, Aug. 23, 1902; Nov. 22, 1902
Gorham	50,000	Geneva & Southwestern	43 How. Prac. 263; 55 N.Y. 135
Greenwich	60,000	Greenwich & Johnsonville	28 Hun. 328; 61 Hun. 622; 92 N.Y. 682; 145 N.Y. 649
Hope	10,000	Gloversville & Northville	78 N.Y. 609; 18 Blatchf. 180
Hume	50,000	Buffalo & Belmont	17 Hun. 374
Lansing	75,000	Cayuga Lake	63 Barb. 105; 36 Fed. 204; 104 U.S. 505; 147 U.S. 59
Lansing	75,000	New York & Oswego Midland	11 Fed. 820; 11 Fed. 829; 14 Fed. 618; 128 U.S. 557
Ledyard	100,000	Cayuga Lake	5 Lans. 89; 2 Hun. 482
Mamakatting	1,000	New York & Oswego Midland	37 Hun. 400; 13 N.E. 937; 106 N.Y. 674
Mentz	30,000	Cayuga Northern	15 N.E. 541; 18 Fed. 52; 19 Fed. 725; 38 Hun. 637; 47 Hun. 46; 108 N.Y. 504; 134 U.S. 632
Northampton	30,000	Gloversville & Northville	120 Fed. 661; 189 U.S. 513
Saratoga Springs	100,000	Saratoga, Schuylerville & Hoosac Tunnel	51 Barb. 312; 46 N.Y. 110
Scipio	25,000	Lake Ontario, Auburn & New York	55 N.Y. 587; 101 U.S. 685
Stockton	34,000	Dunkirk, Warren & Pittsburg	53 N.Y. 128

198

BIBLIOGRAPHY

Primary Sources

Manuscript Materials

1. Municipal Records (principally Minute Books, Common Council Proceedings, and reports of local officials; in the preparation of this study the records of 450 towns were examined.)

2. Private Correspondence

Cornell Papers. DeWitt Historical Society, Ithaca.
Corning Papers. Albany Institute of Art and History, Albany.
Crofts Papers. New York State Historical Association, Cooperstown.
Davenport Papers. Regional Collection of History, Cornell University.
Devereux Papers. Regional Collection of History, Cornell University.
Pliny Fisk Collection. Princeton University Library.
Hickcox Papers. Delaware & Hudson Company Building, Albany, New York.
How Letterbooks. Mott Haven Freight Yards of the New York Central Railroad.
Jervis Papers. John B. Jervis Library, Rome, New York.
Johnstone Papers. Wood Library, Canandaigua, New York.
Kernan Collection. In possession of the Warnick Kernan family, Utica.
Morgan Papers. New York State Library.
Phelps Papers. New York State Library; Delaware & Hudson Company Building, Albany, New York.
Prentice Papers. Delaware & Hudson Company Building, Albany, New York.
Pruyn Papers. New York State Library.
Ramsay Papers. Delaware & Hudson Company Building, Albany, New York.
Rogers Papers. Regional Collection of History, Cornell University.
Seymour Letterbooks. Mott Haven Freight Yards of the New York Central Railroad.
Silvernail Papers. New York State Library.
Gerrit Smith Papers. Syracuse University Library.
Tibbits Letterbooks. New York State Library.
Wadsworth Papers. New York State Library.

3. Records of Railroad Companies (Dividend Books, Directors' Minute Books, Company Correspondence, Stock Subscription Books, Annual Reports, etc.)

The Delaware & Hudson Company. Most of the records of this system are kept in the company's archives at Albany, New York. Considerable recent material, particularly official correspondence, may be found in the offices of the company at 230 Park Avenue, New York City. The records of the following companies in the system were examined: Albany & Susquehanna; Cherry Valley, Sharon & Albany; Cooperstown & Susquehanna Valley; Delaware & Hudson; Glens Falls; Greenwich & Johnsonville; New York & Canada; Rensselaer & Saratoga; Whitehall & Plattsburg.

The Erie Railroad. These records are located in the Midland Building, Cleveland. Document Books, Minute Books, Annual Reports and Mortgage files are all that remain of the old New York & Erie records. The records of the New York & Erie were examined.

The New York Central. The main body of records for New York State lines is located at 466 Lexington Avenue, New York City. Directors' Minute Books for all component companies are in the Secretary's office at 230 Park Avenue, New York City. Sundry material on many early lines is stored in the Mott Haven freight yards at 161st Street in New York City. All records in possession of the New York Central pertaining to the following companies were examined: Albany & Schenectady; Attica & Buffalo; Auburn & Rochester; Auburn & Syracuse; Black River & Morristown; Buffalo & Rochester; Buffalo & State Line; Carthage, Watertown & Sacketts Harbor; Clayton & Theresa; Dunkirk, Allegheny Valley & Pittsburg; Hudson River; Mohawk & Hudson; Mohawk Valley; New York Central; New York Central & Hudson River; New York & Harlem; Potsdam & Watertown; Rome, Watertown &

Ogdensburg; Schenectady & Troy; Utica & Black River; Utica & Schenectady; Wallkill Valley.

The New York, Ontario & Western. The records of this line are located principally in the company's offices at Middletown, New York. Additional records of the company may be found in the First Bank & Trust Company in Utica, the Hayes National Bank in Clinton, and the company's offices at 129 Broadway, New York City. Records of the following companies were examined: Monticello & Port Jervis; New York, Ontario & Western; New York & Oswego Midland; Rome & Clinton; Utica, Clinton & Binghamton.

Printed Primary Materials

1. Contemporary Periodicals and Serials

American Agriculturalist, 1867-1874.
American Railroad Journal (title varies), 1836-1885.
American Railroad Manual for the United States and Dominion, 1873-1874.
Bankers' Magazine, 1846-1880.
Bradstreet's, 1879-1890.
Commercial & Financial Chronicle, 1865-1890.
Contemporary Review, 1891.
Cultivator, 1845-1855.
Financial Review, 1875-1885.
Hunt's Merchants' Magazine, 1839-1865.
Moore's Rural New York, 1865-1875.
Nation, 1870-1885.
Niles Register (title varies), 1833-1848.
North American Review, 1871-1880.
Poor's Manual of Railroads, 1868-1946.
Railway Times, 1850-1862.
Statist, 1874-1885.
United States Magazine and Democratic Review, 1843.

2. Government Publications

New York (county)
  Proceedings of the Board of Supervisors, 1860-1900.
    In the preparation of this book, the records of 55 counties were examined.
    Those not examined were Bronx, Kings, Nassau, New York, Queens, Richmond and
    Suffolk.

New York (state)
  Assembly Documents. 1825-1885.
  Census of the State of New York for 1855. Albany, 1857.
  Census of the State of New York for 1865. Albany, 1867.
  Journals of the Assembly of the State of New York. Albany, 1828-1890.
  Journal of the Constitutional Commission of the State of New York, 1872-1873.
    Albany, 1873.
  Journals of the Senate of the State of New York. Albany, 1828-1890.
  Laws of the State of New York Passed at the Sessions of the Legislature Held in
    the Years 1789-1900. Albany, 1790-1901.
  Messages from the Governors, Comprising Executive Communications to the Legislature and Other Papers..., 1683-1906. Ed. by Charles Z. Lincoln. Albany, 1909.
    11 vols.
  Proceedings and Debates of the Constitutional Convention, 1867-1868. Albany, 1868.
    5 vols.
  Report and Proceedings of the Hepburn Committee. New York, 1879. 5 vols.
  Senate Documents, 1825-1900.
  Special Report on Municipal Accounts by the State Comptroller, 1906-1930.
    Albany, 1907-1931. 25 vols.

United States
  Bureau of the Census, Report of Valuation, Taxation, and Public Indebtedness in the
    United States, Tenth Census, 1880. Washington, 1884.
  Congressional Record, 45 Cong., 3 Sess., Vol. 8 (1879), Washington, 1880.
  Federal Coordinator of Transportation, Public Aids to Railroads and Related Sub-
    jects (Vol. 2). Washington, 1938.
  Interstate Commerce Commission, Decisions of the Interstate Commerce Commission of
    the United States (Valuation Reports). Washington, 1926-1931. Vols. 22, 23, 25,
    27, 28, 30, 31, 33, 34, 35, 36, 38, 39, 43, 46, 97, 110, 116, 121, 125, 130, 133,
    137, 141, 143, 149.
  Senate Executive Document No. 42, 33 Cong., 1 Sess. (1853-1854). Washington, 1855.

    3. Newspapers

Albany Argus, 1840-1853, 1854-1875
  scattered.
Albany Daily Knickerbocker, 1869-1870.
Albany Evening Journal, 1868-1875.
Auburn Citizen-Advertiser, 1940-1945.
Auburn Democrat, 1868-1874.
Auburn Morning News, 1868-1879.
Binghamton Democrat, 1869-1875.
Binghamton Sun, 1869-1875.
Bond Buyer, 1893-1949.
Brookfield Courier, 1946.
Buffalo Express, 1852-1880.
Buffalo Commercial-Advertiser, 1852-
  1880.
Candor Free Press, 1870-1872.
Canisteo Times, 1875-1882.
Cayuga Patriot (Auburn), 1836-1842.
Chenango Semi-Weekly Telegraph (Nor-
  wich), 1865-1882.
Chenango Union, 1865-1880.
Clinton Courier, 1866-1945.
Cobleskill Herald, 1882-1885.
Cobleskill Index, 1869-1880.
Cobleskill Times, 1942-1946.
Cortland Democrat, 1870-1885.
Daily Bond Buyer, 1918-1948.
Delhi Republican, 1868-1881.
Delaware Republican (Delhi), 1869-1885.
De Ruyter Gleaner, 1878-1890.
Dunkirk Evening-Observer, 1890-1903.
Elmira Advertiser, 1875-1882.
Fredonia Censor, 1900-1905.
Freeman's Journal (Cooperstown), 1869-
  1870.
Geneva Gazette, 1865-1875.
Glimmerglass (Cooperstown), 1938.
Greene Chenango-American, 1869-1870.
  1940-1946.
Hamilton Republican, 1869-1875.
Hancock Herald, 1873-1890.
Home & Abroad (Unadilla), 1863-1873.
Hornell Daily Times, 1878-1885.
Hudson Register, 1938.
Ithaca Democrat, 1867-1875.
Ithaca Journal, 1868-1880.

Jamestown Journal, 1875-1880.
Lyons Republican, 1875-1882.
Lowville Journal & Republican, 1880-
  1890.
Manlius Repository, 1869-1875.
New York Herald, 1869-1872.
New York Herald Tribune, 1930-1932.
New York Times, 1865-1880.
New York Tribune, 1873-1880.
Orange County Press (Middletown) 1866-
  1873.
Ontario County Times (Canandaigua),
  1870-1873.
Oneonta Herald, 1866-1875.
Ontario Repository & Freeman (Canandaigua),
  1837-1840.
Oswego Daily Times, 1865-1880.
Oswego Daily Palladium, 1867-1880.
Otsego Farmer (Cooperstown), 1913-1916.
Phelps Citizen, 1887-1897.
Plattsburg Republican, 1869-1880.
Poughkeepsie Eagle, 1870-1875.
Rochester Daily Democrat, 1853-1857.
Rochester Democrat & Chronicle, 1870-1900.
Rochester Express, 1865-1866.
Rochester Times-Union, 1932.
Rochester Union & Advertiser, 1856-1918.
Roman Citizen, 1853-1854, 1894-1895.
Rome Daily Sentinel, 1856-1857, 1880-
  1894.
Schenectady Reflector, 1836-1842.
Schoharie Republican, 1870-1875.
Seneca Falls Reveille, 1873-1890.
Steuben Courier (Bath), 1875-1883.
Steuben Farmers Advocate (Bath), 1875-1882.
Syracuse Daily Courier, 1865-1875.
Syracuse Daily Journal, 1868-1875.
Thousand Islands Sun, 1938-1942.
The Times (London), 1852-1861.
Troy Budget, 1840-1858.
Troy Daily Times, 1851-1856.
Troy Daily Whig, 1834-1856.
Troy Record, 1899.
Troy Times, 1900.
Utica Daily Gazette, 1853-1857.

Utica Daily Gazette & Morning Herald,   Utica Herald Dispatch, 1902-1912.
   1857-1880.   Wall Street Journal, 1931-1936.
Utica Daily Observer, 1875-1912.   Waterloo Observer, 1873-1881.
Utica Daily Press, 1882-1912.   Waterloo Times, 1869-1895.
Utica Evening Telegraph, 1854-1856.   Western New Yorker (Warsaw), 1866-1878.

4. Miscellaneous Works

Address by the Directors of the Albany & Susquehanna Railroad, together with laws
   authorizing Town Subscriptions. Albany, 1856.
Award of the Commissioners Under the Act in Relation to Railroad Corporations in the
   Matter Between the Schenectady & Troy Railroad Company and the Utica & Schenectady
   Railroad Company and the Albany & Schenectady Railroad Company. Albany, 1847.
Hall's Investor's Guide to United States Municipal Bonds; Proving that these Bonds
   Constitute an Exceptionally Safe and Remunerative Investment. London, 1874.
Journal of Proceedings of the First Annual Session of the New York State Grange of
   the Patrons of Husbandry. Held at Albany March 18, 19, 20, 1874. Elmira, 1874.
Remarks by William White, President. The Delaware, Lackawanna & Western Railroad
   Company at the Annual Meeting of Stockholders. New York, 1944.
Report of the Commissioners of the Albany Northern Railroad Loan, Made to the Common
   Council, April 14, 1856. Albany, 1856.
Report of the Investigating Committee appointed by the Town Board of Seneca Falls to
   Examine into the Affairs of the Pennsylvania & Sodus Bay Railroad. Seneca Falls, 1874.
Schenectady & Troy Railroad Company, A Statement. Troy, 1846.

Secondary Sources

Adams, Henry, Public Debts, An Essay in the Science of Finance. New York, 1887.
Adams, Charles, ''A Chapter of Erie,'' North American Review, CXII. (April 1871).
Alexander, De Alva Stanwood, Political History of New York. New York, 1906. 4 vols.
Bagg, M. W., Memorial History of Utica, New York. Syracuse, 1892.
Baldwin, Simeon, American Railroad Law. Boston, 1904.
Beach, Charles, The Modern Law of Railways. San Francisco, 1890. 2 vols.
Beauchamp, W. M., Past and Present of Syracuse and Onondaga County. Syracuse, 1908.
   2 vols.
Birdsall, Ralph, The Story of Cooperstown. Cooperstown, 1917.
Buck, S. J., The Granger Movement. Cambridge, 1913.
Chadbourne, P. A., The Public Service of the State of New York. Boston, 1882. 3 vols.
Clark, Hiram, History of Chenango County. Norwich, 1885.
Clark, Victor, History of Manufactures in the United States. New York, 1929. 3 vols.
Clayton, W., History of Steuben County. Philadelphia, 1879.
Cleveland, F. A., and F. W. Powell, Railroad Promotion and Capitalization in the United
   States. New York, 1909.
——Railroad Finance. New York, 1912.
Clews, Henry, Fifty Years in Wall Street. New York, 1908.
Churchill, John, Landmarks of Oswego County. Syracuse, 1895.
Corey, Lewis, The House of Morgan. New York, 1930.
Curtis, Gates, A Memorial Record of St. Lawrence County. Syracuse, 1894.
Delaware & Hudson Company, A Century of Progress, A History of the Delaware & Hudson.
   Albany, 1929.
Dillon, John, Commentaries on the Law of Municipal Corporations. Boston, 1911. 5 vols.
Donaldson, Alfred, A History of the Adirondacks. New York, 1921. 2 vols.
Doty, Lockwood, A History of Livingston County, New York. Geneseo, 1876.
Durant, Samuel, History of Oneida County, New York. Philadelphia, 1878.
Durant, S. W., and H. B. Peirce, History of Jefferson County. Philadelphia, 1878.
Ellis, D. M., ''Albany and Troy – Commercial Rivals,'' New York History, XXIV (October 1943).
Fairman, Charles, Mr. Justice Miller and the Supreme Court. Cambridge: Harvard University
   Press, 1939.
Gill, Frederick, ''Local Subsidy to the Railroads of New York State,'' Manuscript,
   Cornell University, 1939.

Hammond, Jabez, History of Political Parties in the State of New York. Cooperstown, 1845. 3 vols.

Haney, L. H., A Congressional History of Railways in the United States 1850-1889. Madison, 1908. 2 vols.

Hardin, George, History of Herkimer County. Syracuse, 1893.

Harlow, Alvin, The Road of the Century. New York: Creative Age Press, 1947.

Hedrick, U. P., A History of Agriculture in the State of New York. Albany: New York State, 1933.

Hidy, R. W., The House of Baring in American Trade and Finance: English Merchant Bankers at Work, 1763-1861. Cambridge: Harvard University Press, 1949.

Hillhouse, Albert M., Municipal Bonds, A Century of Experience. New York: Prentice-Hall, 1936.

Hough, Franklin, A History of Lewis County. Syracuse, 1883.

Hungerford, Edward, Men and Iron. New York: Crowell, 1938.

Hurd, D., History of Clinton and Franklin Counties, New York. Philadelphia, 1880.

Jenks, L. H., The Migration of British Capital to 1875. New York, 1927.

——''Railroads as an Economic Force in American Development,'' Journal of Economic History, IV (May 1944).

Johnson, E. R., American Railway Transportation. New York, 1903.

Kessler, W. C., ''Railroads in Madison County,'' New York State History, XXII (January 1941).

Leslie, E. N., Skaneateles, History of Its Earliest Settlement and Reminiscences of Later Times. New York, 1902.

Lincoln, Charles, The Constitutional History of New York. Rochester, 1900. 5 vols.

MacGill, Caroline, et al., History of Transportation in the United States Before 1860. Washington, 1917.

McGrane, Reginald, Foreign Bondholders and American State Debts. New York: Macmillan, 1935.

McKelvey, Blake, Rochester, The Flower City, 1855-1890. Cambridge: Harvard University Press, 1949.

——Rochester, The Water-Power City, 1812-1854. Cambridge: Harvard University Press, 1945.

McMaster, R. B. The Railroad Laws of the State of New York. New York, 1872.

McQuillen, Eugene, The Law of Municipal Corporations. Cleveland: Callaghan, 1945.

Malone, Dumas, ed., The Dictionary of American Biography. New York: Scribner, 1928-1936. 20 vols.

Masten, Arthur, History of Cohoes, New York. Albany, 1877.

Milliken, Charles, A History of Ontario County, New York and Its People. New York, 1911. 2 vols.

Mott, Edward Harold, Between the Ocean and the Lakes, The Story of Erie. New York, 1901.

Murray, David, Delaware County, History of the Century, 1797-1897. Delhi, 1898.

Meyers, Gustavus, History of the Great American Fortunes. New York, 1907.

Peirce, Henry, History of Tioga, Chemung, Tompkins, and Schuyler Counties, New York. Philadelphia, 1879.

Poor, H. V., History of the Railroads and Canals of the United States. New York, 1860.

Powell, Frederick, ''Two Experiments in Public Ownership of Railroads,'' Quarterly Journal of Economics, XXIII (November 1908).

Quinlan, James, History of Sullivan County. Liberty, 1873.

Ringwalt, J. L., Development of Transportation Systems in the United States. Philadelphia, 1888.

Ripley, W. Z., Railroads, Finance and Organization. New York, 1915.

Ruttenber, E. M., History of the Town of Newburgh. Newburgh, 1859.

Schumpeter, Joseph, Business Cycles, A Theoretical, Historical, and Statistical Analysis of the Capitalist Process. New York: McGraw-Hill, 1939. 2 vols.

Scott, William, The Repudiation of State Debts. New York, 1893.

Scoville, Joseph, The Old Merchants of New York City. New York, 1862-1869. 5 vols.

Seaver, F. J., Historical Sketches of Franklin County and Its Several Towns. Albany, 1918.

Shulman, Harry, ''The Demise of Swift v. Tyson,'' Yale Law Journal, XLVII (June 1940).

Simonten, T. C., <u>A</u> <u>Treatise</u> <u>of</u> <u>the</u> <u>Law</u> <u>of</u> <u>Municipal</u> <u>Bonds</u>. New York, 1896.

Smith, James, <u>History</u> <u>of</u> <u>Chenango</u> <u>and</u> <u>Madison</u> <u>Counties</u>. Syracuse, 1880.

Sowers, D. C., <u>The</u> <u>Financial</u> <u>History</u> <u>of</u> <u>New</u> <u>York</u> <u>State</u>. New York, 1914.

Stevens, F. W., <u>The</u> <u>Beginnings</u> <u>of</u> <u>the</u> <u>New</u> <u>York</u> <u>Central</u> <u>Railroad</u>. New York, 1926.

Storke, Elliot, <u>History</u> <u>of</u> <u>Cayuga</u> <u>County</u>. Syracuse, 1879.

Studenski, Paul, <u>Public</u> <u>Borrowing</u>. New York, 1930.

Sylvester, Nathaniel, <u>History</u> <u>of</u> <u>Saratoga</u> <u>County</u>, <u>New</u> <u>York</u>. Philadelphia, 1878.

Van Deusen, G. G., <u>Thurlow</u> <u>Weed</u>, <u>Wizard</u> <u>of</u> <u>the</u> <u>Lobby</u>. New York: Little, Brown, 1947.

Warren, Charles, ''New Light on the History of the Federal Judiciary Act of 1789,''
    <u>Harvard</u> <u>Law</u> <u>Review</u>, XXXVII (October 1933).

Weise, Arthur, <u>Troy's</u> <u>One</u> <u>Hundred</u> <u>Years</u>, <u>1789</u>-<u>1889</u>. Troy, 1891.

Winkler, Max, <u>Foreign</u> <u>Bonds</u>, <u>An</u> <u>Autopsy</u>. Philadelphia, 1933.

Wittke, C. F., <u>We</u> <u>Who</u> <u>Built</u> <u>America</u>. New York: Prentice-Hall, 1940.

Yates, Austin, <u>Schenectady</u> <u>County</u>, <u>New</u> <u>York.</u> New York, 1902.

Young, Andrew, <u>History</u> <u>of</u> <u>Chautauqua</u> <u>County</u>, <u>New</u> <u>York</u>. Buffalo, 1875.

    <u>History</u> <u>of</u> <u>the</u> <u>Town</u> <u>of</u> <u>Warsaw</u>. Buffalo, 1869.